Praise for *The Military Stories You've Been Told ... and the Ones You Need to Hear*

"My dad was a veteran and fiercely patriotic. He served two stints in the Navy before I was born and instilled in me a sense of honor and esteem, in which our military and veterans should be held. But it was not until I was elected to the U.S. Senate that I truly learned there was so much more to appreciate and respect. I learned of the overlooked dedication and sacrifices of military families, particularly spouses and children, and devoted much of my service to eliminating the 'Military Widow's Tax.' In her new book about military families, Jennifer Barnhill brings the stories of military families to life—their struggles and courage, their tragedies and triumphs. In doing so, she not only guides the reader to a greater understanding of these families, and why we should honor them as part of our respect for the military, but relates them to the greater divisions in American society and how we can heal them. This book is a must read for anyone who wishes to get past the vitriol of division in America and back to the common bonds of patriotism that we all share."

—Senator Doug Jones

"Jennifer's book is essential to understanding the military. She makes a compelling case for why supporting the entire military family unit is crucial to a strong nation and shows us what the Department of Defense and policymakers need to do better by taking us inside the lives of service members, their spouses, widows and children. *The Military Stories You've Been Told ... and the Ones You Need to Hear* draws upon Jennifer's vast network of sources, built over decades as a journalist and military spouse, and knocks down long held misconceptions about military life, revealing what this family business is really all about."

—Brianna Keilar, *CNN* Anchor and Veteran Spouse

"A thought-provoking and illuminating guide to the complex world military spouses and their families face, Barnhill skillfully documents and analyzes military spouse history, reclaiming this frequently overlooked narrative. Barnhill also candidly examines military society, addressing the tough realities faced by spouses and families. A military spouse and reporter herself, the author offers an empathetic and deeply researched take on her subject. A must read and an important resource for members of the military community and for civilians seeking a more inclusive understanding of the military experience."

—Heath Hardage Lee, author of *The League of Wives* and *The Mysterious Mrs. Nixon*

"Barnhill's round-up of all the ways things do go wrong is a great reminder that the people who vote for war—civilians often in towns far from battle—must pay attention when service members and their families speak up, and must think about the consequences of those votes."

—Kelly Kennedy, co-author of *The Unit* and award-winning journalist

Military Stories You've Been Told ... and the Ones You Need to Hear

Jennifer Barnhill

EP BOOKS

For permission requests, email the publisher at the address below.

E.P. House
hello@ephouse.co

This is a work of nonfiction. The views expressed are those of the author and of the individuals interviewed.

First edition – October 2025
Paperback ISBN: 979-8-3302-8336-1

PRINTED IN THE UNITED STATES OF AMERICA ON ACID-FREE PAPER

www.ephouse.co
Cover design by Taylor Lisney
Back Cover Photo Credit: Trish Alegre-Smith, courtesy of
Armed Forces Insurance Military Spouse of the Year program

To the hidden all-volunteer
force

Contents

Introduction

Although military spouses have been part of the United States military since the Revolutionary War, military spouse history is not captured in our U.S. history books. Our names are rarely mentioned in military museums. Even today, our modern experiences are not mentioned in stories written about the military, even ones that have a direct impact on our lives.

As a military spouse, this angers me, knowing that so many of my friends have stories worthy of being told and remembered. As a historian, I know history is shaped by those who get to write it. Yes, history is written by the victors—but in a digital age where everyone is a storyteller, whoever tells the best stories wins.

As a writer and journalist, I know that we, as military spouses, have the power to help our community write better military stories—stories that include *all* of us. Unfortunately, it is not as easy as picking up a pen and writing. Because there will always be stories that someone doesn't want told.

Although individual stories help drive change and build connections across divides, they have their limitations. Even when a story is particularly compelling, more often than not, we soon forget it.

We forget it not because it wasn't a good story, but because individual stories often crumble in the face of dominant narratives. The dominant narratives are the ideas our society believes to be true. When a small story comes up against a dominant narrative, our brains don't know how the small story fits, so the small story fades away.

This book seeks to do two things.

First, it serves as a written record of the amazing achievements and harrowing experiences of military families, so they are not lost when newspaper links break and magazine archives disappear.

Second, it is a tool—a smooth stone in the hands of David as he approaches Goliath. Its goal? To take aim at the dominant military narratives we've been told and make way for more complete military stories—stories that include military spouses, parents, recruits, and children. Military stories you need to hear.

My hope is that this book helps you see there is more to the military than what you have been told. The dominant narratives you know serve those in power, not the people who serve. There are countless stories you need to hear, stories of men and women you have never heard about who have changed the military from within. I hope the stories in this book will inspire you to seek out more military stories . . . stories that force you to think about the institution in new ways, both good and bad, because accessing this diversity of experience is essential to understanding the military.

How I Became a Disruptive Storyteller

"You can't go back and change the beginning, but you can start where you are and change the ending."

—often attributed to C.S. Lewis

"You're at the president's table," my friend Tracy said hurriedly as I walked into President George W. Bush and First Lady Laura Bush's private dining room at the George W. Bush Presidential Center in Dallas, Texas. Earlier in the day, I had shaken his hand and instantly forgotten my own name. I was sitting two places away from a man whose presidency left an indelible mark on my military family and the nation. As a journalist, I wanted to ask him about the war on terror; instead, I told him a story.

But first, I have another story to tell you . . .

On our first date, my husband took me to church in his dress whites. It was a strategic invitation not only because he was appealing to my religious upbringing, but because he didn't just take me to church. He took me back in time. When we approached the United States Naval Academy chapel in Annapolis, Maryland, I was surrounded by uniforms.

Inside, I saw both the expected crisp white starched military shirts and slacks, and the "just so" attire of the civilians sitting beside their service members. Although I was working at the Smithsonian American Art Museum at the time, surrounded by Jeffersonian-style architecture and the history of Washington, D.C., the buildings on the USNA campus, known as "the Yard," were impressive. Somehow, his smile and ability to bypass small talk distracted me from the formality and structure of the institution I had entered.

Ironically, what attracted me to my husband was his nonconformity. He has never heard a statement uttered by an authority that he hasn't questioned. He challenged me, an overthinker, to keep overthinking. Years later, it struck me that while we were sitting in that chapel, he was praying to a God that he was not afraid to ask hard questions of, but working in a job that asked him to leave his questions at the door.

By the end of the day, when I said yes to a second date, it may have already been too late. I was starting to fall for someone whose job would demand both of us to become smaller in service of our country. But unlike my Navy midshipman, I swore no oath and got no training. I just bought a blue dress and went on our second date.

We were married two years later.

Saying "I do" to him meant I had to say no to many of my own ambitions. I turned down a full scholarship to pursue a PhD in art history and followed my newly commissioned naval aviator husband to Pensacola, Florida. I quickly learned that the military was not a job, it was a lifestyle. I was infuriated that my husband could not simply ask his commanding officer where we would move next. I didn't understand why life had to be written in pencil and why asking "why" seemed off-limits. We were still in that chapel, living life in a 1950s time capsule, where some hidden authority "knows best." I wanted to know why, but life got in the way.

Six months later, we moved to San Diego, California; the following year, we moved overseas, to Atsugi, Japan, a small town an hour outside of Tokyo. But, within a week of our arrival, he deployed on an aircraft carrier, leaving me to navigate military life alone.

Surprisingly, I fell in love with what military life could be. Even though I missed my husband while he was deployed, I was strengthened by a community of military spouses, mostly women, who made the time apart easier. We tracked deployment dates and planned fun social activities to boost morale while our service members were away. At a time before remote work, most of us couldn't maintain traditional jobs overseas, so life was what we made of it. From the locations we explored to the culture clashes to the wine and Japanese Chūhai, we turned separation into an adventure and showed up for each other when needed.

A shore tour in the desert of Nevada followed. Kid one. Pregnancy. Another tour in Japan. Kid two. San Diego again. Kid three.

Military life was predictable in its unpredictability. I took jobs along the way because a career in art history or journalism seemed out of reach. I blogged to keep my creative juices flowing, cared for my kids, and spent time with other wives, who also resented the sacrifices that seemed expected of us but accepted them as a byproduct of loving our service members.

Then, in October 2017, everything changed. My new friend Esther, one of the members of my military spouse club, was diagnosed with pancreatic cancer. I had barely gotten to know her when she received her diagnosis, but like many new military connections, I liked her at our first meeting. Her two kids were around the same age as mine.

At the time our military spouse club, the unofficial group often tasked with sharing information and resources with military family members, lacked leadership. The desire to help a friend—a fellow "dependent," as the military classifies us—and her family led me to volunteer to be president of our group, something I did not have time for in between raising three under five and working as a project manager to pay the bills.

This organization, while not officially connected to the Department of Defense (DoD), was intended to be a lifeline to military families, providing access to official communication and a sort of initiation into the unfamiliar military lifestyle. From the beginning of my tenure as president, I realized our group was ill-equipped to help Esther. While there were many military and nonprofit organizations her family could turn to for financial assistance and counseling, spouse clubs were the military's stand-in for family and friends. She needed full-time help with day-to-day things like meal prep and child care, things non-military people would only ask of family. We wanted to help her. But to varying degrees, we all needed help. Some were acting as solo parents as our spouses were deployed. Others were struggling to find employment. We were all drowning yet were expected to help keep each other afloat.

Luckily, Esther had a well-established network of friends and family to help meet many logistical needs, so she could go to appointments and attempt normalcy. Our husbands' command leadership was amazing and, in an instant, covered her husband's duties so he could be by Esther's side. It broke my heart to think of others with no support in a new duty station, surrounded by strangers and with nowhere to turn.

Esther's situation forced me to slow down and reevaluate the things I had come to accept about military life. Why did my experience in that church on my first date with my husband feel so *dated*? Why were spouses expected to do so much if we were not part of the military? Certainly, military service is a hard job, but why does his job require me to participate as well?

Because I was trained as a journalist, my first reaction to observing this problem was to find the story. I asked myself, *Why does it feel like the military is living in the 1950s? Am I the only one who feels this way?*

Over the next year, after my kids went to bed each night, I researched military support programs and military-serving nonprofits. I offered to help existing organizations come up with ways to provide practical support to military families like Esther's. I interviewed military and civilian leaders during lunch breaks and on my daily 45-minute commute. I wanted to find out if anyone else was working on improving spouse club programming.

No one was. Circumstances were practically taunting me to start a nonprofit. It seemed like everyone who observed a broken system in the military started a nonprofit. And I was tempted.

But there were so many—too many.

Then a dear friend reminded me, "You are a journalist. Be one." I was not the right person to help every Esther who came my way by providing meals or child care, but I *could* research the hell out of the problem and share what I learned with the world.

So I started writing and published what I learned in a military-focused magazine. My reporting confirmed that, yes, the military relies on spouses as an unpaid workforce.[1] We were systematically expected to volunteer our time in support of our spouses' careers. While the spouses I interviewed were happy to help one another and show community support by joining spouse clubs, the exhaustion involved in this participation seemed universal. For most, juggling family, career, friendships, and military-related volunteering felt expected, no matter how unrealistic. Not only was volunteerism expected and relied upon, it was simultaneously ignored by the military and dismissed as a "social activity," code for "women's work."

I soon learned that spouse groups were just one of the many military family programs that were not prioritized by the military. While these and other military quality-of-life efforts were featured prominently in public-facing memos and discussed during public relations briefings, these programs were practically absent from the DoD's budget. I redoubled my focus and began pursuing my master's degree in public administration to better understand how government is *supposed to* work. In black and white, the DoD budget told me all I needed to know about what our government prioritizes.

The American public has been told that taking care of military families is a top priority. My reporting uncovered countless examples that challenged this narrative.

---

[1] Jennifer Barnhill, "Future Military Spouse Clubs Must Change to Survive," *Military Families Magazine*, https://militaryfamilies.com/military-spouses/future-military-spouse-clubs-must-change-to-survive/.

I learned that military widows were subject to what was known as the "widow's tax,"[2] a bureaucratic policy that prevented surviving military families from receiving earned death benefits for nearly forty years because it was deemed too costly to correct. I learned that: junior enlisted personnel struggled with food insecurity but leaders blamed poor budgeting,[3] not low pay; military children with special needs were being sued by public schools when they fought for access to adequate education[4]; the undermining of military health care[5]; military family housing was uninhabitable but leaders blamed government contracts[6]; female veterans suffered from homelessness and had fewer resources than male veterans[7]; and veterans leaving service felt abandoned.[8] So many military quality-of-life efforts seemed to fall short.

I couldn't help but notice that military service members, families, and veterans felt like an afterthought. But the narratives being told about this community by the DoD kept saying everything was fine.

These narratives said:

- Military quality of life is important but take personal responsibility.
- Service is a calling for the elite warriors.

---

[2] Jennifer Barnhill, "What You Need to Know About the Military Widows Tax," *Military Families Magazine*, https://militaryfamilies.com/military-news/what-you-need-to-know-about-the-military-widows-tax.
[3] Jennifer Barnhill, "A Food Insecurity Crisis Afflicts Military Families," *Military Families Magazine*, July 23, 2019, https://militaryfamilies.com/military-news/a-food-insecurity-crisis-afflicts-military-families.
[4] Jennifer Barnhill, "Military Kids May Be Key to Fixing Special Education," *Military.com*, February 11, 2021, https://www.military.com/daily-news/opinions/2021/02/11/military-kids-may-be-key-fixing-special-education.html.
[5] Jennifer Barnhill, "Looming Changes to Military Medical Care Cause Uncertainty," *Military Spouse Magazine*, December 2019, https://www.militaryspouse.com/news/looming-changes-to-military-medical-care-cause-uncertainty.
[6] Jennifer Barnhill, "Will Tenant Bill of Rights Fix Privatized Military Housing?" *Military.com*, March 28, 2023, https://www.military.com/daily-news/2023/03/28/will-tenant-bill-of-rights-fix-privatized-military-housing.html.
[7] Jennifer Barnhill, "Women Veterans Face Increased Risk of Homelessness," *Military Families Magazine*, February 2020, https://mydigitalpublication.com/publication/?i=646155&ver=html5&p=28.
[8] Jennifer Barnhill, "The Problems with the Military Transition Process Need More than a Band-Aid Solution," *Military.com*, February 6, 2020, https://www.military.com/daily-news/2020/02/06/problems-military-transition-process-need-more-band-aid-solution.html.

- Service members are strong.
- The military takes care of its own.
- The military leaves no one behind.
- If a service member dies in the line of duty, we will take care of their family.
- Military family members are dependents.
- The military community is resilient.
- The military is not political.

I observed these and other messages in news articles and official military channels, in military budgets, spoken by leaders in town hall meetings and behind closed doors, and in marketing materials. Civilian depictions of military life too often glamorized the military lifestyle, flattening the diverse force into two-dimensional caricatures. Official military instructions further restricted what service members shared with the public, making military life seem all the more foreign.

But these messages don't reflect the lived reality of military families.

We can reclaim the military narrative by gaining access to stories that paint a more complete picture.

But before I can tell you some military stories you need to hear, we need to deconstruct the military stories you have been told.[9]

EXAMINING THE MILITARY STORIES WE'VE BEEN TOLD

"Whoever tells the best story wins."
—John Quincy Adams

Back to my story.

I was sitting three seats away from a former president of the United States. At the table with us were members of the George W. Bush

[9] Jennifer Barnhill, "A Military Spouse's Journey From Annoyance to Advocacy," *The War Horse*, May 6, 2020, https://thewarhorse.org/from-annoyance-to-advocacy.

Presidential Center's Stand-To Veteran Leadership Program, who were working to solve some of the military's biggest issues, like veteran suicide and reducing veteran and military spouse unemployment. As we ate dinner, my fellow program participants asked questions about the highs and lows of Bush's presidency and shared a little bit about what brought them to the program.

As we informally made our way around the table, sharing our thoughts and asking questions, a reel of a million interviews with military families began scrolling in my head. I didn't know whose story I should tell. I panicked, but then trusted my gut.

"Sir, I would like to tell you a story," I started. "My dad was in the World Trade Center, in Tower One, the North Tower."

I had a hook, but do not let that mislead you. I am a writer, not a public speaker. I'm not particularly good at telling stories that put me on the verge of tears on a good day, let alone on a day that involves meeting a man whose presidency profoundly impacted my life and our nation. In this state, I committed the ultimate journalistic sin: I buried the lede.

"A month before September 11, my dad's business wasn't doing well. So he moved down roughly twenty floors to a smaller office, due to a financial hardship that would ultimately save his life and the lives of those he worked with."

The story took a distracting turn when I started talking about which floor he was on, trying to describe how his office used to be right below the distinctive band of windows that marked the top third of the World Trade Center, where the first plane impacted. Thankfully, my nervous storytelling did not cause him to lose interest; instead, he asked clarifying questions.

"Yes, sir, he survived. He made it out, after first stopping on a lower floor to call family." I hesitated to tell the entire truth—that my dad knew he should get out of the building because he saw lifeless bodies in the courtyard. Those deaths saved my father's life. But for whatever reason, I felt the need to censor this grim reality for a man who was certainly all too familiar with it.

"I was in college and attended a 9:00 a.m. class, unaware of what was unfolding," I told the table. "By the time I got out of class, both towers had already fallen. I had no idea if my dad was alive or dead. And I had no ability to get a hold of him."

Somehow, I was still stumbling through a story I have told for over twenty years. I don't know if it was because I was speaking to a president or if the fear I had felt that day still had a hold over me. Eventually, I got to my point.

"Your words carried me home that day," I said, trying my best not to cry. "In my frantic state, not knowing if my dad was alive or dead, I decided to drive home from college to wait by our landline phone. And as I drove, I listened to your speech."

> "The search is underway for those who are behind these evil acts. I've directed the full resources of our intelligence and law enforcement communities to find those responsible and to bring them to justice. We will make no distinction between the terrorists who committed these acts and those who harbor them."
> —Statement by President George W. Bush in his address to the nation on September 11, 2001[10]

This is where my decision to tell this personal story, hopefully, started to make sense. In all the chaos of that day, the president's words, confidence, and resolve helped me, even for a brief moment, set aside my worry about the future of our country and focus on my family.

"Sir, your words helped me realize that our military and our leaders had us in hand, and it freed me up to worry about my family and be there for my dad," I said.

---

[10] George W. Bush, "Statement by the President in Address to the Nation," White House Archives, September 11, 2001, https://georgewbush-whitehouse.archives.gov/news/releases/2001/09/20010911-16.html.

And that's exactly what I did. As my dad's train pulled into the station, he stepped out, covered in white ash, and was greeted with hugs and a warm New Jersey pizza. I glanced around at cars in the commuter parking lot, cars whose owners were not coming home. I spent the night curled up on his lap, watching the news.

The attack sent me and the nation into shock. But while we were in shock, America was writing a story about that day. It was deciding what information was important. It was casting blame on villains and identifying its heroes.

The story crafted by Bush put me at ease in the moment, as intended. But his words also sent my future husband to war.[11]

STORIES SHAPE NARRATIVES, AND NARRATIVE SHAPE THOUGHT

The power of storytelling should not be surprising to a journalist—or the daughter of an Irishman. My father likes to tell a lot of stories again and again, a proud holdover from a man who did not need to kiss the Blarney stone to earn the gift of gab. I became a writer because I had stories to tell but couldn't get a word in, so I had to write mine down. In my family, my dad's well-worn tales are expected. His 9/11 story is one he tells annually, one way he ensures our family will never forget.

I have told his story too, through the lens of my experience—the same story I told Bush. Both my Bush interaction and the story I told him are peripheral to my dad's first-hand account of September 11. He was the one who saw bodies when he looked out of his office window. I didn't. His life flashed before his eyes, not mine. And his story can certainly stand on its own. Mine can't. My story is what is known as a complementary

---

[11] Jennifer Barnhill, "My Dinner with President Bush," *The Bush Institute*, February 28, 2024, https://www.bushcenter.org/publications/my-dinner-with-president-bush.

narrative. It doesn't replace his story, and it would not exist without his experience.

Because my dad loves me and understands how hard I worked to be afforded the opportunity to interact with Bush, he may mention my dinner with Bush when he talks about 9/11. If my dad was with a group of people who hated the former president, adding my story to his 9/11 story may provoke the group. He may decide not to tell it to keep the peace. If he is in a group of people who know me and are fans of Bush, he may share a version of his story that includes my interaction. Or he may simply tell the story that includes me to broaden the listener's understanding of that day and how it impacted his entire family, not just him.

With each choice he makes when telling his 9/11 story, he subconsciously assigns value to different facets of the story based on their connection to listeners. This is just one way that we approach personal storytelling. We subconsciously decide which stories are worth telling, and tell different versions of the same story in order to find common ground with audiences.

The same thing happens at a national level. These stories are our public narratives.

NARRATIVE 101

When we think about the word "narrative," we may think about dialogue in a play or an introduction in a written story. Narratives can be big or small. They can be personal or collective. Narratives are the stories we tell ourselves, as individuals or collectively—in the messages our culture produces in media (social and traditional news), public speeches, and popular culture. Our individual narratives shape how we see the world and can be boiled down to two questions: Who am I? How do I fit?

Whether they know it or not, human beings are really good at observing narratives. We are biologically wired to find patterns. We look at a group and try to make sense of it. We ask ourselves: *Who is the majority? Minority? Who is the most successful?* This instinct to categorize has helped us take a glance at a new scenario and assess our risk. If grouping and sorting is our instant reaction to new scenarios, storytelling is what we do to tell ourselves about the categories we have made.

We ask ourselves, *Am I someone who operates with integrity?* If so, when we find ourselves faced with the option to not pay for every item in the grocery store self-checkout, we may tell ourselves, *This is not like me.* If we don't measure up to our own standards, we may feel bad about ourselves. The discovery of accidentally stealing an item that was left in the bottom of our cart may make us question our values. We may choose to go back to the store to return or pay for the "stolen" item. If we don't feel like going back, we may tell ourselves another story: *I usually pay for things, and the price of goods has gone up. The store won't miss the item.* We constantly tell ourselves stories to help us make sense of the world around us.

If I see myself as creative, I may only pursue employment that allows me to flex my creative muscles. If I have to take a job for financial reasons, I may feel as though I've "sold out." If I experienced trauma and see myself as unlovable, then an unusually brief text message can be devastating; what the sender intended to be a quick message could be misinterpreted as confirmation that they really don't like me after all.

The stories we tell ourselves have a powerful impact on how we show up in this world.

Narratives begin as the stories we tell ourselves to influence and justify our actions. When enough people tell themselves the same story, narrative is used to influence and justify how society behaves.

HOW THE MILTIARY IS USED TO SHAPE NATIONAL NARRATIVES

Unlike other academic fields of study, the study of narrative is not hidden away in a classroom; it is accessible to everyone. We can simply step back and observe cultural messages that make up our dominant narratives. These are the messages that are printed in newspapers and repeated by leaders. If we listen carefully, we can watch how narratives are used to justify a wide range of agendas.

Type of Narrative	*Definition*	*Characteristics*	*Military Examples*	*Cultural Examples*
Dominant Narrative	Widely accepted storyline or perspective within a society or community	Mainstream acceptance, often reflects perspectives of those in power (shapes societal norms and beliefs)	The post–World War II narrative in U.S. emphasized economic prosperity, American dream, often downplaying dissenting perspectives	Taylor Swift is one of the most successful music artists of all time
Counter-narrative	Alternative or opposing storyline, challenges dominant narrative	Challenges established beliefs/norms, offers diverse perspectives (seeks to empower marginalized voices)	Civil rights movements in 1960s challenged dominant narrative of racial superiority	Taylor Swift and her cats are trying to brainwash young voters
Available Narrative	Storyline or perspective easily accessible and widely known	Readily available through various mediums, often aligns with dominant narrative, found in mainstream media/ educational materials	Widely accessible narrative of founding of America, often presented in historical textbooks, emphasized how British rule led to the American Revolution	Taylor Swift sings about female empowerment because of experiences in male-dominated industry
Unavailable Narrative	Storyline or perspective not easily	May be suppressed/ overlooked, often related to	Indigenous perspectives on colonization and impact might be	What does Taylor Swift really think? Unavailable

	accessible or widely known	marginalized voices, limited visibility in mainstream media	marginalized or overlooked in mainstream historical accounts	narrative, unless she decides to disclose
Personal Narrative	Individual's unique storytelling reflects personal experiences and perspectives	Subjective, based on personal experiences, varied and diverse, may contribute to counter-narratives or challenge mainstream views	Stories are as varied as the population, some veterans are proud of their service, others resent it	My daughter loves Taylor Swift because when she sings her songs, it inspires her to know if she works hard she can be a singer too
Settled Narrative	Narrative that is widely accepted, stable, and has become ingrained in societal understand-ing	Established and widely acknowledged, often associated with historical or cultural consensus, may contribute to a sense of stability and shared identity	America's participation in WWII was justified to stop Hitler and end the Holocaust	Taylor Swift is a successful musician and entertainer
Unsettled Narrative	Narrative that is in flux, contested, or undergoing reinterpretatio n	Subject to ongoing debate or revision, challenges existing norms and interpretations, reflects evolving perspectives and societal changes	Many question the legitimacy of U.S. involvement in Vietnam, long-term impacts of war, including PTSD, lasting health effects from Agent Orange, and the treatment of veterans	Taylor Swift wants to obtain power/status far beyond the music industry (while she may have this influence, her motivations are mostly unknown)

When a dominant narrative is commonly believed because a majority feels it fits with their personal narratives, it is seen as settled. The majority of the world agrees that the Earth is spherical. This is a settled narrative. Settled narratives are rarely contested.

If someone questions a settled or dominant narrative, they risk being called crazy. Flat-earthers are seen as conspiracy theorists, not people with a different view on the world. While the flat earth theory can be scientifically disproven, there are other settled narratives that are not as fact-based.

My own 9/11 experience offers an example. Bush offered stability to me and the nation when he spoke to the American public with resolve. He called out the enemy and outlined how America and its military were going to respond. He presented the country with a story, identifying the good guys (America) and the bad guys (those who wished us harm), and cast a vision for how we would move forward as a nation after this attack.

Listening to his words on my drive home shaped my 9/11 narrative. Our military was brave. Our leaders were decisive. Americans were justifiably enraged. We would not sleep until justice rained down on the perpetrators.

9/11 also produced positive narratives. New Yorkers smiled at each other. First responders across the nation were treated to free meals. Americans banded together in a touching show of national unity. I told myself that my dad was alive, and I would never allow myself to forget what nearly happened to him that day.

But while Bush's words offered me hope, they also sparked a new national narrative.

This narrative told us we were fighting "terrorists" in a Global War on Terror (GWOT). This pursuit was not limited to those directly responsible for the attacks, Osama Bin Laden and his network. Instead, anyone who threatened America could be a future enemy. This narrative allowed the government to not only go after the immediate perpetrators but also anyone who may act similarly in the future. Whether intentional or not, this narrative gave the government justification to make unilateral decisions about the nation's safety, significantly increasing the power and role of the Executive Branch while reducing individual freedoms in the name of corporate safety.[12]

---

[12] Madeleine Carlisle, "How 9/11 Radically Expanded the Power of the U.S. Government," *TIME*, September 11, 2021, https://time.com/6096903/september-11-legal-history.

Anyone who questioned these sweeping changes was considered anti-American and soft in the face of terror. Those who questioned this dominant narrative, that all actions taken against terrorists were justified, were treated like flat-earthers and conspiracy theorists.

And this narrative ruled for years. When the conversation turned to weapons of mass destruction (WMD) and the 2003 invasion of Iraq, only a few congresspeople objected. According to author and researcher Robert Krebs, who wrote a book about the role American presidents play in shaping the national security narrative, "Once the War on Terror had become well-established, numerous projects were legitimated in its name but few questioned the war itself, as opposed to how it might be waged."[13] To go against the dominant narrative and question this decision was political suicide, so instead of trying to fight the GWOT narrative, politicians debated *how* to fight, not *if* it needed to be fought in the first place.

Immediately following 9/11, we heard about the Taliban and the GWOT on the nightly news. It was discussed in Congress and around the dinner table. The nation talked about military action because 9/11 brought the military to the forefront of everyone's minds. The attacks on 9/11 united the nation, but they also made us fearful. If anyone could board a plane and kill thousands of civilians, would anyone be safe again? We were unsettled and looked to the military and our leaders to help us understand our new reality.

However, as the GWOT dragged on, the American public became less and less familiar with the military. This was about the same time I met my husband and learned about how my dad's experience affected the before faceless soldiers, sailors, marines, and airmen who were tasked with protecting our nation. While America was growing disillusioned with the GWOT, I was given access to a population that was on the front lines. While the patriotic feeling Americans had after being attacked dissipated

---

[13] Ronald R. Krebs, *Narrative and the Making of US National Security* (Cambridge: Cambridge University Press, 2015), 43.

for civilians, for those in the military community, it had become part of our identity.

The nation experienced 9/11 together but the aftermath drove us apart.

By the 2008 election, 63 percent of Americans cited the economy as the most important issue facing the country, with only 10 percent mentioning the war.[14] America had slowly stopped including the military in our national narrative. Americans felt safe at home. The war was far away. The nation told itself it no longer needed the military. While America had moved on from 9/11, the military was still fighting a war that no one wanted to hear about.

RECLAIMING THE MILITARY NARRATIVE

9/11 is just one example of how our nation has used the military to justify political agendas. When it suits the national narrative, the DoD and individual service members are cast as either death dealers or patriotic Americans. During Vietnam, the DoD was seen as "the man" and individual service members were labeled "baby killers."

Following 9/11, service members were seen as a heroic shield of protection. When the nation learned the DoD fought the GWOT based on nonexistent WMD, DoD leaders were not blamed for acting on bad intelligence. Blame was laid at the feet of politicians and intelligence agencies.

Although how America saw service members during Vietnam and the GWOT varied, the dubious justification for war was the same: America entered a war based on a politically outlined premise, service members

---

[14] Carroll Doherty and Jocelyn Kiley, "A Look Back at How Fear and False Beliefs Bolstered U.S. Public Support for War in Iraq," *Pew Research Center*, March 14, 2023, https://www.pewresearch.org/politics/2023/03/14/a-look-back-at-how-fear-and-false-beliefs-bolstered-u-s-public-support-for-war-in-iraq/

found out that premise was unjustified, they told leaders, but politicians did not end the conflict based on DoD intelligence.

Vietnam and the GWOT show how easily the national narrative can turn on military personnel. This happens because, unlike the rest of the nation, the military rarely fights back. They do not interfere with the national narrative for two main reasons. First, individual military service members and families have been told not to tell their stories to the American public. Second, on a larger scale, the military institution is supposed to be apolitical, and with good reason. A partisan military is a dangerous military.

However, the absence of authentic military stories told by service members has left a gap in our national narrative that has been filled by stories told *about* service members by politicians and a handful of high-level military leaders. While these stories present a grain of truth, they are carefully curated versions of reality. The presented reality often serves specific political agendas, agendas that the American public deserves to understand.

WHO IS IN OUR STORIES?

For a long time, I suspected that the American population did not have access to real military experiences. As a freelance researcher and reporter, I wanted to collect data to see if my suspicion was justified.

I started by reviewing the newsletters of the top three military news outlets, *Military.com*, *Military Times*, and *Stars and Stripes*. The newsletters captured a sampling of military news stories the papers deemed to be the most important, designed to educate readers.

I reviewed a total of 158 articles spanning four days of news spread out over a two-week period. I read each article and noted whose words were quoted, specifically appearing inside quotation marks. I noted if they were a service member, military family member, civilian expert, or bystander to the event or topic being covered.[15] Stories were also labeled with categories based on their themes, including war or threat of war, military action, policy, people, and miscellaneous. I also noted the gender of the individuals who were quoted and the gender of the author to the best of my ability. Although not a scientific sampling, to be sure, it was a starting point.

I learned the following:

- Officers were quoted more than enlisted personnel with only one out of ten military quotes being attributed to enlisted personnel. In other words, 90 percent of military statements came from voices that only represent 18 percent[16] of the population.[17]
- Only six stories featured topics covering military families, representing 3.7 percent of the stories published by military media outlets, far from being representative of the overall military community; military families outnumber military personnel (1.4 to one).[18]

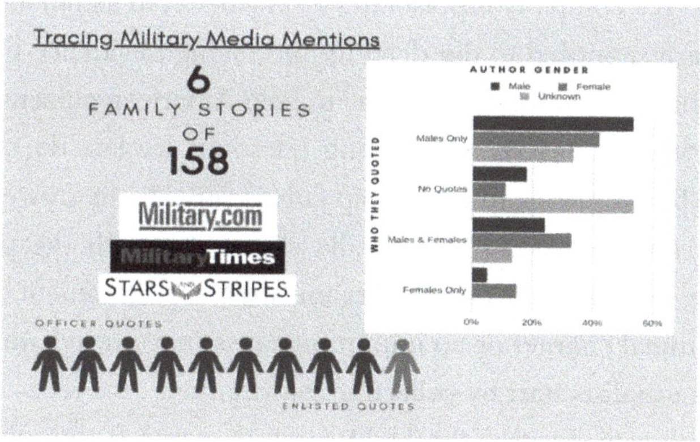

[15] Methodology Note: Some individuals were coded in multiple categories (e.g., veteran and expert). Only quoted sources were counted. Coding included role, presenting gender, and rank; gender was verified when possible, and left unnoted if uncertain.

[16] U.S. Naval Institute Staff, "Department of Defense 2022 Demographic Profile," *USNI News*, November 29, 2023, https://news.usni.org/2023/11/29/department-of-defense-2022-demographic-profile.

[17] Likely because military public affairs personnel are officers.

[18] "The Demographics of Military Children and Families," *Institute for Veterans and Military Families, Syracuse University*, Accessed: August 25, 2025, https://ivmf.syracuse.edu/article/the-demographics-of-military-children-and-families/

My research[19] confirmed what I already knew. Not only were military spouses and children not in the narrative, but service members weren't either. The messages coming out of the Pentagon were not telling the whole story. Instead, they were part of a carefully curated narrative.

IS IT THE MEDIA'S FAULT?

Clickbait is real, and headlines help media outlets sell ad space. These are the sad facts of the industry in which I work. People click on stories about Taylor Swift or Donald Trump because they draw large audiences. Period. The military doesn't draw clicks because the military doesn't have as broad an audience.

When I went to school to study journalism, I was told of the important role I would play. While there were reporters who covered sex scandals and car crashes, the lure of the profession was acting as the country's watchdogs. If a company is poisoning local citizens in its pursuit of profits, reporters are supposed to dig deep to find enough evidence to break the story and bring attention to the topic to help American citizens.

Reporters are tasked with asking questions leaders do not want to answer. When someone in leadership fails to provide an answer or gives a less-than-truthful response, the media shares this with the public. The public may choose to boycott the organization; a government official may pursue criminal charges or an important cause may receive much-needed support. Journalists start by collecting information.

Like other businesses, the DoD carefully controls the information it releases. Information is shared via press briefings or memos by senior leaders. Like civilian media outlets, the DoD releases updates to policies, accident reports, and feel-good news stories. However, unlike the press,

---

19 Reporters' gender influenced source gender: women quoted both men and women, while men largely quoted men, consistent with the Who Makes the News Global Media Monitoring Project (https://whomakesthenews.org/). Beat assignments, however, often dictate source availability and limit source diversity.

which has to present all sides of a story to maintain credibility, the DoD's storytelling is more public relations than a dissemination of facts. If a public official doesn't do his or her job, they can be voted out. If a for-profit company doesn't make a profit, it will go out of business. If the military fails, it doesn't have to close shop. The military PR machine toes a careful line, sharing just enough information to retain the freedom to operate without additional oversight.

Military reporters certainly do push—they ask hard questions of the DoD and submit Freedom of Information Act (FOIA) requests—but are often left with whatever information the DoD chooses to release. Like the DoD, the media performs a duty essential to our democracy. But unlike the DoD, the media industry doesn't have an unlimited budget. It doesn't have the resources to conduct investigative work about every topic that is newsworthy. Local newspapers are shutting their doors daily. Even the Pentagon-funded *Stars and Stripes*' budget is routinely threatened.

In military media, there are only a few outlets and a limited number of reporters. This results in gaps in storytelling. With the emergence of new storytelling methods that utilize social media, there is hope that more individual stories will find their way into the public narrative.

However, service members are often fearful of speaking to the press, not knowing how official restrictions against speaking on behalf of the military may apply to their circumstances. Individuals who live in unsafe military housing conditions may worry that speaking to reporters could negatively impact their careers. Because they live in military housing, their private lives blur with their professional lives. Is telling a reporter about the mold in their child's room a personal story or a violation of their oath to not speak on behalf of the military? This perception makes collecting authentic military stories difficult. The more difficult it is to collect the story, the more time and resources it takes and the more likely it is that the story will be left out of the narrative.

If military service members and families are not represented in the stories told about them, then whose military stories are we hearing? And if we, as American citizens, only receive a highly sanitized version of military life because there are not enough reporters, is the American public really informed about how their tax dollars are being spent? If Americans know nothing of the military lifestyle, they may believe whatever someone in power tells them about it.

HOW ONE PERSON CAN RECLAIM A NARRATIVE

"If I look at the mass, I will never act. If I look at the one, I will."
—Mother Teresa

Dominant narratives are protected by institutions because they stand to legitimize a particular policy, idea, or action. But dominant narratives can change.

"I'm interested in how a narrative switches," Dr. Amy Shuman told me during a phone interview. Dr. Shuman is a retired professor who studied narrative while working in the English department of the Ohio State University. She had been working on a research project that examined how narratives evolve and was asked to speak to a group of teen parents.

"Until then, these teen parents were called 'unwed mothers,'" she said. "We're switching our understanding of them from a concern about whether they're married or not to an age-based concern." The term "unwed mother" intentionally held a negative connotation, Dr. Shuman noted. This negative connotation, however, did not fit all unmarried women who had babies, specifically unwed women in their forties who wanted to become pregnant. Those who used the term rarely called these middle-aged women unwed mothers. These women in their forties forced a split in the narrative. They were unwed mothers but did not fit the narrative of teen parents.

"I went and met with these girls; they were all girls. There were no boys there, even though they're called teen parents," said Dr. Shuman. "I asked the question, which I often asked when I met with groups. I said, 'What's the story?' And they immediately said, 'It's not what you think,'" Dr. Shuman recalled. "I love it when people tell me that. If they say, 'It's not what you think,' there's a narrative that's circulating about them that doesn't fit them. And they're looking for the narrative that does."

The dominant narrative surrounding unwed mothers, who were later referred to as "teen parents," focused on the negative. They were called "unwed mothers" and "teen parents" to shame these girls and women in the hope that they would discourage others from following in their footsteps. According to Dr. Shuman, the stories they often told themselves were: "I'm not going to graduate high school," "My boyfriend is going to leave me," and "I can't go to the prom."

Instead, when Dr. Shuman asked them, "What's your story?" they began to paint a new narrative, saying: "I'm going to graduate high school," "My parents are helping me," "I'm still going to be successful," and "My boyfriend and I are going to stay together."

The narrative shifted from a focus on unwed mothers to teen parents, and these teens wanted to reclaim their narrative. So they did, starting with the messages they told themselves.

When the stories being told about our nation, our community, or ourselves no longer fit, we have the power to change them. And it starts with the stories we tell ourselves.

Like the unwed mother versus teen parent narrative change, the military community is at a crossroads: It can embrace telling better military stories, or it can continue business as usual.

REWRITING THE NARRATIVE

There is a reason our military is generally held in high regard. Many service members embody the ideals of courage, honor, and commitment. Their stories and experiences make the military look good. But inevitably not all military personnel, programs, and stories are good. So the institution, out of fear, minimizes the hard stories. Understandably, it wants to avoid budget cuts, appear strong to adversaries, and maintain a positive public opinion. But in reducing the number and type of stories it tells, the military undervalues and dehumanizes the very people who enable it to function.

Telling diverse and layered military stories threatens the dominant narrative because diverse stories give the public access to the good and the bad.

This book seeks to help the military and civilian communities examine the military stories they have been told by encouraging them to seek out stories that add additional context to the military experience:

Military Stories You Are Told	*A Military Story You Need to Hear*
If the military wanted you to have a family, it would have issued you one	The military depends on military families
No Man Left Behind	POW wives changed international politics
America will not forget the families of the fallen	Military widow(er)s have to tell their stories of loss to ensure the nation keeps its promise
The military takes care of its own	Showing up for the military community requires a nationwide effort
Military families are resilient	Military resilience policies harm families
The military is woke	Military policies serve those who serve our nation
"Be All You Can Be"	Military recruitment relies on word-of-mouth marketing

You will hear about Sybil Stockdale, a housewife who demanded North Vietnamese leaders treat her husband and his fellow POWs safely;

Mouza Zumwalt, a foreign-born military spouse whose experiences influenced how the Navy supported minority populations; Edie Smith, a lady in a yellow hat who walked the halls of Congress for decades, until her friends received their loved ones' military death benefits; Mary Monrose, who was in the right place at the right time to help raise awareness when military families in Hawaii found toxins in their drinking water; Vanessa Ridgeway, a military spouse who demanded her son Tory be given the chance to serve in the Navy despite having autism; and many more.

I could not have imagined as I sat on that cold wooden pew that in choosing to marry my husband, I had started writing my own military narrative. I unknowingly married him *and* the military. And despite the hardships of this life, I was instantly welcomed into a tribe most Americans know next to nothing about.

Although I was a journalist, I was given access to a population that has been told not to talk to reporters and are fearful that telling their stories will harm their loved ones. I have done my best to earn and maintain their trust, helping those featured in this book feel comfortable sharing their stories with the world, while reminding them of the power of their voices. It is a responsibility and a blessing I am proud to carry.

While this book features veteran and active-duty experiences, it is the stories of those on the periphery—military spouses, children, and parents of service members—that are front and center. Their hidden stories are the military stories you *need* to hear.

A Military Story You Need to Hear

Identifying a military story you have been told versus an authentic military story requires you to identify the type of narrative you are hearing. Is it a battlefield story? A personal viewpoint? A family story? No matter the narrative, it's important to pay attention and break it down so you know if you have access to the bigger picture.

Dominant narrative: Highlighting individual service members and their families humanizes the military narrative and therefore weakens the military.

A better narrative: Humanizing the military doesn't weaken the military but reestablishes trust in the institution and gives the nation access to a population it increasingly does not understand or support.

CORPORAL FRED MCGEE: BATTLEFIELD STORY

It was Korea in June 1952. After having taken over from his wounded squad leader, Cpl. Fred McGee held off the enemy so his team, one of the first integrated Army units, could take Hill 528. Despite being shot in the face and leg, he stayed behind to carry wounded soldiers to safety. His actions earned him the Silver Star and two Purple Hearts.

When he returned home, McGee was told his efforts had earned him the Medal of Honor. He was moved when he opened a copy of *Heroic Comics* magazine and saw a cartoon highlighting his heroism atop Hill 528. It read: "528 is just another number on a military map . . . But to the men who fought and died for it, 528 was a bitter reality . . . This is a story of courageous Cpl. Fred McGee!"

But instead of seeing himself, a Black man, McGee saw that the cartoon portrayed the hero as white. And he didn't get the Medal of Honor as promised because it was the 1950s and he was Black.[20]

McGee grew up in a small home in a small town in the Ohio countryside. It was the type of town where everyone knew the good, bad, and ugly behavior of every resident, especially the young ones.

[20] The *Heroic Comics* issue, number 81, was published in 1953 and depicted a real-life adventure of Cpl. Frank McGee—except the magazine illustrators depicted him as a white man. Photo courtesy of the McGee family.

He was one of six children raised by his father after his mother died at the age of forty-seven. Despite this loss, he did not allow resentment to fester. Instead, his pain helped him focus on what really mattered, something that would become the centerpiece of his future life: family. Despite not knowing how to read or write himself, his dad encouraged his six kids to do their best, which is what McGee set out to do.

Getting drafted didn't change his outlook. He showed up to the battlefield as he showed up for life: ready to serve.

"When I was a teenager, I used to play softball in other cities near where I lived," said Robin McGee, his daughter, in a 2023 interview. "They would always tell me, 'You know, your dad's a war hero. There's a comic book about your dad.' I didn't understand at the time because my dad never mentioned it."

When the war ended, McGee was content to have earned the Silver Star and two Purple Hearts. To him, his story of military service was over, as was his fight. And that tracks—in the movies, the story often ends when the soldier steps off the battlefield because once they arrive home and take off the uniform, they are mere mortals again.

But to a military family, service members are not just a body to fill a uniform; they are the person who makes their family whole. We don't fully understand their service, but we try. We ask about these experiences, not because we are necessarily interested in battles or the inner workings of the military. We ask to hear their battlefield stories because we seek to fully understand *them*.

McGee didn't have an easy life, but he did have a positive mindset. He also had a supportive wife who saw both the good and the bad, and helped him move forward.

A HOMEFRONT STORY

"He never discussed the war. He never talked about it at all. The only thing I remember him saying was 'I don't want my boys to go to war. My boys will never go to war,'" said Cornell, McGee's wife, in a 2011 *PBS* interview.[21]

McGee and Cornell got married roughly three years after he stormed Hill 528. As was common with his generation of soldiers, neither he nor Cornell talked about his service much. It was decades before he felt comfortable enough to share stories of service with his family.

Despite not having been married while he was on active duty, Cornell was there for the aftermath. "He would wake up at night, arms flailing and hollering," Cornell told *PBS*. Although PTSD was common among those who had been in combat, it was not something that was well understood or discussed in 1950s America.

Cornell was by McGee's side through it all, trying to navigate an unfamiliar diagnosis. As a stay-at-home mom of five children, she had no formal mental health training. But her lack of training did not matter. She worked tirelessly to help her husband reacclimate to life beyond the battlefield and create a loving home for their family. Their daughter Robin said Cornell kept the family grounded, reminding them of the good even when the reality was hard.

Cornell and McGee's personalities complemented each other. They faced hard things, but always looked forward to a more positive future, so it was impressive that Cornell got him to turn around and look at his past. She lovingly encouraged him to talk more about his military experiences.

The McGees were not afraid of hard things, his past was just one more hard thing. And once he started sharing his story, he began to enjoy storytelling. He was not necessarily comfortable talking about the battle, but he loved remembering his fellow soldiers. Telling their stories was

---

[21] *Long Road Home*, directed by Rick Sebak (Pittsburgh: WQED, 2020), https://www.pbs.org/video/wqed-documentaries-long-road-home.

McGee's way of keeping his buddies alive. His family listened to his stories and learned to retell them too.

A MILITARY FAMILY STORY

"He was not going to *not* help others. That's what he does," said Robin. "That time he was on the Hill, his number was called and he had to save people's lives. He didn't think about his own life. He just thought, 'I have to do this,' and that's what he did."

"As a Black man, he was denied so many things," Robin continued. "And not a lot of Black men got the Medal of Honor. We had to talk him into it." She knew that despite McGee's pride in serving and his love for his fellow veterans, he would not feel comfortable leading a campaign to get the Medal of Honor. So his family helped him. He served because it was asked of him. But his family knew that correcting this wrong would mean a lot, not only to McGee but to other service members of color who were similarly denied military honors.

"When people who were Black and brown fought in wars before civil rights, it would have been very difficult for them to be recognized at the highest level," said Brandi Jones, his granddaughter, who is a military spouse just like her mother before her and her grandmother before her.

The Medal of Honor is the highest level of military honor. This honor comes with benefits—a monthly pension and special retirement pay—and honors that the nation was not yet comfortable bestowing upon Black soldiers. Today, historians, advocates, and families like the McGees have led the charge to write Black service members back into the history books.[22] This systemic racism impacted McGee's life, but it did not change his actions. When he told his story to his family, he did not gripe or complain. He just told it.

---

[22] "Honor Deferred: Black Veterans and the Medal of Honor," *The National WWII Museum*, February 1, 2023, https://www.nationalww2museum.org/war/articles/honor-deferred-black-veterans-and-medal-honor.

McGee's children and grandchildren started their campaign by collecting as much evidence as they could to plead his case and prove that his actions were indeed worthy of the medal. A key piece of evidence was *Heroic Comics* issue 81, which featured his story on the cover. The 1950s was the golden age of comics, and military comic books were used as recruiting tools, featuring characters like Captain America as a means to promote patriotism.[23] As evident by the title of the magazine, *Heroic Comics* focused on showing the bravery and honor of those who were drafted to fight.

These *Heroic* men were the quintessential military service member. McGee's actions fit the bill, but his skin color did not. *Heroic Comics* was not a history book; it was designed to entertain and promote military service. Although it is impossible to know if McGee was whitewashed intentionally or accidentally, the result of making him white in the comic was the same: Promoting the actions of a white man would sell more comics and recruit more white men to join the ranks. In the 1950s, the American public was told a military story that said only white men could be military heroes. McGee's story proved that was not true.

Brandi made it her mission to tell his story to anyone who would listen. A military spouse herself, Brandi knew the importance of telling her pap's story and correcting the injustice he faced. She now does this for a living, working with a military nonprofit called Secure Families Initiative (SFI), whose mission is to help protect civil rights for all military families and to help encourage military families to engage in the political process.

"Even though this happened to my pap, he always showed his pride and love for his country," Brandi said. To his family, his story was not over; it just needed to be rewritten. In helping him rewrite it, they became part of it. Brandi's professional experience helped the McGee family tell his story at the highest levels of government.

---

[23] Eric Milzarski, "This Is Why WWII Troops Are to Thank for the Rise of Comics," *Military.com*, October 19, 2018, https://www.military.com/undertheradar/2018/10/19/why-wwii-troops-are-thank-rise-comics.html.

TAKING MILITARY STORIES BEYOND THE BATTLEFIELD

The McGee family petitioned their congressional representatives to take up his cause, reaching out to Congressman Bill Johnson of Ohio in 2019. Armed with the initial research provided by the McGee family, Johnson launched a congressional inquiry.

Tragically, McGee died in 2020. But his story did not end with his passing. Instead, Brandi and her family collected over one hundred pages of evidence of his actions, something that was required to prove his case, as those who could have confirmed his story had already died.

"At that time we were working on this, my grandfather—I remember there was a period where if he would have received the Medal of Honor, he would have been either the first or second Black man to ever receive it [while] alive," said Brandi. Despite serving in every American conflict since the Revolutionary War, only ninety-six Black service members[24] have been awarded the Medal of Honor, representing less than three percent of awardees.

After receiving the evidence presented by the McGee family, Congressman Johnson petitioned the Secretary of Defense, Lloyd Austin, for review. Secretary Austin recognized McGee's heroism in Korea and agreed he should be posthumously awarded the Medal of Honor. However, because so much time had passed, the DoD could not right this wrong on its own. McGee's nomination also needed congressional approval—which it received when it was included in the 2023 National Defense Authorization Act.[25] All that was left was a presidential signature, which the McGee family got just days before President Biden left office.

---

[24] As of January 2025, only ninety-six Black service members have received this honor. "List of African-American Medal of Honor Recipients," *Wikipedia*, last modified January 2025, https://en.wikipedia.org/wiki/List_of_African-American_Medal_of_Honor_recipients.
[25] H.R. 7776, 117th Cong. (2022), https://www.congress.gov/bill/117th-congress/house-bill/7776/text.

McGee was posthumously awarded the Medal of Honor on January 3, 2025, over seventy years after he earned it.[26]

"These are missing stories, and they're actually history, American history," said Brandi. "I've been sharing the story for probably ten years, wherever I would go. But in that moment, when I saw that [Secretary of Defense] letter, I felt relieved that it wasn't going to die with me." Cpl. Fred McGee has a story worth telling. His heroism on the battlefield is uncontested, even the Secretary of Defense said so. So why did his story go untold for so long? First, his status as a Black man who was an American war hero was not a story the military wanted to tell in the 1950s. Second, McGee himself did not want to relive his battlefield experiences. Third, he was a humble man who did not want to boast. He wanted to move forward, not backward.

Why did he finally decide to tell his story?

His wife's loving support helped him get through the darkest days; it was Cornell who helped him feel safe enough to tell his story, which helped him heal. At the same time, the leadership skills he learned in the military told him it was his duty to protect his fellow service members, on and off the battlefield. He decided that telling his story would encourage fellow veterans to share theirs. This emotional safety, motivation to support others, and his family's belief in him has kept his story alive all these years.

The McGee family represents three layers of military stories: a battlefield story, a spouse story, and a military family story. Their experiences are just some of the stories you need to hear to better understand what you have been told about the military.

---

[26] "7 Soldiers From Korean, Vietnam Wars Receive Medals of Honor," *U.S. Department of Defense*, August 23, 2023, https://www.defense.gov/News/News-Stories/Article/Article/4021420/7-soldiers-from-korean-vietnam-wars-receive-medals-of-honor/.

MORE MILITARY STORIES YOU NEED TO HEAR

Cpl. Fred McGee's story was powerful, but like other valuable stories it went untold for years because it was not yet seen as worthy. Because there will always be stories that someone doesn't want told.

The military stories we are told begin as a diverse collection of personal experiences, but are filtered along the way by politicians, media, and the DoD who reshare stories they want to promote and minimize those they do not. The curated military stories that reach the public are often set on the battlefield, because war is the business of the military. Versions of these stories are retold in movies, in the news, and in statements put out by the DoD. And despite being incomplete, Americans consume these curated tales.

My son, like other eight-year-old boys with military fathers, is currently obsessed with all things related to World War II. On his birthday, he lined up all his trucks flush with his area rug to form a line in preparation for battle. Using his wooden IKEA table and chair, he positioned the German bunkers on high ground. Invisible wires led from the enemy bunker to obstacles sprinkled across what he told me was Omaha Beach, the site of a particularly hard-fought American battle during the D-Day invasion of Normandy. There is something about battlefield stories that fascinates my young son, and kids of all ages. To risk one's life in support of one's country and a cause that is bigger than oneself is powerful.

As a young girl, I wasn't drawn to battlefield stories. Although my dad drilled in the dates of the bombing of Pearl Harbor (December 7, 1941) and the D-Day invasion (June 6, 1944), I didn't relate to the stories the way my son does. I could recognize the importance of military service, but I was not drawn to hearing stories of combat. I simply could not see myself in battlefield stories, and I had not been given access to stories I could relate to.

My son is fascinated with the battlefield because it is so foreign to his lived experience. In his reenactments, death is sanitized—no blood, no gore, just *rat-tat-tat* and *pew pew pew* until an action figure falls to the floor. He has not seen war movies that paint a more realistic image of the cost of war. For him, it is fantasy, a cool heroism to which he wants to aspire. By the time he is old enough to understand, perhaps he will no longer hold the battlefield in such high regard.

The mystery of the battlefield is powerful. We see it as a test of strength and courage. Some, like McGee, rise to the occasion and perform heroically. But many do not wish to relive these moments of horror and death by telling their stories. Others are prohibited from sharing their battlefield experiences if the operation was classified. The battlefield story is alluring because it is not an accessible story.

I can't say I relate to McGee's experiences, either on the battlefield or at home. I can begin to understand how it may have felt coming home, reliving his battlefield experiences, and dealing with mental health struggles. But I can't put myself in his combat boots. I can admire them, but I can't understand.

I begin to understand when Cornell enters the story, describing her best efforts to support her husband as he relived his trauma night after night. I can relate to his daughter Robin and granddaughter Brandi wanting to honor his legacy. Their shoes and stories are familiar to me, not just as a military spouse and woman, but as someone who has not served.

Most Americans will never serve in the military. They can't relate to the battlefield experience. But they can relate to supporting a loved one, making military families vital to understanding military service.

If families are essential to service members and their stories are more accessible to the average American, why do we only hear battlefield stories?

The easy answer is families are not part of the DoD. They did not swear an allegiance to serve or to keep silent.

The reality is, in our military community, there is a hidden all-volunteer force: military families. We, like Cornell, Robin, and Brandi, are essential to our service members, but for many reasons we are left out of the collective military narrative. How and why did this happen?

FAMILIES POSE AN EXCEPTIONAL PROBLEM

I first met Michelle Norman over the phone in 2019, the year she was awarded the title of Armed Forces Insurance Navy Spouse of the Year. I was interviewing her for an article I was writing about the military's Exceptional Family Member Program (EFMP). EFMP is designed to help military families with a spouse or child who has special needs be stationed in locations that can accommodate their unique medical and educational needs.

I was told I needed to talk to Michelle by a mutual friend whose child was also enrolled in EFMP. Michelle's daughter Marissa was born prematurely, resulting in twenty-one unique diagnoses that impact her learning. Certainly, the Normans had medical hurdles to overcome, but it was the public education system that posed the greatest challenge for their family. In our interviews, I learned that Marissa, a minor, had been sued by the Virginia Beach school district. I had not realized that a school district could sue a child, let alone a military child.

Over the course of a few phone calls and hours of research, I learned that the American public education system is underfunded and, as a result, it underserves American children. It is not a system that was built with the mobility of military families in mind.

When a child with a learning or developmental disability is in need of specialized instruction or services covered under the Individuals with Disabilities Education Act (IDEA), that child's caregivers work with educators to formulate a plan called an Individualized Education Program (IEP). These plans are legally required to be customized to the individual needs of the student. This process requires teachers to monitor students and schools and doctors to conduct evaluations to assess a student's eligibility. This process can take months, eating into a significant chunk of the child's academic year. If the caregivers don't agree with the plan the school puts in place to support the student, they must pursue legal action to force a school to make adjustments.

The trouble is that military families have to restart this process every two to three years—every time they move to fulfill military responsibilities. Their kids feel these delays, and families often do not have the will to fight it out in court.

By the time I met the Normans, they were in the middle of a contentious battle with their daughter's school district. Instead of giving up and taking what they got from the district, the Normans pushed back, both for their daughter and for the other military families who could not afford the fight. The Normans filed for due process, not because they wanted to make a stink, but because this is the only avenue open to parents with a child needing special education services.

Michelle, along with three other military mothers of children enrolled in special education, founded an organization called Partners in Protecting the Rights of Military Children in Education (PiP) with the goal of raising awareness about what military special education families face. A few months after forming PiP, Michelle was asked to testify before Congress about her experiences with EFMP—and she was not alone.

On February 5, 2020, she appeared beside Austin Carrigg, another military mother with a child with multiple medical diagnoses. Austin also founded a nonprofit within months of her testimony, Exceptional Families of the Military (EFM).

Austin's adopted daughter, Melanie, was born with Down syndrome and a congenital heart defect that would land her in the hospital just three days after she joined their family. Melanie had open-heart surgery at just eight weeks old. Austin and her husband hoped the military's health insurance, TRICARE, would help make one thing in their life more manageable—not easy, but not hard. This didn't happen. Instead of finding an easy button, the Carriggs hit brick wall after brick wall.[27]

While their daughter was in the hospital, Austin's husband was told it was time to move to a new duty station across the country—or voluntarily separate from the Army. At a time when they should have been caring for their daughter, they were fighting the duty assignment process, asking if Austin's husband could serve his country in a location that had the medical support his family needed.

This would not be the only time the military would try to send the Carriggs to a duty station that did not have the medical care Melanie needed. Because they relocated during the COVID-19 pandemic, they did not get specialty referrals in their new location for six months. This disruption of care resulted in Melanie suffering a catastrophic stroke that nearly took her life and left the entire right side of her body paralyzed.

Both Michelle and Austin didn't want other families to have to fight alone, so they founded PiP and EFM to give families a voice. PiP focused on special education and EFM focused on helping military families access medical care.

What struck me during my early interviews with Michelle and Austin was how many layers of hardship EFMP families face. They fight school districts to ensure their kids are properly supported. They fight the military to ensure they are stationed in locations that have the medical resources to support their needs. They have to fight TRICARE, the military medical insurance program, to get referrals, authorizations, and reimbursements.

Why did these busy mothers of children with high needs feel compelled to form nonprofits with all that they already had on their plates?

This community was so tired of fighting their individual battles that no one was telling their story. When presented with the opportunity to share

---

[27] Austin Carrigg's Testimony Before the Subcommittee on Military Personnel: "The Exceptional Family Member Program: Are the Military Services Really Taking Care of Family Members?" 116th Cong., 2nd sess., February 5, 2020, https://docs.house.gov/meetings/AS/AS02/20200205/110469/HHRG-116-AS02-Wstate-CarriggA-20200205.pdf.

their experiences, Michelle and Austin seized the chance to tell not just their own stories, but to elevate the stories of their community. And those stories opened the door for change.

Despite not having a child in special education or in EFMP, I was moved by all they had been through. I am a military mother who has lived through deployment separations and dealt with military insurance. None of what I experienced was easy, but it wasn't anything compared to EFMP parents.

So I did what no journalist should ever do. I got involved. I joined PiP in February 2020 to help them create a communications strategy and make the experiences of military children in special education more accessible. I shared the lessons I had learned while interviewing and reporting on military Gold Star Families, those who lost a loved one in the line of duty. I later became PiP's lead researcher and helped institute an annual survey, partnering with the Ohio State University, that helped add context and scope to the stories we were sharing.

We got good at telling these stories, and within three years saw federal legislation from the DoD, Congress, and the Department of Education (ED), all aimed at tackling the problems PiP and EFM highlighted. Our PiP data was cited by the White House.[28] Our government and military community were finally starting to pay attention to military families with special needs.

Like any "overnight success," change was gradual, then sudden.[29] This is exactly what happened with the EFMP narrative.

EFMP hadn't made national news headlines for decades, despite being established in 1979. Media mentions jumped in 2016, after the government asked military families to provide input via the Federal

---

[28] "Strengthening America's Military Families," The White House, September 2021, https://bidenwhitehouse.archives.gov/wp-content/uploads/2021/09/Strengthening_Americas_Military_Families.pdf.

[29] The idea of slow then sudden change was first introduced to me by my pastor, Mark Batterson, of National Community Church.

Mark Batterson, "Gradually, Then Suddenly," *National Community Church Audio Podcast*, January 7, 2024, https://podcasts.apple.com/us/podcast/national-community-church-audio-podcast/id80219293?i=1000641072582.

Register, the official government site that tracks agencies and regulations, about how it could improve the program. Although family voices found their way into the narrative, they were not unified until 2020, when the nonprofits founded by Michelle and Austin, PiP and EFM, were formed. These organizations were formed for different reasons, but they found success because telling stories forms new communities.

The stories were clear and backed with data: Families wanted change, and they wanted it *yesterday*. Although individual families had been asking for help for decades, they were not heard until their collective voices were too loud to be ignored.

I had confirmed my suspicion about how change happens within the military: *tell stories, bring data.*

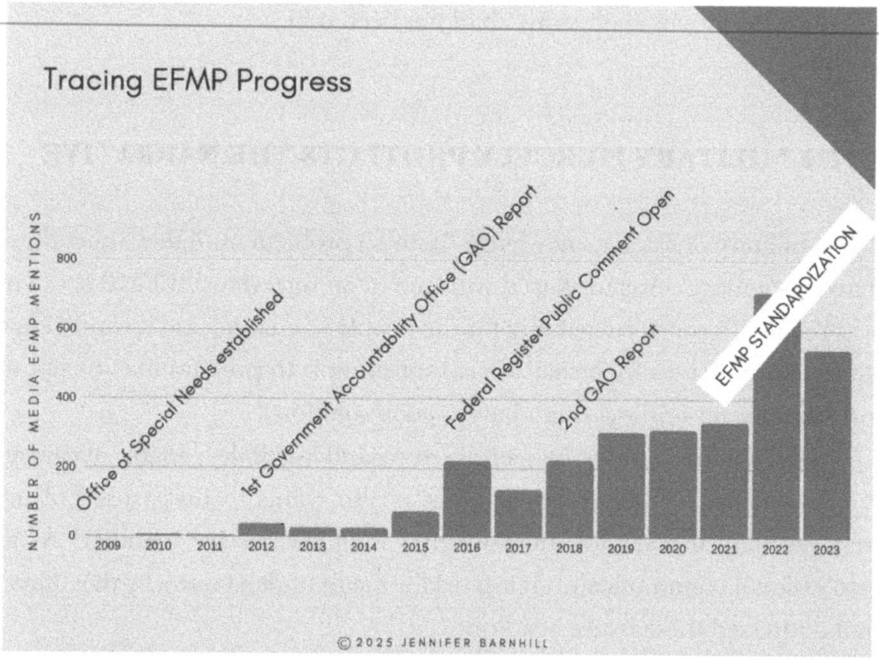

In 2023, I wanted to quantify this storytelling strategy. EFMP advocates helped me piece together a timeline. I looked at key moments in the program and compared them to the number of times EFMP was mentioned in Google news stories each year (see chart on previous page). It is far from proper research, but it did reveal an imperfect pattern.

The more military families told their story, the more often the public heard it. Obviously, that's how storytelling works. But it was groundbreaking for a group of people whose stories had been ignored for decades.

Before PiP and EFM began their work, EFMP families were routinely gaslighted. The Normans and Carriggs were just individual families, and the issues they faced were seen as such. They were made to feel that their problems were something that should be expected as a byproduct of the life of special needs parents. However, data showed that the military programs and benefits designed to help families actually made their lives *harder*, not easier.

And this is why their stories had not been told.

THE MILITARY FIERCELY PROTECTS THE NARRATIVE

"The military doesn't acknowledge there's a problem until they think they have a solution," Austin shared with me in an interview. "EFMP is often so broken, it's so overwhelming for the people in charge, and it would cost so much money to fix it that the easiest thing is to pretend like it's not a problem because [they] don't have a good solution."

The military wants to be seen as strong and infallible, capable of caring for its people, including families, but it also wants to divest itself of its responsibility to care for anyone other than the service member. As a professional communicator, it is hard for me to understand why they have not addressed these issues head-on.

- EFMP family stories are objectively compelling: Why would a school sue a child?
- EFMP family solutions are reasonable: Standardize EFMP across

service branches and provide legal support for families.

The Normans' story and the story of the transformation of the story of the transformation of this program could easily make the military look bad. Why would the DoD not try to help this population sooner? The hardships faced by military special education students and families are made harder because of the military lifestyle.

Families were not asking the DoD to wave a wand and fix the entirety of special education; they just wanted to be able to go into an EFMP office and get the same quality service from one location to the next. The DoD knew the program was flawed for decades, but only made improvements when it was mandated to do so after families brought their concerns to Congress.

It is easy to say that the DoD is tasked with fighting and winning wars, not worrying about the problems of military family members.

But if programming exists, why would the military not work with EFMP families to identify weaknesses in a program? It could easily say it can't change federal law because it can't. It could easily say it didn't have the funding to improve the program because it doesn't. But instead of sharing these and other honest realities, the DoD avoided the conversation altogether.

Because the DoD can't control the military family narrative, it attempts to minimize the scale of military families' concerns by casting them as squeaky wheels when expressing frustration or concern. The reality is military families like the Normans and Carriggs are not squeaky wheels, they are whistleblowers trying to correct a military program that isn't working. Telling their stories was key.

WHY AMERICANS NEED TO HEAR THESE STORIES

The United States military is the most powerful in the world, spending nearly $850 billion in 2024, which represented 12 percent of all federal spending and over 50 percent of all discretionary spending. The military has an international presence in roughly eighty countries around the world, wielding incalculable influence.

This is one reason many service members run for Congress after leaving the military. They have had a peek behind the curtain and unique boots-on-the-ground insights into how military budgets are distributed and orders are followed. Alarmingly, this representation has been on the decline since the formation of the All-Volunteer Force.[30]

Americans deserve to understand how Congress and the DoD are spending taxpayer dollars. Reading a story about the military budget doesn't tell the public if that money has been well-spent, just that it has been spent. If those who are on the front lines of this fighting force cannot use their voices and Congress is increasingly unfamiliar with military service, this power could be abused.

But in a digital age, narratives can be changed by individuals without money or political power.

According to researcher Robert Krebs, a dominant narrative can be replaced if those who are guarding it find themselves in any of the following situations:

- *Leaders can't "read the room" and tell themselves the narrative is settled when it's not.* ("People only serve in the military because they want to serve their country." Reality: There are many reasons people serve.)
- *Leaders aren't in a position to solve the problem being discussed.* ("If we ask the public about a program we can't fix, like EFMP, we will look

---

[30] Drew DeSilver, "New Congress Will Have a Few More Veterans, but Their Share of Lawmakers Is Still Near a Record Low," *Pew Research Center*, December 7, 2022, https://www.pewresearch.org/short-reads/2022/12/07/new-congress-will-have-a-few-more-veterans-but-their-share-of-lawmakers-is-still-near-a-record-low/.

bad." Reality: EFMP already looks bad.)

- *The story they want to tell is too hard to "sell."* ("Military service is inherently hard; nothing we can do will make that palatable." Reality: While partially true, not trying to improve broken systems is a waste of taxpayer dollars.)
- *They don't wish to engage or interact with the public, so they are seen as distant and irrelevant.* ("We are above engaging in public discourse." Reality: No public institution is above public accountability.)[31]

In recent years, the DoD has lost the support and trust of the American public[32] and the military community[33], partially because it has not been able to keep up with the way human beings communicate. It sends out press releases only after they have slowly passed through the chain of command. Its messages are crafted by senior leaders who are tacticians, not public relations or communications experts.

The door is open for new and better stories that go far beyond the battlefield.

HOW MILITARY FAMILIES CAN SHAPE THE NARRATIVE

Today, not all heroes have to storm beachheads; some fight cyber wars.[34] The battles my son recreates from his bedroom floor are becoming all the more mythological as warfare changes. No matter what war looks like,

---

[31] Ronald R. Krebs, *Narrative and the Making of U.S. National Security* (Cambridge: Cambridge University Press, 2015), 66–67.

[32] Mohamed Younis, "Confidence in U.S. Military Lowest in Over Two Decades," *Gallup News*, July 31, 2023, https://news.gallup.com/poll/509189/confidence-military-lowest-two-decades.aspx.

[33] Corie Weathers, *Military Culture Shift: The Impact of War, Money, and Generational Perspective on Morale, Retention, and Leadership* (St. Paul, MN: Elva Resa Publishing, 2023).

[34] Less than half of 1 percent of Americans have experienced combat.
Kim Parker, Ruth Igielnik, Amanda Barroso, and Anthony Cilluffo, "Deployment, Combat and Their Consequences," *Pew Research Center*, September 10, 2019, https://www.pewresearch.org/social-trends/2019/09/10/deployment-combat-and-their-consequences.

there will always be a story that takes place beyond the battlefield that the American public knows nothing about.

When Michelle and Austin told the stories of EFMP families, people took notice and positive changes occurred. While not perfect, many aspects of EFMP were improved, theoretically freeing service members from having to battle bureaucracy at home and enabling them to focus on their jobs.

The needs of military families aside, telling layered stories that include experiences of military families, friends, and agencies brings the American public into the story. It gives eight-year-olds like my son something to aspire to, and adults with no military connection a way to understand military life.

Far from weakening our military, humanizing the military stands to strengthen the bond between the American public and the military community by welcoming our neighbors into the homes of those who serve their nation. There, they will see the love spouses and children have for their service members and their desire to honor that service. They will see why generations of families choose to serve and why families who bear heavy burdens like the Normans and Carriggs fight to be able to serve rather than giving up and getting out.

When we only praise battlefield heroics but forget the home front, we strip service members of their humanity. In the following chapters, we will unpack the military stories we have been told and introduce stories the nation needs to hear, reclaiming some of that lost humanity.

Rewriting the military narrative doesn't mean we upend an institution, but present stories it can't ignore.

If the Military Wanted Service Members to Have a Family

"Corporate capitalism's historical separation between its public and private work spheres has constructed all wives' unpaid work as invisible and socially irrelevant. The military takes full advantage of this separation, treating each estranged wife as if she had never performed its institutional work, but had been rendering a mere personal service to some inconsequential man."

—Weinstein & White (1997)[35]

Erin Morris is an Army reservist and veteran who became a "dependent" in 2015. "That transition was drastic because one day I was Captain Erin Morris, lawyer," she said, and "the next day, I was Chief Stern's wife."

Erin is not alone in feeling like an outsider within her own community. "We have different last names, and you think that's not that drastic," she said. "Except I'll never forget this: I went to the vet on post because we were getting ready to move to Germany and we had a cat that had to get

[35] Christie C. White and Laurie Weinstein, *Wives and Warriors: Women in the Military in the United States and Canada* (Westport, CT: Praeger, 1997), 45–46.

a certificate. I went to the vet, and I will never forget the sign-in sheet. It said something like 'date and time of appointment, name of pet, service member name and ID expiration date.' It never once asked me for my name."

Nearly a decade has passed since Erin transitioned from a service member to a dependent and she's still processing this change of status. "I'm still mad about how horrible that felt, that I didn't even have a name on a base where just the other day I was an officer," she said.

Dominant narrative: If the military wanted you to have a family, they'd have issued you one. Military families are dependents and a burden on the military.

A better narrative: The military depends on military families. We are a military family unit.

The narrative that says military families are "dependent" on the military has been circulating since the Revolutionary War. At that time, military families were known as "camp followers" and "hangers-on."[36] Even the future president, General George Washington, had opinions about camp followers. In 1777, he wrote to Governor Jonathan Trumbull, stating that camp followers, especially those who were pregnant or had children, were a "clog upon every movement." He went as far as to recommend "getting rid of all such as are not absolutely necessary" and forbade any additional families to join their ranks.[37]

While Washington's concerns about the impact families had on military operations may have been valid in a Revolutionary War setting, modern military families have not advanced much beyond the narrative he perpetuated. These camp followers may have been the first (but not the

[36] Walter Hart Blumenthal, *Women Camp Followers of the American Revolution*, 1994 ed. (New York: Ayer Company Publishers, Inc., 1994), 48.
[37] John C. Fitzpatrick, ed., *Writings of Washington*, vol. 9 (Washington, DC: Government Printing Office, 1938), 17.

last) to observe the narrative of "If the military wanted you to have a family, it would have issued you one."[38]

The phrase first appeared in print when Marine Corps wife Mrs. Reiland of Wichita, Kansas, wrote a letter to the editor of *Time* magazine in 1956, stating, "As they told my husband, while he was on active duty: 'If the Marine Corps wanted you to have a wife, they would have issued you one.'"

Subsequent generations of leaders, service members, and military spouses have repeated the phrase, reinforcing the notion that families are a burden upon the military, not an asset. The narrative has even permeated military terminology. Military spouses and children are referred to as "dependents" on military paperwork.

Like all narratives, the idea that military families depend on the military is based on a sliver of truth. In the mid-1900s, military spouses did not look much different from their civilian counterparts. The majority lived lives as stay-at-home wives and mothers. They moved with their husbands and faced many challenges. Wives depended upon their husbands to bring home the bacon. Having a steady job that paid well made a man a more attractive partner. Women were in charge of taking care of the household, and children were expected to be seen but not heard. Military life closely aligned with those societal norms.

However, the 1970s changed many things for women, inside and outside the military community. Women were not allowed to have credit cards in their name before 1974 and couldn't access birth control outside of marriage before 1972. In the prewar 1940s, women's workforce participation was 24 percent.[39] In 1948, it went up to 32.7 percent,[40] and

---

[38] "Letters, Nov. 19, 1956," *TIME*, November 19, 1956, https://content.time.com/time/subscriber/article/0,33009,867235,00.html.
[39] "Employment of Women in War Production," *Social Security Bulletin* 5, no. 7 (July 1942): 4–5, https://www.ssa.gov/policy/docs/ssb/v5n7/v5n7p4.pdf.
[40] U.S. Bureau of Labor Statistics, *Women in the Labor Force: A Databook – Report 1092* (Washington, DC: U.S. Department of Labor, April 2021), https://www.bls.gov/opub/reports/womens-databook/2020/home.htm.

in 1970 to 43 percent.[41] In 2024, it was up to 57.6 percent.[42] Women also started contributing to their household incomes at higher rates, with women contributing 26.6 percent of total household income in 1970 to 37.5 percent in 2018.[43]

Women started joining the military too, with the rate of females on active duty increasing from just 3 percent in 1973 to roughly 15 percent in 2010.[44] The military had begun to welcome female recruits, incrementally changing gendered policies and finally opening up all jobs to women by 2016.

Military spouses also experienced these cultural shifts, and, in some cases, helped steer positive policy changes.

THE SUPREME COURT CALLS MILITARY SPOUSES "DEPENDANTS"

In December 1970, Air Force Lieutenant Sharron Frontiero filed a legal complaint against the Secretary of Defense, Elliot Richardson, a complaint that in just three years would find its way to the Supreme Court. Frontiero had petitioned the Air Force for benefits for her husband and was denied. Despite being a full-time student, her husband did not meet the Air Force criteria of what was considered a dependent.

At the time, Air Force regulations required female service members[45] to prove that their husbands were financially dependent on them for more

---

[41] "Women in the Labor Force, 1970–2009," *U.S. Bureau of Labor Statistics,* January 5, 2011, https://www.bls.gov/opub/ted/2011/ted_20110105_data.htm.
[42] "Data Deep Dive: A Decline of Women in the Workforce," *U.S. Chamber of Commerce,* June 26, 2024, https://www.uschamber.com/workforce/data-deep-dive-a-decline-of-women-in-theworkforce.
[43] U.S. Bureau of Labor Statistics, *Women in the Labor Force: A Databook* (Washington, DC: U.S. Department of Labor, 2020), table 25, "Contribution of Wives' Earnings to Family Income, 1970–2018," https://www.bls.gov/opub/reports/womens-databook/2020/home.htm.
[44] Eileen Patten and Kim Parker, "A Snapshot of Active Duty Women," *Pew Research Center,* December 22, 2011, https://www.pewresearch.org/social-trends/2011/12/22/a-snapshot-of-active-duty-women.
[45] LGBTQ+ families were not officially recognized by the DoD until 2011.

than 50 percent of their support to qualify for spousal benefits. However, the female spouses of male service members automatically received benefits without needing to provide proof. The benefits in question included an increased housing allowance that accounted for an increased number of people in a household, medical and dental benefits, and access to shop at the military commissary and exchange.

The case reached the Supreme Court, where a young Ruth Bader Ginsburg, representing the American Civil Liberties Union, argued against the policy, calling it unconstitutional gender discrimination. Ultimately, the Court ruled eight to one that the DoD had discriminated against female service members.[46]

The Frontiero case set a legal precedent that paved the way for gender equality in the U.S., with civilian women benefiting from the ruling in incalculable ways.

This ruling, while significant for American women, did not help military spouses move away from the narrative that said they were a liability to the military; it codified them as dependents. But, because the ruling and subsequent payments to all married service members were seen as a positive change, the dependent narrative was not challenged. In fact, our role as supportive members of the military was soon going to earn us presidential recognition.

POLITICIANS CALL US FAMILY

President Ronald Reagan established the first Military Spouse Day[47] on May 23, 1984, saying, "As parents and homemakers, they preserve the cornerstone of our nation's strength—the American family." This came a few years after the administration asked the services "to determine

---

[46] "Frontiero v. Richardson," *Oyez*, accessed August 25, 2025, https://www.oyez.org/cases/1972/71-1694.

[47] "Proclamation 5185—Military Spouse Day, 1984," *U.S. Statutes at Large* 98 (1984): 3583–3584, https://www.govinfo.gov/content/pkg/STATUTE-98/pdf/STATUTE-98-Pg3583-2.pdf.

[appropriate] levels of women" in the military and reduced its recruitment goals for women,[48] a policy referred to as "womenpause."[49]

Reagan, like most politicians, used the military to serve his party's narrative. He believed emphasizing the family would help the American economy, saying, "If we strengthen families, we'll help reduce poverty and the whole range of other social problems."[50]

By bringing military spouses to the forefront, Reagan showed that a strong family strengthened our military and national security. At a time when social programs were seen as handouts, the Army quickly adopted the Reagan administration's family focus, emphasizing the need for quality-of-life programming to support the "Army family."

Programming, rather than being labeled a handout, was now seen as an essential component of operational readiness. Military families received new benefits, service members received military promotions, and military spouses received public thanks for their volunteerism. While this offered some spouses legitimacy for their unpaid labor, working military spouses could not "earn" this reward.

Tensions bubbled over during an Air Force Blue Ribbon panel investigation focused on "Spouse Issues."[51] The committee found "two wives of senior officers at Grissom Air Force Base in Indiana had been pressured to quit their outside jobs."[52]

The 1988 report highlighted the fact that the "two-for-one" model, where a service member serves in uniform and his wife volunteers her time on the home front, was no longer sustainable within the changing cultural

---

48 Pete Earley, "Army Lowers Its Goals for Recruitment of Women," *The Washington Post*, August 27, 1982, https://www.washingtonpost.com/archive/politics/1982/08/27/army-lowers-its-goals-for-recruitment-of-women/87050ff1-3ee9-4c6f-a359-1eb73d004276.

49 Bernard Rostker, "The Role of Women in the All-Volunteer Force," in *I Want You!: The Evolution of the All-Volunteer Force*, 1st ed. (Santa Monica, CA: RAND Corporation, 2006), 559–90, http://www.jstor.org/stable/10.7249/mg265rc.22.

50 Ronald Reagan, "Radio Address to the Nation on the American Family," broadcast from Camp David, MD, December 3, 1983; transcript available from the Ronald Reagan Presidential Library & Museum via the National Archives, accessed August 26, 2025, https://www.reaganlibrary.gov/archives/speech/radio-address-nation-american-family.

51 *Air Force Blue Ribbon Panel Report: Spouse Issues* (Washington, DC: U.S. Air Force, 1988).

52 "Air Force Says Wives' Jobs Are Up to Them," *The New York Times*, March 20, 1988, https://www.nytimes.com/1988/03/20/us/air-force-says-wives-jobs-are-up-to-them.html.

climate. They could no longer factor in spouse volunteerism when making promotion decisions. The panel reported what all military spouses already knew: "It is all right for the husband of a military woman to work in the civilian community, but if the wife of a military man works, she is often perceived as shirking her responsibilities to the Air Force family."[53]

The Supreme Court decision told the world that military spouses were dependents. Reagan's policies told military spouses that they should be *proud* to be dependents, a message that didn't align with the evolving role of the military spouse—a spouse who was now willing to sue the DoD to separate themselves from unofficial military duties.

The military was no longer able to give a service member a bad rating if they had an "unsupportive" wife, but it would come to realize it did not have to use the carrot when another stick still existed. If it minimized the role of military spouses and the resources available to them, spouses would be forced to step up to help each other. The military could still pay the service member and get the wife for free.

"DEPENDA": HOW WORDS CONTROL THE NARRATIVE

One of the ways to control a narrative is to curate the words used to describe a person, idea, or event. The military calls military spouses and children "dependents." The word has its roots in English and French; to depend is "to hang from." This word, by its very definition, implies that there is a strong versus weak relationship present. Dependents hang from those they depend on.

The message the word conveys is:

- Military service members must be strong enough to hold the weight of their family members.
- The burdens presented by military dependents must be light.
- If the service member is not strong enough or if families ask too

[53] *Air Force Blue Ribbon Panel Report: Spouse Issues* (Washington, DC: U.S. Air Force, 1988), 11.

much, the military lifestyle will break the military family unit.

When this strength-to-weight ratio is balanced, families are labeled resilient. If they can't manage their problems on their own, military family members are seen as dependents, bedraggled camp followers who are a strain on military resources.

Erin Morris was only valuable to the military as long as she wore the uniform. It reinforced this message by calling her a "dependent" on official paperwork. This is just one way the DoD has fed the narrative that military families are a burden.

Changing terms on paperwork may seem insignificant, but big changes usually start small.

In October 2022, I wrote an op-ed for *Military.com* challenging the dominant narrative that military spouses depend on the military.[54]

The article sparked significant attention, and I was asked to become a columnist for the publication. One unexpected response came from then–Secretary of the Army Christine Wormuth, who personally reached out to discuss the piece and better understand military families' concerns.

Notably, she was the only service secretary to do so. When she asked me what the Army could do to help, I urged her to remove the word "dependent" from all military paperwork. Because we can't get people to care about military family problems if they don't see us as people in the first place.

If you call a group of people "dependent," then anything you do to help them is a handout, not an operational necessity. If you treat them as equals and see them as people, you may be forced to care. And if you care, you may be compelled to put your money where your mouth is.

---

[54] Jennifer Barnhill, "Could Military Spouses Fix DoD's Recruitment Problem?" *Military.com*, September 19, 2022, https://www.military.com/daily-news/opinions/2022/09/19/could-military-spouses-fix-dods-recruitment-problem.html.

VETERANS AND SERVICE MEMBERS SLANDER SPOUSES

> "The Air Force wife was stunned. She had allowed a photo of herself with her husband and children to be posted on a website. Soon, an anonymous commenter labeled them 'the fat family.' Other online trolls doubled down on the nastiness in a stream of intense, crude insults about each family member's appearance. Even more shocking: The online troll who initiated the online attack, a Facebook profile revealed, was an Army colonel."
> —"'Dependa' Bashing: Mudslingers Stun Military Spouses," written by Karen Jowers for *Military Times*.

"I think a lot of military members were sick and tired of seeing military spouses advocate for themselves. They thought we should be quiet and shut up," said retired military spouse Angie Drake. "The idea of a dependa has been around for a long time. The internet made it much easier to make the concept go a little more viral. People were getting individually attacked and I think they still are."

Angie shared that based on her observation, the term "dependa" peaked in 2015. Dependa is a derogatory term used by the military and veteran community to mock military spouses. At that time, she and a group of fellow spouses were fed up with the bullying and collaborated on releasing a series of articles on the topic to raise awareness. Sadly, it didn't do much to reduce the frequency of service members and veterans labeling military spouses as dependas.

By using the term "dependent," the DoD officially undervalues military spouses. When veterans and service members use the term "dependa," they intentionally demean military spouses. It's like calling a woman a "Karen."

A more colorful word used to describe military spouses includes the term "dependapotamus." This term would often be accompanied by photos of obese military spouses in skimpy clothing and is defined by Wiktionary as "a servicemember's partner (especially a [stay-at-home mom]) who behaves in a parasitic manner, especially by taking advantage of their partner's status to demand beneficial treatment."[55]

Although female spouses are the primary targets of dependa bashing, male spouses are not immune to these attacks. Jeremy Hilton, the 2012 Armed Forces Insurance Military Spouse of the Year, even stepped up to shame the shamers by writing an article that appeared in the *Huffington Post.* In the article, "The Pentagon, Misogyny, and Cyber Bullying," Jeremy wrote:

> "In his *Washington Post* piece, Dave Duffy, a retired Army officer, connected the action of a military spouse, who he says acted poorly in his smoothie establishment, to the larger issues of having an 'entitlement attitude' and worsening civilian-military relations (a rather large leap). Carl Forsling, an active-duty Marine Corps officer, started his opinion piece with an unnecessary hunter-bear-rape metaphor to describe the decision to re-enlist. That provocative opening quickly spiraled into a stereotype-fueled argument that placed military spouses as enemy number one. However, other than an 'Army Wife: Toughest Job in the Military' bumper sticker, Forsling cited no specific examples, facts, or research supporting his claim. His main purpose for writing seemed to be to air a grudge against military spouses. Both officers' weak logic, not surprisingly, led to weak arguments. Whatever points they were trying to make regarding entitlement got lost in the authors' willingness to stereotype the 1.1-million-member community of military spouses."[56]

Jeremy was responding directly to an article titled "Military Families Need to Get Over Their Sense of Entitlement," written by Carl Forsling, a retired Marine Corps officer, for the online military publication *Task & Purpose.*[57] Entitlement is the belief that one deserves something special,

[55] "dependapotamus," *Wiktionary*, accessed August 25, 2025, https://en.wiktionary.org/wiki/dependapotamus.
[56] Jeremy Hilton, "The Pentagon, Misogyny and Cyber Bullying," *HuffPost*, April 6, 2015, https://www.huffpost.com/entry/the-pentagon-misogyny-and-cyber-bullying_b_7065266.
[57] Carl Forsling, "Military Families Need To Get Over Their Sense Of Entitlement," *Task & Purpose*, March 25, 2015, https://taskandpurpose.com/news/military-families-need-to-get-over-their-sense-of-entitlement..

often an unearned benefit or status. The "entitled dependa" narrative is one that portrays military spouses as using service members to take advantage of military discounts, health care, and pay while offering the service member little in return.

As Jeremy points out, Forsling did not cite real military spouse entitlement but instead furthered existing stereotypes by speaking in generalities, a technique that distances readers from the subject. Without specific evidence to paint a more realistic picture of who military families are, we care less about them.

This narrative distancing is frequently used to undermine counternarratives. The author's "proof" that spouses are entitled only pointed to satirical articles. They cited the *Duffel Blog's* "Pentagon Releases Preliminary Military Spouse Rank Chart,"[58] playing up the stereotype that military spouses "wear rank" or live through the accomplishments of their spouses, and a phony letter written to *Military.com's* Ms. Vicki, a former advice columnist for the publication, that stated:

> "Ms. Vicki, I was told that Army wives are paid a monthly stipend just for being a wife at a minimum of $800. The amount is supposed to increase based on rank. Mine should at least be $1,000. Could you please let me know who to talk to so I can discuss this issue? I have not seen any of this money, and it's been two years now. I'm used to nice, expensive things, and my husband promised my father that he would take care of me just like he did when I was living at home."[59]

When a narrative is widely held, it can be used to excuse a lot of bad behavior. Instead of undermining the contribution of spouses by citing evidence, Forsling's opinion piece did not substantiate his accusations. On the other hand, an opinion piece that promotes a counternarrative (e.g., the military depends on those it calls "dependents") would have to be

---

[58] "Pentagon Releases Preliminary Military Spouse Rank Chart," *Duffel Blog*, October 5, 2022, https://www.duffelblog.com/p/pentagon-releases-preliminary-military-spouse-rank-chart.
[59] "Ask Ms. Vicki: Where Is My Army Wife Pay?" *Military.com*, July 12, 2013, https://www.military.com/spouse/relationships/where-is-my-army-wife-pay.html.

flawless, citing reputable sources and making articulate and logical arguments. Forsling presented his opinion as fact and did not feel the need to prove his case.

The piece was further legitimized because it was published by *Task & Purpose*, which is considered a reputable source within the community and a favorite of military service members. The opinion piece was also published under a news banner, only indicating that it was opinion at the very bottom of the article.

Although protected under the First Amendment and an extension of Forsling's freedom of speech, *Task & Purpose*'s inclusion of the piece reinforced the negative stereotype of spouses.

Even civilians have bought the message that military spouses are dependas. In 2022, Netflix released the romantic drama *Purple Hearts*, a movie about a woman who pursues a service member to obtain military benefits.

No one from the DoD stood up in defense of the Army family or military spouses *because when military families don't fit into the DoD's narrative or align with their agendas, the DoD remains silent.*

PAINTING A BETTER PICTURE

The military spouses, male and female, who were on the receiving end of dependa bashing fought hate by sharing their own experiences to drown out the stories being told about them within the military community. By telling their own stories, they hoped to paint a picture absent of entitlement.

While Angie Drake and other spouses called out the dependa narrative publicly, other military spouses were pushing back more quietly. Some saw the conversation as unnecessary drama and intentionally distanced themselves from the military lifestyle. Others avoided any sense of entitlement by leaning into their individual passions and careers and participating in expected volunteerism less.

When spouses tried to come out and confront the dependa narrative, citing data to prove their cases, they faced backlash based on anecdotes. In asserting their independence and owning their stories, they were violating the dominant narrative that sees military spouses as dependent and a burden on the institution.

Silence from the DoD, combined with online bullying, was enough to undermine the counternarrative that the military is dependent on military spouses, not the other way around. The DoD protects the narrative by allowing dated terms to remain and bad behavior to go unchecked, all while allowing spouses to police their own actions. For instance, if a spouse speaks up and points out that the military relies upon the unpaid labor of military spouses, they are told not to complain, someone else will step up to volunteer. Because they do not want to make their service member look bad, they avoid making a stink. But if no one speaks up, the expectation of unpaid labor remains unchecked.

The reality is the military itself wants to avoid being seen as dependent upon anything or anyone, and it will fight those who say it isn't strong enough to hold its own weight.

DATA SHOWS THE DOD DEPENDS ON FAMILIES

OFFICER SPOUSE VOLUNTEERISM OFFSETS SHORTFALLS IN ENLISTED PAY

The very first military party I ever attended was a change-of-command party in Tokyo, Japan, while my husband was assigned to a helicopter squadron with Carrier Air Wing 5. My husband and I navigated at least three train transfers before ultimately finding our way to the restaurant where the party was being held. Every sign was shockingly neon while every corner held an authentically Japanese architectural flourish—the traditional and the modern living side by side.

We were there to celebrate the departure of one commanding officer, welcome a new one, and do so in style. This was the first of many military traditions I would experience in my time as a military spouse.

I would later learn that parties were also thrown to celebrate the commanding officer's wife—a COW party. This tradition is unique to the naval aviation community, both the pilots you see flying the fixed-wing jets in *Top Gun* and the real heroes, helicopter pilots. The other service branches and communities have their own versions of these parties and social obligations.

To celebrate the COW, junior and senior officers' spouses will decorate the COW's home with cow-themed decorations and host a black-and-white cow-themed party. All officer spouses are invited and, in most cases, are expected to give the COW a gift. These gifts are usually cow-themed: cow aprons, cow dish towels, and porcelain cow figurines. If there is a black-and-white cow print version of something, then it's worthy of being a COW party gift.

These parties are hosted by the Officer Spouse Club (OSC), a dues-paying 501(c)3 nonprofit organization. The OSCs I have been part of set aside some of their annual budget, generated by dues and fundraisers, to pay for these celebrations. Why celebrate the spouse of my husband's boss? She has unofficial but essential duties that often go unrecognized by the military at large.

"In November, Michael took over as commanding officer, so I'm also a COW, and [the squadron] is deployed. And it is a nightmare. My life is a slow-rolling nightmare right now," Navy spouse Rebecca Ivory, PhD, shared with me in a 2022 interview. "Every day I wake up and at some point in the day I have to decide whether it's more important to be my husband's wife and do squadron stuff or do my dissertation stuff."

The doctoral project in question? Studying the efficacy of mental health interventions on Navy SEALs' chronic pain and trauma symptoms.

The squadron "stuff" included sending messages via phone trees, hosting morale-boosting events, and building a sense of community on the home front.

Commanding officer spouses are a lot like First Ladies: They are not officially required to perform any functions. Yet there are dozens of manuals, updated regularly, that instruct modern-day military spouses on how they can support their service members by supporting the institution. The manuals focus on social obligations, family-focused programs and initiatives, and praising the work of families. Neither First Ladies nor military spouses are legally obligated to perform any functions but are relied upon by the organizations and initiatives they choose to support. For instance, in 2011, First Lady Michelle Obama and Second Lady Dr. Jill Biden founded a program called Joining Forces to elevate the issues faced by veterans and military families so that political leaders would be well-informed about how they could help.

After Obama left office, the program was shuttered. Second Lady Karen Pence also worked to support military families, but in a less formalized way. When Joe Biden took office, First Lady Dr. Jill Biden revived Joining Forces and its brighter spotlight. As of early 2025, neither First Lady Melania Trump nor Second Lady Usha Vance has made any indications that they would take on a program in support of military families.

When our government relies upon unpaid labor, its absence is felt. To understand what happens in the absence of military spouse volunteerism, we have to measure the contribution. In 2001, researcher Dr. Margaret Harrell, a Navy spouse herself, wanted to determine whether there had been a diminished reliance upon military spouse volunteerism after the 1988 Blue Ribbon panel report said the two-for-one model was no longer official policy.

Dr. Harrell found that instead of declining, both formal and informal expectations for officer spouses increased, especially for senior Army leaders. Attaining this level of leadership is the gold star (literally) that

Army officers are trained to want. Similarly, military spouses are conditioned to want their significant other to receive this type of promotion.

In the military, you promote up or you get out. Assuming a military family does not want to leave the service, they will do everything they can to get a good rating on periodic fitness reports, called a FITREP in the Navy and an Officer Evaluation Report (OER) in the Army. Getting a good rating, or "good paper," is required to be promoted. This pressure is felt more as seniority increases.

Despite the Blue Ribbon panel prohibiting including military spouse volunteerism in service member promotion calculations, the perception that military spouse involvement has an impact persists. But senior spouses like Ivory feel like they have no choice but to volunteer; there are duties that, if left undone, would cause harm to the commands their spouses were tasked with supporting.

As part of her research, Dr. Harrell interviewed 105 spouses to better understand their experiences. She found that not only were military spouses relied upon to support their peers, they were also intentionally or unintentionally recruited as volunteers to offset the shortfall in enlisted service member pay. Her research report "Army Officers' Spouses: Have the White Gloves Been Mothballed?" reads:

"In an environment of decreasing budget dollars, officers' spouses are perceived as an easy solution for addressing the problems faced by enlisted spouses. Indeed, at many locations, volunteerism is valued at millions of dollars each year."[60]

Dr. Harrell examined the value of volunteerism in Fort Stewart, Georgia, which, as of the 2020 Census, is the home to roughly 15,400 service members and 16,000 family members.[61] Dr. Harrell estimated that in 1997 alone, volunteer labor by military spouses in Fort Stewart saved

---

[60] Margaret C. Harrell, "Army Officers' Spouses: Have the White Gloves Been Mothballed?" *Armed Forces & Society* 28, no. 1 (2001): 55–75, http://www.jstor.org/stable/45346907.

[61] *Fort Stewart Military & Family Support Center*, Military OneSource, accessed August 25, 2025, https://installations.militaryonesource.mil/in-depth-overview/fort-stewart.

the government $4,175,817. This figure assumed spouses' volunteer hours were paid at minimum wage, which was $3.25 per hour in 1997.[62] Their 1,284,866.77 hours are worth roughly $9.3 million in 2025 paid at our current minimum wage of $7.25,[63] or $1,210 donated per person.[64]

If we assume Dr. Harrell's findings are still representative of the roughly 1 million military spouses today,[65] this group of "dependents" donates over a billion dollars, or $1,205,160,000, of time and labor to the military *annually*. This is not a scientific assessment because truthfully the data isn't good; but it does give us an idea of the estimated contribution of military spouse volunteers and should inspire us to ask for better data. While this is nowhere near the over $850 billion FY2025 defense budget,[66] it is a lot of free labor and it's just the labor we have been told about.

If the DoD is tracking volunteer hours, it is not publicizing them. Because if it tracked how dependent it was on military families, it may disrupt its narrative. So I submitted many Freedom of Information Acts (FOIA) requesting that the Air Force, Army, and Navy provide the total number of volunteer hours it has tracked to obtain more up-to-date information. The only branches that responded to my FOIA requests with actual data were the Navy and Army.

---

62 Federal Reserve Economic Data (FRED), "STTMINWGGA," Federal Reserve Bank of St. Louis, accessed August 25, 2025, https://fred.stlouisfed.org/series/STTMINWGGA.

63 U.S. Department of Labor, "Minimum Wage," accessed August 25, 2025, https://www.dol.gov/agencies/whd/minimum-wage.

64 This assumes that 50 percent of service members at this location are married, following current demographic patterns: National Academies of Sciences, Engineering, and Medicine, *Demographic and Military Service Characteristics of Military Families*, National Academies Press, 2019, https://www.ncbi.nlm.nih.gov/books/NBK547615/#:~:text=The%20family%20status%20of%20service,and%2039%20percent%20have%20children.

65 U.S. Department of Defense, *DoD Military Spouse Demographics and Employment Report*, September 12, 2018, https://trumpwhitehouse.archives.gov/wp-content/uploads/2018/09/DoDMilitarySpouseDemographicsandEmployment_20180912.pdf.

66 Congressional Budget Office, *Long-Term Implications of the 2025 Future Years Defense Program*, Publication 61017, November 2024, https://www.cbo.gov/publication/61017#:~:text=The%20proposed%20budget%20for%20DoD,2024%20(excluding%20supplemental%20funding).

NAVY OMBUDSMEN—UNPAID MEMBERS OF THE COMMAND "TRIAD"

In addition to the other spouse groups available to Navy spouses (officer and enlisted clubs and Family Readiness Groups), the Navy officially supports families through its ombudsman program. Originally created in the 1970s to give Navy wives a voice, the program has evolved into a more structured—though still unpaid—role.[67]

Ombudsmen are usually the spouse of a senior non-commissioned or commissioned officer within the unit. They are the official military family representative, working with the commanding officer (CO) and executive officer (XO) as part of the command "triad." They relay official information, connect families to resources, and report trends affecting the command climate. Their reports help the Navy track family concerns and their work "represents a huge cost savings to the Navy than if these were paid positions."[68]

The total number of Navy ombudsmen as of December 2022 was 1,714, supporting roughly 376,000 Navy spouses and children,[69] which equates to one person supporting roughly 220 people.

---

[67] OPNAVINST 1750.1 was instituted by former Chief of Naval Operations (CNO) Zumwalt in a memo, entitled a Z-Gram in 1970 (Z-Gram #24; 14 September 1970).

[68] U.S. Department of the Navy, Navy Family Ombudsman Program Manual, 2016, https://ffr.cnic.navy.mil/portals/76/Family_Readiness/Documents/Ombudsman%20Program%20Manual%202016.pdf.

[69] U.S. Department of Defense, *2020 Demographics Profile of the Military Community*, Military OneSource, 2020, https://download.militaryonesource.mil/12038/MOS/Infographic/2020-demographics-active-duty-navy-families.pdf.

Ombudsmen Volunteerism

Year	*Average Monthly Hours*	*Total Hours*	*Hours per Month per Ombudsman*	*Estimated Annual Value ($35/hour)*
2019	19,594	235,123	11.4 hours	$8.2 million
2020	20,554	246,643	12 hours	$8.6 million
2021	14,777	177,322	8.6 hours	$6.2 million
2022 (Jan 1–Oct 31, 2022 only)	13,671	136,712	8 hours	$4.8 million

Source: FOIA response. Media Relations: Navy Installations Command HQ received on December 8, 2022. More recent data may be available but was not captured in this FOIA request.)

While this data is striking, it is likely incomplete. Ombudsman hours are logged on a website that requires a common access card (CAC) to log in, a card that is only issued to official military personnel. Because military spouses can't access this system, this data is tracked by the ombudsman, then submitted to Navy personnel to enter, likely resulting in data loss.

The ombudsman program quietly reinforces a contradictory narrative. Navy spouses are important enough to have a program designed to support them, but not important enough for the program to be funded.

THE ARMY RIVALS THE NAVY

Some branches of service have acknowledged the needs typically fulfilled by military spouse volunteerism over the years by funding positions to do what otherwise would be a volunteer's job. One example is the Army's 2019 change from Family Readiness Groups (FRG) to Soldier and Family Readiness Groups (SFRG). FRGs are spouse clubs that are not separated by rank. However, just because the Army tasked service members with overseeing these groups in 2019 doesn't mean volunteerism is not needed.

Army Average Monthly Volunteer Hours

FY2017	*FY2018*	*FY2019*	*FY2020*	*FY2021*
91,929	142,719	810,009	58,112	19,060

Source: FOIA response. Data pulled by United States Army Installation (Management Command (IMCOM), received on February 24, 2023. More recent data may be available but was not captured in this FOIA request.)

Army data from 2017 to 2021 shows fluctuating volunteer hours, with an unexplained peak of 810,009 in 2019 before plummeting during COVID-19. Using an estimate of $35 per hour, these documented hours saved the Army more than $471 million over five years—nearly half a billion dollars.

The Marine Corps is also looking for ways to cut costs. For decades, it paid civilian Family Readiness Officers, who managed the Unit, Personal, and Family Readiness Program (UPFRP), ensuring families were informed, connected, and prepared for the challenges of military life. By staffing these roles with civilians who did not have to move every few years, the program offered Marine families consistency and specialization. In 2025, it was announced that funding for this program would be reallocated, and the duties will be reassigned to a Marine, likely as a collateral duty, taking them away from their warfighting mission.[70]

However, these official roles are just a fraction of the unpaid labor provided by military spouses. Many contributions go untracked. Books like

[70] Oriana Pawlyk, "Marine Corps Doing Away With Civilian Family Readiness Officers, Limiting Jobs for Military Spouses," *Military.com*, March 14, 2025, https://www.military.com/daily-news/2025/03/14/marine-corps-doing-away-civilian-family-readiness-officers-limiting-jobs-military-spouses.html.

The Army Spouse Handbook by Ann Crossley reinforce these unspoken expectations. In its over 400 pages, fifty-four pages cover entertaining; thirty-eight pages outline how to extend/receive invitations; thirty pages are dedicated to social graces; and thirty-eight pages delineate the roles of those married to commanding officers, noncommissioned officers, and general officers.[71] And these admonitions were not from the 1950s, they were cited in the 2019 *updated* Handbook.

Declining to participate in these traditions isn't without consequence. "Plenty of people don't [volunteer]," said Erin Paulus, Army spouse of twenty years. "If I choose not to participate, the role or the expectation only transfers to the next spouses in line—it doesn't disappear."[72]

"There was one commanding officer's wife in particular who had asked me if I wanted to be the president of the [Officer Spouse Club]," said Loren Marner, Navy spouse. "At that point, I had decided I was not going to volunteer anymore. I had four children and a lot on my plate."

When the commanding officer of her husband's unit came up to Loren at a party and said, "I heard that you are taking a [spouse group] position," instead of correcting her husband's boss, she said yes, she was going to volunteer with the spouse group.[73]

Although spouses like Loren said yes, they didn't do so because they wanted to. Rather, they were politely bullied into it. The DoD doesn't have to set aside a sliver of its multi-billion-dollar budget to fund these positions because tradition has laid out the expectation. They are told the work they do is essential, but not as essential as the "real" work of the military. It is "non-operational" work. It is social. It is women's work.

---

[71] Ann Crossley with Ginger Perkins, *The Army Spouse Handbook* (New York: Rowman & Littlefield, 2019).

[72] In 2021, I conducted an informal survey to better understand the role of military spouse groups. I subsequently conducted over thirty interviews of military spouses aimed at understanding their motivations for volunteering in support of the military community. Detailed survey findings: https://www.linkedin.com/pulse/2021-military-spouse-group-survey-findings-jennifer-barnhill.

[73] Ibid.

A POLICY OF RELIANCE

In addition to helping their service members perform their duties by holding down the home front, hosting events, and boosting morale, military spouses also serve the DoD by being the primary caregivers to military children. While not every service member has children, roughly 51 percent of military personnel do.[74]

Because so many service members are also parents, the DoD insists they have a family care plan[75]—a documented strategy outlining how their children will be cared for if they deploy at a moment's notice or are working 24-hour shifts. This policy is designed to maximize the readiness of the force, ensuring that caregiving responsibilities don't interfere with operational duties.

While logical, these plans reveal a hidden narrative: The DoD relies on military spouses to provide care at no cost to the military. According to Army policy, if the soldier is a parent, they must create a plan—unless they are married to an "able-bodied" military spouse. The contributions of spouses go far beyond the donated volunteer hours; the DoD has codified its dependence on military spouses as part of its official policy.

While civilian couples also struggle with finding child care, service members work long hours and often need 24-hour care—care that the DoD is not capable of providing through internal child care programs, where waitlists are six to seven months long.[76] While the DoD offers funding assistance to families so they can get care in civilian markets, the compensation doesn't always cover the cost of 24/7 care, a type of care not easily found in the civilian market.[77]

---

[74] U.S. Department of Defense, *2022 Demographics Profile of the Military Community*, Military OneSource, 2022, https://download.militaryonesource.mil/12038/MOS/Reports/2022-demographics-report.pdf.

[75] U.S. Department of Defense, *Caregiver Support During Military Deployment*, Military OneSource, accessed August 25, 2025, https://www.militaryonesource.mil/resources/millife-guides/caregiver-support-during-military-deployment/.

[76] U.S. Government Accountability Office, *Military Child Care: DoD Efforts to Provide Affordable, Quality Care for Families*, GAO-23-105518, February 2023, https://www.gao.gov/assets/gao-23-105518.pdf.

[77] Kristy N. Kamarck, *Military Child Development Program: Background and Issues*, Congressional Research Service Report R45288, March 19, 2020, https://sgp.fas.org/crs/natsec/R45288.pdf.

In the absence of care, the cost is borne by military spouses who are forced to step away from jobs or take less competitive employment to account for additional flexibility.

Unless the military is prepared to prohibit service members from having children or adjust deployments and work schedules to mirror civilian jobs, child care will be a national security and readiness issue—an operational function that has largely been outsourced to military spouses.

This reliance is very similar to the unpaid, invisible household labor performed by American women. It is estimated that unpaid caregiving performed in America is valued at one trillion dollars annually.[78] Except, in the military community, male military spouses are also expected to perform unpaid labor. At times we assume nearly 100 percent of home front responsibilities—grocery shopping, laundry, cleaning, caregiving, etc.

Despite its quantifiable value, the narrative surrounding "women's work" is largely negative. Not only does it not have actual monetary value, but it is also a type of work that actually has negative value.[79] This negative value is experienced when a spouse is shamed for staying home to raise children or alternatively shamed for working outside of the home. Military spouses feel this negative value when they perform unpaid labor for the military and are called dependas by members of the very institution they are supporting.

Despite the negative personal impacts on spouses, the DoD knows spouses will continue to step up in support of the one they love.

---

[78] Katherine Gallagher Robbins and Jessica Mason, "Americans' Unpaid Caregiving Worth $1 Trillion Annually; Women Provide Two-Thirds of Care," National Partnership for Women & Families, June 27, 2024, https://nationalpartnership.org/americans-unpaid-caregiving-worth-1-trillion-annually-women-two-thirds-work.

[79] Linda Babcock and Sara Laschever, *Women Don't Ask: The High Cost of Avoiding Negotiation—and Positive Strategies for Change* (New York: Bantam Books, 2007), 49.

IS THE DOD TOO GREEDY?

Claudia Goldin won the Nobel Prize in Economics for her groundbreaking research on the evolving role of women in the workforce. Her work also explored how couples divide responsibilities, revealing that one partner is often more likely to take on what she calls "greedy work"—work that demands long hours, inflexible schedules, constant availability, and a willingness to drop everything for work. When couples try to balance life together, one partner typically ends up supporting the other's greedy employer—often by absorbing additional responsibilities at home.

Before women began to enter the workforce en masse in the 1970s and 1980s, greedy jobs were commonplace. Men worked long hours to prove their worth to their employer. While social progress moved forward, workplace expectations didn't adapt. Women took on more demanding professional roles, often without the workplace accommodations that supported family life.

Maternal leave helped some, as did the introduction of remote work in recent years. But at its core, industry expectations remained greedy, built on the assumption that someone, usually a woman, would be at home taking care of the home front, an equally greedy workplace.

Goldin's work uncovered the primary hurdle to achieving the elusive work-life balance: time. Greedy jobs don't care about work-life balance.

If ever there were a greedy boss, it would be the United States Armed Forces.

Civilian employers don't think work-life balance is their responsibility, nor does the military think families are its responsibility. However, civilian employers rarely, if ever, ask for the free labor of the spouses of their employees. However, the DoD depends on this labor. The DoD makes military families its problem each time it accepts the unpaid labor of military spouses. It has always relied upon our contributions, and it always will. It knows this, but military spouses don't.

When someone marries a service member, they unknowingly enter the greediest of institutions. Military spouses do so in total ignorance of what will be expected of them. *I need to pick up a sick kid because he has a training exercise. I have to wake up with my toddler at midnight because my husband, a pilot, needs a minimum amount of sleep because otherwise his life and the lives of his crew could be put at risk. My need for communication puts the mission at risk.* Military spouses don't know that this institution will condition them to make choices that put their own health and careers on hold to serve the mission. And their careers pay the price. Military spouses have suffered staggeringly high unemployment rates—roughly 20 percent—for half a century.[80] In 2017, the DoD reported roughly 39 percent of spouses were out of the workforce entirely,[81] significantly more than what would be expected in a similar civilian population (roughly 24 percent). Many are not unemployed or out of the workforce by choice.

In a 2019 DoD survey, active-duty military spouses who were out of the workforce were asked why they were not looking for work and presented with sixteen responses, including:

- I do not want to work
- I cannot find any work that matches my skills
- I want to be able to stay home to care for my children

The number one reason cited for military spouse parents was wanting to stay home with their children (41 percent). However, the number one reason military spouses *without* children said they were not looking for work was "other," at 28 percent.[82]

---

[80] *Navy Wifeline Survey, 1970: Profile of Wives Surveyed.* Documentation provided directly to the author.
[81] U.S. Department of Defense, *2017 Active-Duty Spouses Overview Briefing*, Military OneSource, 2017, https://download.militaryonesource.mil/12038/MOS/Surveys/Survey-Active-Duty-Spouses-2017-Overview-Briefing-MSO.pdf.
[82] U.S. Department of Defense, Office of People Analytics, *2019 Survey of Active Duty Spouses (ADSS)*, July–November 2019,
https://download.militaryonesource.mil/12038/MOS/Surveys/ADSS1901_MOS-Briefing-508-Revised.pdf

This got my "spidey sense" tingling. As a researcher, when I see "other" as the most commonly selected choice, I assume one of two things: either the population being surveyed is so diverse that a consensus is unlikely, or the survey question was poorly constructed. While both are possible, it was hard not to notice that an obvious choice was omitted—the demands the military places on military families, namely service members' unpredictable work schedules and deployments. It didn't give spouses the choice to indicate that it was the demands of military schedules that cost them professional opportunities.

But military spouses know the truth. They are expected to support their service members' greedy careers at the expense of their own.

WHY THE DOD PROTECTS THE NARRATIVE

The DoD protects the dominant narrative that it is strong enough to carry the load, no matter how heavy. Military leaders are overtasked, so many distance themselves from military spouse support efforts so they don't have to admit to failing a critical, yet unfunded, mission. It protects the narrative by officially calling military spouses dependents, minimizing spouse contributions.

Individuals within the military—service members, veterans, and even military spouses themselves—also protect these narratives when they wield the term "dependa" to shame spouses into silence. Whether they are conscious of this or not, the DoD and cyberbullies behave the way they do because if they were forced to publicly admit they needed military spouses, their perceived strength would be diminished.

Just as unpaid household labor sustains American society, military spouse unpaid labor sustains the military. If either were to disappear, both systems would face a reckoning.

"We need two incomes to be comfortable," said Air Force spouse and military food insecurity advocate, Heather Campbell over a Zoom interview. "We have a Department of Defense that runs our military as if somebody is at home handling things—the dog, the house, the kids, the car—but pays military families as if they are every other family that has a second income. And I think we're really to this breaking point in our community where we have to decide, are we a one-working-parent and one-at-home-parent institution? Or are we a dual-working institution?"

The military cannot have it both ways. It can't say that families are essential yet call them "dependents."

The second it owns up to its dependence, it would have to publicly admit that the average employed enlisted spouse loses $9,500 a year in income. Officer spouses lose roughly $27,000 annually. This amounts to an average loss of nearly half a million dollars in individual spouse income over the course of a twenty-year military career.[83] The losses for spouses who are out of the workforce entirely are far higher. Leaders would rather increase service member pay, get a political win and ignore what its own research has confirmed: marrying into the military does "permanent" damage to the earning potential of military spouses.[84] It would have to admit military spouses are the hidden all-volunteer force, saving our nation billions of dollars annually. It ignores this because restructuring America to value unpaid labor is an undertaking that feels hopeless.

If the DoD wants to get ahead of this narrative, it should start by calling military families "teammates" instead of "dependents." It should stop online bullying in its tracks by holding service members online to the same conduct standards they are held to in person. Instead of referring to families as "unissued baggage," publicly recognize military spouse contributions as operational, not just social. And for goodness sake, do not assume a military spouse is the family care plan. Invest in child care infrastructure as if operational duties rely upon it, because they do.

---

[83] U.S. Department of Defense, *The Fourteenth Quadrennial Review of Military Compensation, Volume IV: Dual-Income Military Households* (January 2025), 67, https://militarypay.defense.gov/Portals/3/Documents/QRMC-14-Vol_4_final_web.pdf#page=67.
[84] Ibid.

How *you* can change this narrative: Normalize saying no to obligatory volunteerism. Don't consume stereotypical military content that reinforces the narrative that military families are dependas.

How military spouses can change this narrative: Tell your stories. Write your local newspapers, offer to share at your child's school, church or local community group. Insist that media coverage goes deeper than capturing smiles at homecoming events. Share the good and the bad of military life. Doing so will combat the stereotype that says military families are "dependents." Say no if you are asked to volunteer if you don't want to say yes. The only way the expectation of volunteerism will be removed is if we stop saying yes.

How the DoD can change this narrative: Tell more military family stories alongside battlefield stories in museums and in statements released. Remove "dependent" from all military forms. Follow the logic outlined in your Fourteenth Quadrennial Review of Military Compensation that recognized the financial sacrifices made by spouses. Rather than debating how to account for lost spouse earnings through service member compensation, which only indirectly benefits spouses, properly fund the essential support programming currently supported by military spouse volunteers; in other words, put your money where your memos are and pay those who perform the essential labor that benefits the institution. Invest in childcare infrastructure with oversight. Remove red tape from provider applications and reimbursement processes to maximize available care providers and encourage civilian participation.

No Man Left Behind

"Go, Blackburn, go!" shouts Staff Sergeant Matt Eversmann, sending Army Private First Class (PFC) Todd Blackburn out of the airborne Sikorsky UH-60 helicopter.

"RPG!"

In an instant, the Black Hawk tilts to evade the rocket-propelled grenade, saving the lives of the crew but plunging Blackburn into a free fall sixty feet in the air and disappearing into a swirling cloud of brown dust and debris.

The Battle of Mogadishu had begun.

As the wife of a former Navy helicopter pilot, I have sworn to never rewatch *Black Hawk Down*. The 2001 movie, based on the book of the same name, is a painful and honest example of the military embodying its "no man left behind" narrative.

In 1992, America was in Somalia as part of a United Nations (UN) peacekeeping effort called Operation Restore Hope. However, a year later, America's role in this mission had shifted from providing food and supplies to establishing a stabilizing force in the area. This meant American troops were engaging in missions focused on fighting an enemy who was disrupting their peacekeeping efforts.

Things began to escalate when President Bill Clinton ordered an Army unit called Task Force Ranger to conduct the mission Operation Gothic Serpent in August 1993. The mission was straightforward and only supposed to last thirty minutes if successful. Army Rangers were supposed to enter Mogadishu, Somalia, and capture two lieutenants of Somali warlord Mohamed Farrah Aidid.

But things quickly started to unravel when two Army helicopters were shot down by rocket-propelled grenades and ground forces were pinned down. Special forces that were sent in to assist their fellow service members and ensure no man was left behind also took heavy fire. The 15-hour battle ultimately took the lives of eighteen Americans.[85]

Despite technically achieving the mission objective—capturing the Aidid lieutenants—both the initial mission and the recovery efforts were seen as failures. They were made worse by the very public desecration of the bodies of American service members by Somali forces. Human beings were dragged through the streets amid cheering and dancing. A photo capturing Somalis' abuse of American Staff Sergeant William David Cleveland helped win photojournalist Paul Watson a Pulitzer Prize but lost America its citizens' support for what was supposed to be a humanitarian mission.

Americans were horrified to see the bodies of their soldiers being desecrated by the very people they were sent to help. They supported sending rescue teams to aid those who were pinned down after the failure of the initial mission, but they were dismayed that the military was put in that position in the first place.

When someone joins the military, Americans recognize that those individuals are putting their lives on the line. Our collective hope is that

[85] NPR Staff, "What a Downed Black Hawk in Somalia Taught America," *All Things Considered*, NPR, October 5, 2013, https://www.npr.org/2013/10/05/229561805/what-a-downed-black-hawk-in-somalia-taught-america.

America's leaders make decisions to protect our nation's interests while not unnecessarily risking American lives. Americans expected our military to honor its promise—to leave no man left behind—but the Battle of Mogadishu forced them to confront the cost.

Just days later, Clinton ordered a stop to all aggressive actions against Aidid, deciding it was not worth the further loss of life and the resulting loss of public support for America's peacekeeping efforts in the area. America ended the conflict and prisoners of war were returned, but a price had been paid.

No man left behind is a great ideal, said America, if the mission justifies the cost.

Dominant narrative: Americans want our military to honor the promise of "no man left behind." Rigorous military training and effective negotiations by our government will ensure that America keeps that promise.

A better narrative: No American wants to leave a man behind. When faced with complex or wicked problems, leaders may choose *not* to honor "no man left behind." It takes the individual advocacy of those who have skin in the game to ensure that no service member is left behind.

WHAT DOES "NO MAN LEFT BEHIND" MEAN TO THE DOD?

When someone signs up to fight and possibly die for their country, there is an understanding that they are joining a cause bigger than any one person. They are signing up to be a part of a team.

Membership comes with benefits and preparation, including intense training and camaraderie imbued with a sense that no matter what someone "has your six"—military speak for having your back. This assurance is an essential part of the bargain. It is a hard sell to ask Americans to put their lives in harm's way without also assuring them that their government will do everything within its power to mitigate the risks posed to them.

And if the worst should happen, if a service member is injured in the line of duty or captured by the enemy, the military will do whatever it takes to leave no man behind.

But why has the military embraced this narrative? And how does the military assure service members, their families, and the nation that it will uphold its end of the bargain?

In addition to the peace of mind that this narrative provides service members, it is a sound military strategy. If the enemy has access to American personnel and their intelligence, leaving a man behind puts national security at risk. This is why the military trains its personnel to withstand captivity at Survival, Evasion, Resistance, and Escape (SERE) school, a program designed to prepare service members should they be stranded behind enemy lines or captured. In addition to providing concrete survival training, SERE trains service members to abide by a code of conduct that offers a framework under which they should operate if captured as a prisoner of war (POW).

The Code of Conduct is a non-legal military code that governs the conduct of all service members. Article III instructs service members to disclose only their name, rank, and service number to captors, and to do everything within their power to resist capture and attempt escape. Article II states that, "If in command, I will never surrender the members of my command while they still have the means to resist."[86]

The DoD equips service members with the code and survival training, empowering them to resist and evade capture to the best of their abilities. It instructs service members on what they should do but not *how* to do it.

---

[86] Executive Order 10631, "Code of Conduct for Members of the Armed Forces of the United States," issued August 17, 1955, codified at 20 FR 6057, 3 CFR, 1954-1958 Comp., p. 266, amended by EO 11382 (Nov. 28, 1967) and EO 12633 (Mar. 28, 1988), accessed via National Archives, https://www.archives.gov/federal-register/codification/executive-order/10631.html.

The Soldier's Creed says, "I will never leave a fallen comrade."[87] Similarly, the Airman's Creed says, "I will never leave an Airman behind."[88] Despite not publicly adopting this narrative across all the DoD, it is widely understood to be the accepted ethos of not just active-duty service members but Americans in general. No one wants to see an American left behind enemy lines.

The military has operationalized its promise to leave no man behind. There are dedicated special operations units and mission sets, Combat Search and Rescue (CSAR), which have the purpose of extracting and rescuing fellow service members from behind enemy lines.[89] The Defense POW/MIA Accounting Agency's tagline is "Fulfilling Our Nation's Promise." The group is dedicated to identifying the remains of fallen service members decades, if not centuries, after they lose their lives.[90] The military institution does not wish to leave a man or woman behind, but how does the military execute this ethos when forced to make impossible decisions with limited resources.

This is the crux of what is called a "wicked problem." Americans like being seen as the world's heroes but don't want to see soldiers being dragged through the streets of Somalia. We take pride in our ability to bring our troops home, but we don't want to be in a situation that requires a rescue. We believe America is the greatest nation in the world. We cheer when our country wins gold at the Olympics or when we feed starving Somali children. But we don't like seeing other countries beat our athletes and we certainly don't like it when those we are trying to help hurt us.

Wicked problems are distinctly different from other problems in that they do not have a single correct answer. Government officials are

---

[87] U.S. Army, "Soldier's Creed," Army Values, accessed August 25, 2025, https://www.army.mil/values/soldiers.html.
[88] U.S. Air Force, *The Airman's Creed*, accessed via Air Force Retiree Services, 2016, https://www.retirees.af.mil/Portals/53/documents/LIBRARY/THE%20AIRMAN'S%20CREED.pdf?ver=2016-10-28-142543-513.
[89] George Galdorisi, "Leave No Man Behind," *CNN*, June 9, 2014, https://www.cnn.com/2014/06/09/opinion/galdorisi-leave-no-man-behind/index.html.
[90] Defense POW/MIA Accounting Agency, homepage, accessed August 25, 2025, https://www.dpaa.mil.

generally not focused on finding win-win solutions; they accept the necessity of finding the best lose-lose compromise. These compromises are designed to appease a narrow majority but often are aimed at pleasing their own constituency. Honoring the promise to leave no man behind is a wicked problem because the decision to use military force always has a cost.

The Battle of Mogadishu was a perfect example of how "no man left behind" can quickly go from a promise Americans want to see kept to a wicked problem that redirects American foreign policy. America pulled out of Somalia five months after the battle, and the remaining UN forces followed a year later.

The dominant narrative is flawed because it presumes "no man left behind" is only the responsibility of the military or the government. In reality, executing this ideal is the business of the entire nation. After the Battle of Mogadishu, Americans lost their taste for the loss of American life. Pulling out of Somalia seemingly solved that problem. Until the next battle.

"No man left behind" is a great ideal, but honoring this promise requires more than just military training. Military special operations and special forces, and search-and-rescue teams can go in and get the job done. American diplomats can negotiate for the release of hostages. Getting people out of harm's way is the easy part. The hard part is ensuring the military and government leaders who send our military into harm's way honor this promise. Because history tells us, when tasked with this wicked problem, the government may choose to cover its ass.

FROM NEXT OF KIN TO THE LEAGUE OF WIVES

It was a fall day in the middle of COVID-19 when I opened a hardbound book wrapped in sleek library cellophane. Upon a recommendation from a friend, I picked up *The League of Wives: The Untold Story of the Women Who*

Took on the U.S. Government to Bring Their Husbands Home by Heath Hardage Lee. As I turned the pages, I found myself transported back to Coronado, California, a Navy town I once called home, and into the welcoming home of fellow Navy spouse Sybil Stockdale.

Admittedly, before picking up the book, I only knew about the Vietnam POW narrative from the lens of the male POWs. Because my husband is in the military, and because my dad watched war movies like other dads watch sports, I had seen a few documentaries on Vietnam. I knew that service members-turned-politicians like John McCain and Sybil's husband had been abused and tortured by the Vietnamese for years before being released at the end of the war.

When I read the description of Sybil and the other POW/MIA wives, something resonated in my soul. As a woman, I rarely pick up a history book and feel as though it captures my story. It is even rarer to feel that as a military spouse. Despite not having a personal connection to the military, the author had found a narrative that had been forgotten, not just in American culture but even within my own military spouse community. I had been a military spouse for over ten years, I had visited Vietnam's infamous Hoa Lo Prison, nicknamed the "Hanoi Hilton," during my husband's first tour in Japan, yet I knew nothing about the League of Wives or Sybil.

Lee's book documented the POW experience, a lesser-known narrative, but she told it from the point of view of their military spouses. A historian and museum curator, she got wind of the story after coming across the diary of a family friend, Phyllis Galanti, whose husband Paul was a POW. Through Phyllis's papers, Lee unearthed a network of women who had formed the National League of Families of American Prisoners and Missing in Southeast Asia in the 1960s. These women, led by Sybil, put pressure on the U.S. government to bring their husbands home from Vietnam.

"I always try to pick projects where I have no connection," Lee shared with me in an interview. "The disconnects [in the story] are very obvious when you come in knowing nothing."

The flaw she detected?

The dominant narrative of the return of the POWs from Vietnam did not give credit where credit was due. It was at Sybil's dinner table in a suburban dining room, not a war room, where the real Vietnam POW rescue mission was launched.

Sybil met James (Jim) Bond Stockdale while he was attending the Naval Academy in Annapolis, Maryland, in 1946. In their joint memoir, *In Love and War*, Sybil recalled that if she had been a bit taller, she may not have married him. She and her friend Bebe had been set up on a side-by-side blind date by another friend. When confronted by a tall Marvin Scoggins and a short Jim Stockdale, height decided their fate.[91] They got married the following year.

Fast forward to the mid-1960s and Stockdale was the Carrier Air Group Commander in charge of an air wing at the start of the conflict in Vietnam. He had been flying over the Gulf of Tonkin that summer. He refuted a key piece of intelligence related to the war—that a report of an attack by the Vietnamese had never taken place.

What he reported could have saved countless lives, had it been considered. Instead, President Lyndon B. Johnson went on TV on August 4, 1964, and told the American public that two U.S. ships had been attacked by the Northern Vietnamese. The Tonkin incident was the justification the Johnson administration needed to escalate the Vietnam War.[92]

---

[91] James B. Stockdale and Sybil Stockdale, *In Love and War: The Story of a Family's Ordeal and Sacrifice During the Vietnam Years* (New York: Harper & Row, 1984), 42–43.

[92] Encyclopædia Britannica, "How Did the Tonkin Gulf Resolution Result in the Escalation of the Vietnam War?," video segment *From Vietnam Perspective* (1985), accessed August 26, 2025, https://www.britannica.com/video/response-Lyndon-B-Johnson-attack-patrol-boats-August-1964/-244303.

Just over a year later, on September 9, 1965, Stockdale's A-4 Skyhawk was shot down over enemy territory. He would soon be transported to the infamous Hanoi Hilton, where he was held captive for nearly eight years, four of which were in solitary confinement. During his imprisonment, he and other prisoners were held under the worst of conditions and were subject to torture at the hands of their captors.

While common knowledge today, these violations of the Geneva Conventions were not something the American public was aware of in the mid-1960s. They knew that military personnel were held captive, but the POW issue was not front-page news.

This was intentional.

Because it was an unpopular war, the narrative surrounding Vietnam POWs and the military was controversial. The plight of the POWs was seen as an extension of the war effort, not a separate problem the American population needed to concern itself with. America did not want American service members to be held prisoner, but it left the military and government to honor the promise of no man left behind.

There was no public outrage about the POWs' treatment because the public wasn't told about the torture. Like with the Tonkin incident, the Johnson administration decided to withhold this information. But the Johnson administration wasn't the only powerful group that knew the POWs were being tortured.

Sybil learned that her husband was still alive when she received his first letter from Vietnam in April 1966, seven months after having been shot down. After reading those first letters, Sybil immediately knew something was off; he referenced names of people Sybil did not know, as if they were family members. "How could most of Jim's letters be so natural and astute sounding, and those parts be so crazily mixed up? Maybe they were just momentary lapses. But even as I thought it, I knew it didn't make sense," Sybil wrote in the book *In Love and War*.[93]

[93] James B. Stockdale and Sybil Stockdale, *In Love and War: The Story of a Family's Ordeal and Sacrifice During the Vietnam Years* (New York: Harper & Row, 1984), 130.

She soon realized Stockdale had intentionally sent her a coded message that revealed the names of a few fellow aviators imprisoned in the Hanoi Hilton whose survival was previously unknown. Sybil, working with Navy Commander Robert Boroughs—known by the POW wives as Mr. POW—soon began exchanging a series of coded letters with Stockdale, gathering valuable intelligence that she shared with the Navy and State Department. It was through these letters that Sybil and the other POW wives would learn that their husbands were being tortured in the Hanoi Hilton.

At first, the POW wives responded as expected, relying upon the advice from DoD leaders while leaning on each other for support. They were good military wives who wanted to keep to the tradition of following the chain of command and trusting that the government would ensure their husbands would not be left behind.

According to Lee, "Sybil continued to wrestle daily with the thought of going to the press with her story about Jim's torture. Her entire career as a Navy wife told her *not* to say anything and to keep her opinions to herself. But Sybil was an avid student of history, and what she found in her deep dive into the brutal communist treatment of prisoners of war was clear-cut. She decided that 'a constant, gruesome pattern was clear, and I had to conclude that the worst way to influence the enemy to accord our men humane treatment was to keep quiet about the truth.'"

As the most senior wife in the League of Wives organization, it was Sybil's decision to speak out that ultimately gave the other wives the freedom to as well.

"They had to fight not only the North Vietnamese Communists who were torturing their husbands, but their own government, their own military institutions, to get justice," Lee told me in an interview. After years of being told to play by the rules and keep quiet, these accidental feminists had enough.

According to Lee, what pushed these wives over the edge was the Johnson administration's refusal to acknowledge that their husbands were being tortured by the Northern Vietnamese. They correctly believed a public acknowledgment would pressure their torturers to abide by the Geneva Convention and make life better for their husbands. The women, of course, wanted their spouses to be home, but they were more concerned with stopping the 16-hours-a-day torture sessions they knew were happening. Instead of getting these men humane treatment by using their leverage, politicians had been focused on optics-first silence, not people-first action.

"By 1966, the government fully knew what was happening," Lee shared in an interview. Their government's policy of silence felt like abandonment to the POW wives. Ultimately, the women reached out to the media, the only avenue left to them. By sharing their story with the world, they found a way to leverage public outrage, helping to bring an end to the unpopular war. After a shift in leadership in the intervening years, in May 1969 President Richard Nixon's administration finally got on board with the plan to go public.[94] It was the same year that Stockdale reported prisoners were "fighting hard" to resist.

In August 1969, Stockdale was caught writing a letter to his fellow prisoners. Communication between prisoners in the camp was forbidden. Rather than be the reason other prisoners were tortured, according to Stockdale he slit his wrists in protest, to "stop the flow" of torture.[95] He was later told the camp authority was investigating the possibility of improving living conditions.

---

[94] Nixon made the following remarks following a 1969 meeting with League members: "What I have assured these very courageous women is that, first, in reaching a settlement of the war, that an integral part of any settlement that is agreed to must be a settlement which is satisfactory on the prisoner issue and, second, that clearly apart from reaching an overall settlement of the war that this Government will do everything that it possibly can to separate out the prisoner issue and have it handled as it should be, as a separate issue on a humane basis."
Richard Nixon, "Remarks Following a Meeting With Wives and Mothers of Prisoners of War and Servicemen Missing in Action in Vietnam," December 12, 1969, Roosevelt Room, White House, *The American Presidency Project* (hosted by University of California, Santa Barbara), accessed August 26, 2025, https://www.presidency.ucsb.edu/documents/remarks-following-meeting-with-wives-and-mothers-prisoners-war-and-servicemen-missing-in-action-vietnam.

[95] James B. Stockdale and Sybil Stockdale, *In Love and War: The Story of a Family's Ordeal and Sacrifice During the Vietnam Years* (New York: Harper & Row, 1984), 356.

While Stockdale was putting up a fight in the Hanoi Hilton, Sybil was working hard to get the POW story out, even appearing in the *New York Times* on July 31, 1969. Many more media opportunities followed that summer. By the spring of 1970, public awareness of the torture of POWs "increased dramatically."[96]

Stockdale reported that his torturers began to show signs of weakness in early 1970, and by the fall the Hanoi Hilton "felt like Easy Street." The timing of the cessation of the torture of prisoners is noteworthy. The coordinated resistance led by Stockdale and his second-in-command, Jerry Denton, was significant, but so were the stateside efforts of Sybil and the League of Wives.

Both Stockdales contributed to the improvement of the treatment of POWs. He was ultimately awarded the Medal of Honor. His citation read, "Rear Adm. Stockdale resolved to make himself a symbol of resistance regardless of personal sacrifice. He deliberately inflicted a near-mortal wound to his person to convince his captors of his willingness to give up his life rather than capitulate."[97]

It is only fitting that the nation honored Stockdale for his selfless leadership during his captivity. His name appears on Navy buildings, ships, and statues. Upon reflecting on the Stockdale legacy, Martin L. Cook, retired Admiral Stockdale Professor of Professional Military Ethics at the Navy War College, noted that the Stockdale name is often bestowed upon anything that is meant to recognize ethics, leadership, and character.

However, Cook did not believe that this association was reflective of Stockdale's leadership in command roles or even a reflection of his character, but rather in his willingness to tell his story and go public about his captivity.

"No other great Navy leader and no other former prisoner of war went on to write, think, and speak as widely and deeply about the meaning of all he had been through as did Stockdale," Cook wrote about Stockdale in

---

[96] Ibid., 372.

[97] Congressional Medal of Honor Society, "James B. Stockdale," accessed August 26, 2025, https://www.cmohs.org/recipients/james-b-stockdale.

the *Naval War College Review.*[98] Many others were tortured and exemplified leadership in the same conditions, but the public is familiar with Stockdale, not Denton, because of his willingness to speak up.

Stockdale's post-release public commentary presented a new "no man left behind" narrative. His leadership famously highlighted the downsides of optimism, citing that the men who hoped to get out by Christmas would "die of a broken heart."

Rather than looking at the glass half full, Stockdale focused on stoicism, something he went out of his way to study while at Stanford University. While withstanding torture, he focused on controlling the controllable: his actions and thoughts. Optimism was toxic in the Hanoi Hilton because the POWs could not control the *if* and *when* of their release. Furthermore, Stockdale did not cite his rigorous military training as being as essential to his survival as the personal development and education he pursued on his own time.[99]

Sybil and the League of Wives' original plan similarly sought to control the controllable, working within established guardrails and the chain of command. But like her husband, she was forced to question what she thought was controllable, and she ultimately changed immovable institutions like the Navy and the federal government.

GOING PUBLIC WITH THE LEAGUE'S STORY

The POWs' safe return was a direct result of the individual strength of the service members and their wives' go-public campaign. One reason many people are unaware of the contributions of these women is because this narrative has been unofficially contested for decades by the women

---

[98] Martin L. Cook, "Reflections on the Stockdale Legacy," *Naval War College Review* 65, no. 3 (Summer 2012): 9, Gale Academic OneFile, https://link.gale.com/apps/doc/A299257196/AONE?u=anon~2f4430d&sid=googleScholar&xid=772186e1. Accessed February 22, 2025.

[99] Ibid., 12.

themselves, who minimized their own efforts; by their husbands, who felt emasculated by their wives' new role as their own powerful hostage negotiators; and by a society that wanted to move on from Vietnam. Despite having made real advancements in the accepted roles held by women, this narrative is still being contested over fifty years later.

Contested narrative: Despite testimony that this "go public" strategy was the brainchild of Sybil and the League of Wives, political leaders claimed credit for the safe return of the Vietnam POWs.

The dominant narrative surrounding the POWs' return is that of America honoring its promise to ensure no man is left behind. This narrative cannot comfortably coexist with the contributions of these women because the League's efforts highlighted the inaction of the Johnson administration, the inability of the military to act without the support of the Department of State, and the desire of the Nixon administration to be on the "right side" of the POW issue.

While there were certainly members of all of these organizations who wanted to bring the POWs home and help the League, the institutions tasked with bringing the men home had competing agendas. Rather than honoring their promise, they allowed their personal policies and mission objectives to interfere with the rescue.

By contrast, the League of Wives did not let anything stand between them and their mission. They would do anything to bring their boys home. This is why they were able to accomplish what the men in power couldn't or wouldn't do.

"They were treated like mavericks—thorns in the side of a strictly men's-world problem," said Stockdale in a 1990 talk in their hometown of Coronado. "[They were told], just keep calm, ladies, don't worry your little heads, we have a secret plan for a quick victory; sorry you're not cleared to hear it."[100]

So why is it that the League ladies have been left out of the POW narrative?

In May 1973, after the POWs had been released, Nixon raised a glass and toasted not to the POWs, although he certainly honored them, but to the wives and mothers of the POWs. On a night dedicated to these military heroes and the honored promise that none of them would be left behind, the president designated the League the "First Ladies of America."[101] The commander in chief had recognized the unofficial yet essential role these military spouses played.

Sybil was later honored with the Navy's Distinguished Public Service Award, the only spouse of an active-duty officer to ever receive this honor.[102]

Although the League was a quiet part of the POW narrative, it is not surprising that these more traditional pearl-wearing women weren't front-page news. The decade between 1965 and 1975 was full of attention-grabbing headlines. Vietnam War protests, a sexual revolution, race riots, moon landings, and Woodstock's sex, drugs, and rock and roll punctuated a period of change. These women weren't in the narrative because America wanted to move on from Vietnam and so did they. While Americans may not have vilified the POWs as they had other service members who returned from war, they didn't fully celebrate them either.

"That generation of ladies was taught that their names should only be in the paper three times: birth, marriage, and death," said Lee. "It was shameful to get other coverage." And military wives, who were told to keep

---

[100] Vice Admiral James B. Stockdale, "Armed Forces Appreciation of Coronado," May 2, 1990, *Coronado Public Library*, accessed August 26, 2025,
https://coronadolibrary.org/DocumentCenter/View/1284/Armed-Forces-Appreciation-of-Coronado-by-Vice-Admiral-Jim-Stockdale-1990-May-2-at-Coronado-Library.
[101] C-SPAN, video, "Paul Galanti," accessed August 26, 2025, https://www.c-span.org/video/?c4665020/user-clip-paul-galanti.
[102] Academy of Achievement, "Admiral James B. Stockdale, USN," *Achievement.org*, accessed August 26, 2025, https://achievement.org/achiever/admiral-james-b-stockdale/#biography.

quiet for so long to avoid tarnishing their husbands' reputations and costing them promotions, no longer had justification for speaking up.

Even though many highly respected POWs, like Stockdale, Denton, and Galanti, were very proud of the work their wives did on their behalf, some men felt ashamed of not being the hero of their own story.

"Even in their own households, for various reasons, sometimes ego, sometimes PTSD, the husbands didn't want to recognize them," said Lee, during an interview. "I think they saw it as emasculating. I think they felt like they should have been able to rescue themselves and how embarrassing that a woman, that their wife, had to rescue them." While no one would contest their heroism, Lee believes many POWs felt threatened by the new roles their wives had taken to ensure their safe return.

Some POW wives divorced their husbands. Others, like the Stockdales, allowed their experience to bring them closer. Rather than hiding from Sybil's contribution, Stockdale's pride in his wife grew all the more. Together, they published a book called *In Love and War*, in which they chronicled their parallel experiences. Together, they ensured that no POW would be left behind or forgotten. Jim Stockdale passed away in 2005 and Sybil in 2015. Their story and determination to ensure that no man is left behind did not die with them. Their narrative was just waiting to be unearthed by a modern audience.

The contributions of the League women are undisputed. Their advocacy helped raise awareness of the torture of their husbands, which caused the public to put pressure on the government to end the war before a victory could be established. America's military narrative was left unsettled. Were those who fought in Vietnam brave or pawns to a political agenda? Did America abandon its promise to leave no man behind, only to have the wives of those left behind pick up the pieces?

CARRYING ON THE LEGACY: HONORING THE LEAGUE

Ensuring no service member is left behind matters most to those who have skin in the game: military families and service members themselves. The League of Wives pushed the POW torture narrative to the forefront despite having no obvious source of political power. The League was a "family organization"[103] fueled by their members' willingness to do whatever it took. But just because they had the power to elevate *a* narrative doesn't mean *their* narrative was elevated.

Today's military spouse knows the magnitude of what the League did because it doesn't take much for us to imagine having to do it ourselves.

"Trying to live your life day to day and raise your kids and really have no communication or knowledge about your spouse for an indefinite amount of time—it's like running a marathon and they moved the finish line," said Alexia Palacios-Peters, military spouse and chair of the League of Wives Memorial Project (LWMP), whose mission was to erect a statue honoring the League in Coronado, California, the birthplace of the League and the home of the Stockdales. "For these women, there was no end in sight."

Alexis, a Coronado resident, could easily imagine what it must have been like for Sybil and the other League ladies, walking their coded Hanoi-bound letters to the mailbox, passing by happy, shiny people heading for a beach day in the glistening San Diego sun. Life moved on outside their doors, but remained at a standstill inside.

"Every time they met, there were always different ladies at Sybil's Coronado dinner table, stuffing envelopes or talking about what they were going to do in prepping for the next thing," said Alexis. "It was a small but

---

[103] Michael J. Allen, *Until the Last Man Comes Home: POWs, MIAs, and the Unending Vietnam War* (Chapel Hill: University of North Carolina Press, 2009), accessed August 26, 2025, https://epdf.pub/until-the-last-man-comes-home-pows-mias-and-the-unending-vietnam-war.html.

mighty team." And it all started with thirteen women sitting around Sybil's table.[104]

That is what Brad Willis, founder of LWMP, envisioned when he assembled the board for the LWMP after viewing an exhibit on the League's efforts in fall 2019. Willis, like many Coronado residents, knew the Stockdale story. As an author, filmmaker, and award-winning foreign news correspondent, he even accompanied former POW Senator John McCain and Senator John Kerry when they returned to Vietnam in 1990.

But it was in his capacity as Coronado Commissioner of Public Art that Brad got the idea of creating a statue to honor the League. After reading Lee's book, he filmed a documentary on the topic as one way to honor the wives' story. He approached Lee to gauge her interest.

"Between Brad and the designers he had in mind, Chris and Elizabeth, and the rest of the board, was such an incentive to participate," Lee shared. She noticed that there were many similarities between the League she had researched for years and the modern military spouses working to honor them. She found herself surrounded by a team with a similar determination as the original League, united around a common others-focused cause, to establish the first statue in the nation to honor military spouses. And like the League, the LWMP got the job done in no time, designing, approving, fundraising for, and installing a statue in under four years.

THE STATUE

Lee's 2019 book had reawakened the League's narrative and came out on the heels of other books that focused on lesser-known stories, including Margot Lee Shetterly's *Hidden Figures: The American Dream and the Untold Story*

---

[104] James B. Stockdale and Sybil Stockdale, *In Love and War: The Story of a Family's Ordeal and Sacrifice During the Vietnam Years* (New York: Harper & Row, 1984), 145.

of the Black Women Mathematicians Who Helped Win the Space Race, which was ultimately made into a film in 2016.

Members of the LWMP knew the time was right to present a new hidden narrative. But how to honor the members of the League, some of whom were still alive? Would it be enough to tell their story on a plaque, following the lead of the POW/MIA memorial in D.C.? Or was it important to show the women themselves? Would these women even want there to be a statue built in the first place?

These were the questions faced by the LWMP team and design committee, which was composed of historians, military spouses, veterans, and Coronado locals who knew the Stockdales, along with their sons, Taylor and Sid, serving as advisors.

"I was told very specifically in the beginning of this work that Sybil did not want a memorial or any kind of honor to herself only. She always emphasized the group," said Christina Bagaglio Slentz, LWMP co-chair and Navy veteran and spouse. "I think it underscores what a good leader she was. Any good leader recognizes that what he or she has brought forward is really the result of the group."

At a time when statues across America were being pulled down, the LWMP wanted to put up a statue that highlighted an untold narrative by both naming women and attributing their success to their collective efforts. The LWMP designed the memorial in close collaboration with artists Christopher Slatoff and Elisabeth Frederickson Pollnow, who attempted to honor Sybil's desire to focus outside of her solo efforts, with the statue both pointing to the "she" (individual participation) and the "we" (unified coordination) that was an integral part of understanding their small Coronado-based organization.

The memorial is a bronze sculpture featuring four female figures; the only identifiable figure is that of League founder Sybil Stockdale. The other three women are intentionally unidentifiable, representing the national movement that was the historic League of Wives. The four women face forward, with the figure of Sybil at the center, signifying her leadership and determination. Sybil's figure is, for this reason, the tallest and most prominent. The women are stepping forward on an upward slope, signifying their uphill battle and their transformation from passivity to action. Normally, artwork features an odd-numbered composition; however, the missing "fifth person" in the League of Wives memorial is understood to be today's military spouse and those to come. The gap invites the viewer to step into the League's story as they approach to read the plaque describing the League.

"There were several folks who argued that only Coronado figures should be on the statue," recalled Christina. And top of the list of who should be featured was Sherry. Her husband, retired Vice Admiral Edward Martin, was imprisoned in the Hanoi Hilton alongside Jim, and Sherry was an invaluable League member.

"I'm Sherry Martin. Sherry, like the wine," Christina recalled her greeting at their first meeting in May 2023. This was the first time the ladies would be given the chance to see the maquette, the small-scale mock-up of the statue, and share their reactions. Because the LWMP board wanted to incorporate feedback from League members, they held regular lunches with the ladies to discuss the memorial.

"I was a little nervous," said Christina. "I didn't know how she would take it. We explained how Sybil was the only person identified, and the other three ladies were symbolic of all the women around the country. She loved it. She pointed to the lady to Sybil's right and said, 'Oh, she's so cute. She has short hair. I had short hair back then.'"

Sherry wasn't advocating to be identified in the statue; she was happy the League's collective efforts were being honored at all. Nevertheless, she saw herself in the figures that were there. "That's our goal; everyone can look at the statue and see themselves or their family member in it," said Christina.

THE VOTE

On July 19, 2022, League supporters traveled to Coronado, the birthplace of naval aviation, to see if the city would accept the statue. Some League ladies lined the chamber, including ninety-year-old former member Pat Mearns.

Despite all the positive intentions and feelings shared about the project, it was not a slam dunk. The LWMP had to fight an uphill battle, with one council member voicing the minority concern of the community. He believed in the value of honoring the League but believed the memorial statue belonged in D.C., beside other national monuments that honor service members.

Despite this hesitation and a two-hour delay due to a heated pickleball vs. tennis debate, the motion passed, and the room celebrated. Upon the conclusion of the vote, Pat, in typical League lady fashion, approached the city council members. She went right to the only reluctant council member and shook his hand.

Earning this victory confirmed for the LWMP that military spouses helped honor our nation's promise to ensure no man is left behind—and the public needed to know about it.

MAKING HISTORY

The statue honoring the League was dedicated in Coronado's Star Park on June 21, 2024. It is the first public monument in our country to honor military spouses and their service to our country. The fact that this is the first shouldn't be too surprising, given that as of 2021 only 6 percent of U.S. public statues are of women.[105] In a time when many historical statues

---

[105] Sierra Rooney, "Commemoration of an Epoch: Monuments to the Women's Suffrage Movement in the United States," *Panorama: Journal of the Association of Historians of American Art*, Fall 2021 (7.2), accessed August 26, 2025, https://journalpanorama.org/article/commemoration-of-an-epoch/#marker-12556-6

are being torn down, erecting a new statue sends a message: The contributions of military spouses are valuable.

I had the honor of serving on the steering committee of the LWMP,[106] and I was able to bring my then eleven-year-old daughter to the dedication. Despite being the youngest person in attendance by far, she knew she was experiencing something special.

Before the ceremony started, we had the opportunity to meet with members of the League and their families. Many memories were shared—some sad, others uplifting. One moment that stood out was an interaction my daughter had with Page Rander, who had grown up as a military kid. Now an adult, Page is the youngest daughter of Andrea Rander, an Army POW wife and one of the few Black women who helped lead the League of Wives. Page shared a memory of what it was like to be a POW kid.

She told my daughter the story of another POW family, saying, "One lady, she had a daughter a little younger than you," said Page. "People were noticing that the girl's dad was not around, and someone asked her where he was. [The POW's daughter] said, 'Oh, he's in prison.' Of course, when you say 'prison', people think he's done something bad." Page was telling my daughter the story of one POW family, but in doing so she highlighted the disconnect POW families felt. The American people did not understand. It was up to the POW families, children included, to set the record straight. "Then [the POW's daughter] said, 'Oh no, not that kind of prison. He's been captured by the enemy.'"

As Page shared the story of the POW experience through the eyes of a military child, I saw a hidden narrative come alive in my daughter's blue eyes. She saw herself in Page's story. What would she have done if her dad was in that situation? What would she say to a peer who misunderstood

---

106 The LWMP was led by Alexia Palacios-Peters and Christina Bagaglio Slentz, founded by Brad Willis, with Cathy McJannet, Mari Fries, Navy Lieutenant Grace Kording, Nancy Schrum, Sally Ann Zoll, Millie Creager, USNR Commander (Ret.) Cherie Collins, Gail Bardin, Heath Hardage Lee, Kalee Thomas, Navy Captain (Ret.) Holly Nappen, Amy-Kestleloot-Steward, Mary Danaher-Sikes, Doug St. Denis, and myself on the Steering Committee.

that her dad was not a criminal, but being held captive in service of his country?

Honoring the League does not simply honor the women who fought for the safe return of their husbands, it honors the contributions of those who come after. It's the brief story Page shared with my daughter. The statue, like the League ladies themselves, forces the world to confront the fact that there is more to the "no man left behind" narrative than the stories they've been told.

REWRITING THE "NO MAN LEFT BEHIND" NARRATIVE

Winston Churchill is rumored to have said, "History is written by the victors." When Vietnam's POWs were released, the world saw the military planes that flew them home. They heard that government negotiations secured their release. The government and the military had acted.

But America wasn't told about the government's delays and inaction. Instead, the government took full credit for the League's efforts because they needed the political win. The wives had "won" their only operational objective: their husbands' safe return. But this is a rewriting of history and a minimization of the League's efforts.

Our government only worked to get the POWs home when public pressure to act was so high it had no other choice. It was "going public," as the League called it, that forced the government's hand. From a public relations standpoint, anti-war protests were common. What was uncommon was to receive negative press from a pro-military group. The League supported the war effort, but not the abandonment of their husbands. They didn't go on television to bash military leaders or political policy. They were masters of diplomacy. They simply told the brutal truth about their husbands' torture and allowed the American public to draw their own conclusions.

After the POWs were released, the women went back to life as usual, and the government benefited from their relative absence from public life. They could write whatever history served them. And they did.

Political and military leaders have robust processes that document their written words and actions for posterity. Their weekly agendas and letters are saved in archives as historical artifacts. It is easy to suppose what leaders were thinking or feeling, because their words are documented and searchable. Every event invitation is saved; every meeting notepad is preserved. While the wives were quoted in articles here and there, what we know about them and their experiences comes from their letters—if they chose to share them, and if anyone cared to preserve them.

Unlike the government, because the League ladies did not publish their strategy in bringing their POWs home, they are often painted as reactionary wives, not passionate strategists. If the League women only appear as love interests or supporting characters to their imprisoned husbands, the dominant narrative remains.

While relationships were certainly the motivation behind their advocacy, these women performed operational tasks that the military and government could not. They first reacted with emotion upon learning the news of their husbands' imprisonment and torture, but later tested strategies to get the job done and brought their husbands home. They didn't spend all day at home crying; they strategized how best to gain allies, going back to the drawing board when needed and applying the lessons learned to future decisions. Some operated as unofficial American spies. All of them acted as head of household for an indeterminate period of time.

As a military spouse, I can tell you that when my husband was deployed, I became a different person. I would worry about him. Did he fly that day? And if so, did he land safely? To function, I had to come up with strategies to get by. I would keep my phone by my side at all times, but I would also keep busy to distract myself. I would focus on caring for my children so I wouldn't miss him as much. I focused on the feelings of my children so I wouldn't have to feel my own.

These women did all this and more. They likely adopted similar coping strategies to protect themselves and function as they waited for their husbands' safe return. These women loved their husbands, but I would suggest that they were not starry-eyed in their actions. They somewhat begrudgingly took on a role that asked them to professionalize their personal heartache. They had to talk to Congress and reporters about their worst nightmare, answering all manner of personal questions to raise awareness of their cause.

Like their husbands, they had a mission that needed to be accomplished. They organized themselves to accomplish it.

Scholars confirm that Vietnam marked the beginning of the grassroots movement that put pressure on the government to expand its commitment to the retrieval of fallen service members[107] and honor its promise to leave no man behind. The League is finally getting the recognition it deserves as a direct result of Heath Hardage Lee's *League of Wives*, Taylor Baldwin Kiland and Judy Silverstein Gray's *Unwavering: The Wives Who Fought to Ensure No Man is Left Behind*, Kristin Hannah's *The Women*, and the LWMP statue.

But why did the League have to exist in the first place? And why has their story been separated from the Vietnam POW narrative for so long?

WHY THE DOMINANT NARRATIVE HAS BEEN PROTECTED

"No man left behind" is a nice promise that every American wants to keep, until they are faced with competing priorities. In the Battle of Mogadishu, the American public did not want to pay the price of humanitarian missions; American lives were more valuable. The public did not want to send in troops to save any more downed Black Hawks.

---

[107] Caroline Alexander, "Across the River Styx: The Mission to Retrieve the Dead," *Letter from Vietnam*, *The New Yorker*, October 25, 2004, 44–51.

During Vietnam, the POWs were nearly forgotten by the American public, which not only didn't want POWs, but didn't want soldiers, the draft, or the war at all. The government didn't want to talk about POWs and make an already unpopular war less popular. So the League's accomplishments were allowed to fade.

Today, we have the opportunity to modernize the story we have been told about how America keeps its promise to leave no man behind. By including the stories of Sybil Stockdale and the League alongside the Vietnam War and the POW narrative, we will help honor them and better understand what it takes to ensure no man is left behind.

But first, we have to recognize that all the military stories we have been told are just *part* of the story. Behind the story we are told, there are military families on the home front doing the work to protect the ones they love. Sometimes this is as simple as loving our service members. Other times, like Sybil, we must push our pearls to the side and force the government to act by going public with the problems we are facing. Sometimes, military spouses are the only ones who know the full story.

How *you* can change this narrative: Realize you, as an American, already have skin in the game. Invest in learning about the holistic military family experience. Read their stories and say their names. When you care about individuals who serve and their families, you can help keep the promise of "no man left behind."

How the DoD can change this narrative: Tell stories of the League of Wives and other historical military spouses who have positively impacted the military, and own your past mistakes. Admitting you need help honoring this promise isn't admitting weakness; it gives Americans a way to serve.

We Will Not Forget the Families of the Fallen

I knew Theresa's name long before I met her.

Her husband, Landon Jones, like my husband, flew the MH-60S Seahawk helicopter, the Navy's version of the Army's Black Hawk helicopter, and was stationed in Japan in a world before smartphones.

On Facebook, we saw pictures of the Joneses going out with friends we had just met at our new favorite stomping ground. Their names were in stories told by those who came after, giving them near-legendary status. We might have been good friends if we had arrived a few months earlier. But our friendship was never meant to be lighthearted.

When we finally connected, it was under the worst possible circumstances. On September 22, 2013, Jones's helicopter landed on the destroyer *USS William P. Lawrence* and was chained down to the deck as the pilots began performing their standard landing checks. Because the ship was traveling at such a high speed, ocean water crashed above the flight deck, hitting the still-moving rotor blades.

The damage was catastrophic. While official reports go into many complex details, my husband said the shaking was so violent it tore the helicopter apart. The helicopter, with Jones and his copilot, Chief Warrant Officer Jonathan S. Gibson inside, fell from the flight deck into the Red Sea.

The Navy went on high alert and began rescue efforts. But on the home front, wheels started turning as well.

UNOFFICIAL PANIC

Any time there is a "mishap," which is what the military calls any unplanned event that results in personal injury or property damage, the military initiates a specific chain of events. Because Navy ships are essentially small cities in the middle of the ocean, they can turn off all outbound communication to quiet the chatter that often results from conflict or accident. This is known as "River City."

From the family point of view, when this happens, your texts and emails go unread. Families know that something has happened, but without a way to get ahold of anyone, they are left in the dark. This is done to prevent panic. Word travels quickly when accidents happen aboard ships, and those waiting for the safe return of their loved ones often go into full panic mode.

Theresa first learned that her husband's squadron had been involved in a "mishap" while she was breastfeeding their newborn son. She had been scrolling Facebook when she saw a post by the Navy that said, "Navy helicopter crashes in Red Sea."[108] She didn't know exactly where he was at the time, but when she clicked on the link, it told her that his squadron was involved. She was in the middle of a nightmare of unknowns.

---

[108] U.S. Department of Defense, "Update: Navy Helicopter Crashes in Red Sea," *Defense Visual Information Distribution Service*, accessed August 26, 2025, https://www.dvidshub.net/news/114075/update-navy-helicopter-crashes-red-sea.

As a military spouse, she knew what it was like to be in the dark, but not when the stakes were this high. It turned out that his family happened to be visiting Theresa. They leaned on each other as they awaited news.

Theresa's experience highlights the fact that for military families, it doesn't take an actual notification of an accident to send the home front into a tailspin. Younger generations of military families, who have grown up with the ability to reach a loved one at a moment's notice, feel this panic any time communication is disturbed because it is assumed that something has happened.

Older generations within the community see this panic and may dismiss it as an overreaction. They were not able to reach their loved ones for months, there was no FaceTime, no email, no texting. Maybe the service member could call using the ship's phone if they had a calling card and the available free time. Maybe they would write a letter. Because they have not experienced it, they don't understand. Notification processes are slow to modernize, to the detriment of younger generations of surviving family members.

When Theresa finally received an update, it was on social media. A friend forwarded a Navy public affairs notification that the search and rescue efforts in the Red Sea had been suspended, commenting, "Devastated. Please pray for our dear friend and her boys. A pilot wife's worst nightmare come true." In our community, when a search is called off, we know the implication: there were no survivors.

Theresa commented on her friend's post, "I didn't know that yet."

Forty-five minutes later, she got the knock on the door and the official notification that her husband was dead.[109]

---

[109] Jill Qualters, "Racing Facebook: A New Challenge for Military Spouses," *Keep Calm and Have a Cosmo*, March 2014, http://keepcalmandhaveacosmo.blogspot.com/2014/03/racing-facebook-new-challenge-for.html.

Dominant narrative: If you die in the line of duty, a grateful nation will take care of your family.

A better narrative: Death is part of military service. We train and mitigate these risks, but if service costs a life, we will ensure the family is not forgotten. Their feedback will guide us in honoring our promise, correcting these issues will take top priority, above other budget line items.

HOW A MILITARY COMMUNITY PROCESSES GRIEF

Theresa had experienced the worst 24 hours of her life.

Feeling helpless to support someone I had not officially met, I, like others in the helicopter community, posted a squadron patch with a black line through it on my Facebook page. This small gesture of solidarity is intended to indicate that our community has experienced a loss. I sat in a Nevada Starbucks and cried with another military spouse friend who knew Theresa better. Every year since, I see friends post about Landon Jones and I think about Theresa.

I finally had the chance to speak with her in 2019. I reached out to her after being asked to write an article about something called the "widow's tax." It was the second article I ever wrote about military family issues.

At the time, I wasn't looking to cover topics that touched on death or surviving spouses; it was so far off my radar and infinitely beyond my comfort zone to have to confront this type of loss. My husband had been in a helicopter crash in 2011, in which all of the rotor blades broke off and a tree went through the front window, nearly impaling his copilot. Everyone walked away from the crash.

Talking about death felt wrong. My guilt was palpable. I didn't have to suffer as Theresa and others did. My husband walked away, but hers didn't. I was not yet ready to confront those feelings. How would I talk to her about the worst day of her life and not offend her? At minimum, how could I avoid making it worse? Would I give my feelings of relief away?

Theresa was the only surviving spouse I felt comfortable enough reaching out to directly without ever having spoken before. I didn't feel up to the task of reaching out to others. I suppose my editor asked me to write the article because it talked about loss alongside death benefits and congressional budgets, things that seemed too dry for some but were right up my alley.

I soon found that at the heart of this topic was something less mournful, but just as devastating. It's a story that has stuck with me because of what it has taught me as a human being: that only those who have never experienced loss are afraid to talk about death. And our discomfort comes at a cost to those who have already paid more than their fair share.

Since Landon's death, Theresa has had to recount the story of her husband's accident countless times. She has had to tell reporters that her two-month-old son never met his father, how something called the widow's tax prevented her from accessing earned survivor benefits, and how a Trump administration tax policy cost their family thousands of dollars.[110] Today, she is *still* forced to talk about how the military is failing to live up to its promise to take care of survivors.

This chapter is not just about individual service members who lost their lives and the families who have to go on without them. It is about how the military treats death beyond initial notification: the living death experienced by their surviving spouses and children.

In his second inaugural address to the nation, President Lincoln vowed the nation would "care for him who shall have borne the battle and for his widow and his orphan."[111] These words are inscribed on the walls of the

---

[110] Jeremy Herb, "Military Families Could See Tax Changes under Trump Budget," *CNN Politics*, April 26, 2019, https://www.cnn.com/2019/04/26/politics/military-families-tax-change-trump/index.html.

[111] National Park Service, "With Malice Toward None: Lincoln's Second Inaugural Address," *National Park Service*, accessed August 26, 2025, https://www.nps.gov/articles/000/-with-malice-toward-none-lincoln-s-second-inaugural.htm.

Lincoln Memorial and seen by millions each year. But few, if any, check to ensure we are keeping our nation's promise.

Theresa's story opened my eyes to how I had failed members of my own community. My reporting helped educate me about the lengths surviving families must go to collect earned benefits. Rather than make their loss easier, the military seemed to make their loss harder.

Although bureaucracy and red tape are expected within the military community, I did not expect to see widows forced to parade the stories of their husbands' deaths before the media and Congress to enact change. I certainly had no idea that individuals like Theresa had been fighting to access earned benefits for forty years.

Theresa Jones opened my eyes. Edie Smith helped me connect the dots.

THE POWER OF LOSS

Edith "Edie" Smith's house is settled in a normal neighborhood in northern Virginia. To anyone driving by, they would not have any idea that this little old lady with a southern drawl has held our country's highest leaders' feet to the fire.

Knowing I was coming for our interview, she laid out her binders containing newspaper clippings and photos. Framed mementos lined her mantle, and virtually every surface. These trophies marked every victory and setback experienced in her thirty years of fighting a war with bureaucracy.

"I never leave these out like this," she said, gesturing at the binders and photos. I stopped at her coffee table and saw it: a black Sharpie in a shadowbox. Also inside the frame was a photo of Edie and South Carolina Congressman Joe Wilson. Edie smiles as he has his arm over her shoulder, posing in front of military jets and a large American flag. He's behind a partition, in the inner circle, Edie on the other side. The photo celebrates their win.

In the photo on the previous page, they are at Joint Base Andrews in Prince George's County, Maryland. Moments before, President Trump used Edie's Sharpie to sign into law the 2020 National Defense Authorization Act (NDAA), a must-pass bill that funds the military. To not sign would be political suicide, so it's signing often feels like a formality. But for Edie and the roughly 65,000 other surviving spouses,[112] the December 2019 bill signing felt like a day that would never come.

As Edie and I sat and looked over her collection of memories, it was the first time in all my reporting related to the widow's tax that she was front and center. She had been in the background of all my interviews and photos for months, but she was in or behind every picture. In the White House, in congressional offices, Edie was everywhere. She met Republicans and Democrats—anyone who was willing to take up a cause.

"You need to talk to Edie Smith," was the admonition I heard time and again as I researched the widow's tax. While I didn't get to speak to her during her final push to repeal the "tax," I knew Edie was the one who could tell me how a group of survivors finally changed the minds of Congress and the military. Her methods were not formalized, but they were practiced. She had dealt with this type of bureaucracy before.

It all started for Edie when her husband, Vincent Smith, underwent quadruple bypass surgery at the age of forty-three, just 6 weeks after his

---

[112] Veterans of Foreign Wars, "Defense Act Ends 'Widows Tax'," *Veterans of Foreign Wars*, March 2020, https://www.vfw.org/media-and-events/latest-releases/archives/2020/3/defense-act-ends-widows-tax.

retirement from the Marines. He became eligible for Medicare, but this new eligibility meant he could no longer receive his earned military medical benefits. This was Edie's most personal standoff with something called "concurrent receipt," but it wouldn't be her last.

WIDOW'S TAX/CONCURRENT RECEIPT 101

Concurrent receipt is a 19th-century congressional rule that says you cannot receive more than one source of government funding for the same thing.[113] If you are eligible to receive more than one source of funding, any overlapping funds must be "offset," or withheld, despite being earned. Some in Congress categorized this as double-dipping.

Let's use Social Security as an example. Traditionally employed Americans pay into Social Security through income that is automatically deducted from paychecks. This payment will be returned to them (or a surviving spouse) upon retirement. Those who have an employer that also offers retirement benefits may expect to get both Social Security *and* their company's retirement benefits.

The military offers retirement pay to eligible service members. Service members can also elect to buy into something called the Survivor Benefit Plan (SBP). SBP is a benefit that the service member pays into that guarantees survivors access to their military retirement benefits after their death. SBP is paid for like an insurance payment and is deducted from the service member's monthly retirement paycheck. The highest SBP payment for a spouse is calculated at 55 percent of the service member's retired pay; for example, if their retired pay is $1,000 per month, the spouse would receive around $550 per month.

If a service member pays the ultimate price and dies in the line of duty, the military offers families a Dependency and Indemnity Compensation

[113] Kristy N. Kamarck and Mainon A. Schwartz, *Concurrent Receipt of Military Retired Pay and Veteran Disability: Background and Issues for Congress*, CRS Report R40589 (Washington, DC: Congressional Research Service, June 16, 2025), https://crsreports.congress.gov/product/pdf/R/R40589/16.

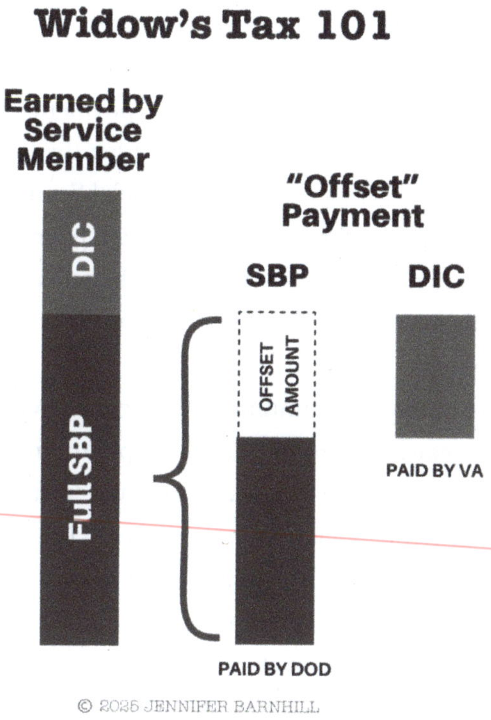

(DIC), paid out by the U.S. Department of Veterans Affairs (VA). This monthly payment essentially indemnifies the military from liability for the service member's service-related death.

You might assume that if a service member died in the line of duty, their spouse would be entitled to collect Social Security, as would any citizen, plus all eligible military retirement and death benefits. But that would be incorrect.

After the death of their loved ones, active-duty military survivors had to pay the "widow's tax." Although their spouses paid into SBP and died in the line of duty, they were not eligible to collect both payments in full. Their payments were being offset (withheld). Here is an example:

SBP Estimated Payment: $2,500/month
DIC Estimated Payment (as of December 2024): $1,653.07/month
Offset (SBP – DIC) = $846.93
What they should have been paid (SBP + DIC) = $4,153.07/month
What was paid (offset amount + DIC) = $2,500/month[114]

[114] Some survivors were also eligible for Special Survivors Indemnity Allowance (SSIA) that paid them a few hundred dollars to offset cost of living increases.

While the widow's tax was a slap in the face for survivors, it was just one more concurrent receipt issue Congress had to address.

Before 2008, military members who paid into SBP had their payment offset when they became eligible for Social Security payments.[115] They served in the military and paid into the SBP, but didn't get the full benefit because they, like most employed citizens, paid into Social Security.

This withholding was seen as unfair because these two payments were not for the same thing. It denied veterans the same benefits that were available to civilians. If citizens could collect pensions *and* Social Security, why couldn't service members collect both?

The government and military community knew concurrent receipt regulations and offsetting earned income was unpopular and seemed unfair, but because correcting these issues was expensive, it did not act. Veterans fought to overturn the Social Security offset. However, both Congress and the veteran community left military widows and widowers to figure out how to deal with their offset on their own. They said it was an unfortunate policy oversight, shrugged their shoulders, and moved on.

THE GOLD STAR FAMILY NARRATIVE

Before being asked to write my first widow's tax article, I did not know much about what a Gold Star spouse was. I had heard of the organization Blue Star Families; the name Blue Star refers to the blue stars many military families put in their windows, with each star representing a family member who is currently serving on active duty. But even I, as a military family journalist, barely knew what the blue stars represented; I suspect most Americans don't.

Kate Horrell, "Understanding the SBP-DIC Offset," *KateHorrell.com*, February 25, 2021, https://www.katehorrell.com/understanding-sbp-dic-offset/.

115 Kate Horrell, "Debunking 4 Survivor Benefit Plan Myths," *Military Officers Association of America*, accessed August 26, 2025, https://www.moaa.org/content/publications-and-media/news-articles/2024-news-articles/finance/debunking-4-survivor-benefit-plan-myths/.

The Gold Star designation is given to the family of a service member who lost their life while serving in the U.S. military. When I learned about the meaning behind those gold stars, I wondered how many times I walked by ribbons on a front door or in the rear window of a car without knowing I had passed by someone dealing with unimaginable loss.

While researching the widow's tax, I interviewed many nonprofit experts and political leaders, including the repeal's biggest advocate in Congress, Senator Doug Jones, a Democrat from Alabama.

But the most important people I spoke to were the survivors themselves. Some called themselves Gold Star spouses, some called themselves widows, and some were simply survivors. They used different phrases to describe themselves, but were united in their passion to both tell the stories of their loved one's death and to tell the world about the injustices they were facing as a result of their loss. They shared that neither they, nor their spouses, were aware of the offset until their loved one's death.

Their narratives, like Theresa's, started with a story of the loss of a service member but focused on their ongoing battle with bureaucratic injustice. They were not just Gold Star families who experienced loss and moved on; they were dragged back into hardship while trying to access earned benefits—benefits they needed to survive.

Imagine that the worst possible thing you can think of happens to you. You find out via Facebook that the search for your missing husband has been called off; then, you get a knock on the door and learn he's dead.

You are rushed through a pile of unfamiliar paperwork you have to try to digest and sign. You are grieving and unable to fully process what is happening. Then, you find out that the benefits you and your spouse thought you would receive in this situation are being withheld.

THE IMPACT OF THE WIDOW'S TAX

"Surviving spouses are military spouses first," Ashlynne Haycock-Lohmann told me in an interview. Ashlynne is the deputy director for government and legislative affairs for the Tragedy Assistance Program for Survivors (TAPS) and has been advocating for surviving families for decades.

In addition to her role at TAPS, Ashlynne is the Gold Star daughter of Army Sergeant First Class Jeffrey Haycock, who died while training to deploy in 2002, and Air Force veteran Nichole Haycock, who died by suicide in 2011. Ashlynne is all too aware of the cost surviving families pay.

"They'll never make up for that lost income," she said of surviving spouses. "And our military families generally do things like military retirement as the household retirement plan [because] most military spouses will never be able to work a career that they can actually retire from."

Military spouse unemployment has been a problem since the 1970s. Active-duty military spouses move every two to three years, have to take part-time opportunities, have gaps in their resumes, tend to be underemployed in order to stay in the workforce while facing overt and subtle forms of employment discrimination because employers see them as a risky hire.

Despite this being a well-documented problem, military spouse unemployment (the percentage of those who are looking for but not finding work) has not improved over the past half century. It has remained stagnant at around 20 percent—five times the national average. When these unemployed or underemployed spouses suddenly find themselves as the sole breadwinners, they are already at a professional and economic disadvantage. This makes any loss of income significant.

How could this happen? How can we not protect the families of those who pay the ultimate sacrifice? It is easy to say that this is red tape. But the reality is there is a disconnect between the active-duty community and surviving spouses. No one wants to think about what it is like to lose someone that they love, so survivors are pushed outside of the community, leaving them to fight this battle alone.

Veterans' groups too did not always welcome survivors because family members are not veterans. The active-duty community did not want to have to confront the reality that they could die too. Military families didn't want to think that they could one day become Gold Star family members. In the absence of established support, survivors took on the responsibility of doing their own advocacy. Some founded and worked for organizations like TAPS, while others became unpaid lobbyists.

Edie pointed to a picture of herself and a group of surviving spouses wearing yellow hats while walking the corridors of Capitol Hill, back in a time when anyone could just walk up and request a meeting with their representative. "When you represent Gold Star wives, they have that hat—and all the young people hate that hat," she said. "It tells people who you are. You don't have to walk up to anybody and say, 'I'm a widow.' So I bought one and wore it. Did I like it? No!"

Edie never went to Capitol Hill without wearing her hat and her signature color, red. She recommended that I choose my own signature color if I wanted to be memorable in the ever-evolving Congressional landscape.

For decades, the yellow hats made survivors instantly recognizable. Before marketing and branding was something the average person concerned themselves with (as in, before influencers and social media), Gold Star widows were branding their loss. They didn't need to prove themselves each time they took a meeting; their predecessors had done that for them. They each had a unique story to tell, but the goal was the same: "Axe the tax."

"[Congressional representatives] would smile and be really nice, get their pictures taken with us so they could put it on their newsletter or on the wall, and send us on our way," Gold Star spouse Kathy Prout recalled. "And then they would do nothing."

Kathy's husband, Rear Admiral James Prout, crashed in the mountains of New Mexico in his F/A-18 Hornet in 1995.[116] Kathy found that no matter how compelling their stories of loss were, initially these widows could not get anyone to take up their cause. They were told that fixing the widow's tax would cost too much money.

To get Congress to do anything, it needs to be pressured to do so. Because military survivors represent a sliver of our nation's population, they are like the tiny residents of Whoville in Dr. Seuss' *Horton Hears a Who*, their entire world the size of a speck of dust on a flower in Horton's path. Their stories existed and were important but took effort to hear.

Edie Smith and the other gold hat-wearing widows just could not compete with agencies that had all the money in the world to bend the ears of Congress and the DoD. Survivors felt as though they were talking to themselves. It took just one woman to unite their voices.

"With privacy laws, you can't find anybody. You can't find another widow unless somebody says, 'I know somebody,'" said Kathy during one of our first conversations in 2019. So Kathy formed a Facebook group to gather surviving families in one place, something she says she wishes she had done much sooner.

"I am a teacher," Kathy said, and she taught the survivor community how to organize and unify. She developed a plan of the week that she shared with the online community, like canvassing a certain state or focusing on the Senate or House Armed Services Committee or appropriations committee. Everybody in the group was responsible for calling their own congressperson and senators weekly to remind them about the widow's tax repeal.

"We walked the halls of Congress," she said. "We developed fact sheets with congressmen, outlining what committees they are on, phone numbers, staffer names." And they used this information to create a

---

[116] Kristin Davis, "Learn About This MOAA Awardee's Long Fight to Repeal the 'Widows Tax'," *Military Officers Association of America*, accessed August 26, 2025, https://www.moaa.org/content/publications-and-media/news-articles/2021-news-articles/learn-about-this-moaa-awardees-long-fight-to-repeal-the-%E2%80%9Cwidows-tax%E2%80%9D/.

grassroots advocacy army. Their weapons were their stories, and their only armor was their hats.

They had help in the form of nonprofit organizations that represented a larger number of active-duty military and veterans, and their families, including TAPS, Veterans of Foreign Wars (VFW), National Military Family Association (NMFA), Gold Star Wives of America, Military Officers Association of America (MOAA), and others.

But they also had a champion: Senator Doug Jones. Having won a special election, he had nothing to lose other than his next election. He was a Democrat in Alabama; many would say he knew he'd lose. He was free to vote each day as if he'd never hold office again because he knew he might not. So he voted with his conscience and passionately took up the cause of Gold Star families.

This left a group of widows, organizations like TAPS, and the Democratic senator of a Republican state educating Congress and the military community about the injustice of the offset. Widows met with leaders and told their stories to reporters—or anyone else who would listen—until their yellow hats couldn't be ignored. And they did the legwork.

"For every dollar they gave to us, they had to take one dollar away from somebody else, some other program, and nobody wanted to give up their dollars," said Kathy. Although the benefits were earned, concurrent receipt allowed the government to not have to set aside the money to pay families. Surviving family members had to fight for Congress to put their earned benefits back in the budget. "So the budget part was really difficult. I went to the budget people over in the Senate, and they said, 'Nobody ever comes to see us.'"

Notably, said Kathy, they couldn't figure out where SBP came from. They knew the military retirement trust fund had money. Because SBP is an insurance benefit that must be paid into, it generated income for the DoD. It was "finding" this money, Kathy said, that ultimately *offset* the cost of the offset.

The Gold Star families told their stories, they found the money, and they got Congress on board. It took forty years, but survivors finally got unanimous support. The widow's tax was formally repealed when the NDAA was signed into law on December 20, 2019. It took three years for the offset to be fully phased out and for families to see full payments, but the 40-year battle with the widow's tax was over.

Despite this amazing step forward, I'm still talking to Theresa Jones about her fight for survivor benefits. Not because she's unhappy with the progress that has been made, but because she is still fighting.

Correcting the widow's tax was just one battle in the war to hold America accountable. The narrative that says our nation takes care of widows and orphans relies upon the widows and orphans to fight so that we keep our promise.

We are still talking about Landon Jones and the aftermath of his death because the survivor benefits Theresa has fought so hard to receive to support herself and her two sons will be forfeited if she chooses to remarry before her 55th birthday.

"I don't get remarried because I would be penalized financially," Theresa told me in a 2023 interview. Because Theresa was only thirty-three when her husband died, repealing the widow's tax only solved part of the problem she faced.

STILL FIGHTING: THE REMARRIAGE PENALTY

Marcie Robertson met her husband, Army Sergeant First Class (SFC) Forrest Robertson, when they were in preschool. They dated throughout high school, then married a few days after 9/11 at a DMV within a JCPenney department store. Their new military marriage was tested by the war in Iraq, the birth of children, and countless wartime deployments.

"I remember talking to him on that Friday . . . I could just hear the smile in his voice. He was happy. He was doing what he wanted to do," she told me in an interview. Just two days after that November 2013 call, Marcie learned her husband was killed in combat in Afghanistan.

"In February of 2014, right before Valentine's Day, I got my first letter asking me to verify that I had not remarried," said Marcie. This letter would be an annual reminder to her—and to all survivors who receive death benefits—that if she wanted to remarry, her happiness would cost her.

According to current law, if a Gold Star or surviving spouse remarries before the age of fifty-five, they will lose their survivor benefits,[117] including SBP, DIC, Tricare health coverage, access to VA home loans, and much more. The average total loss amounts to roughly $4,000 in payments per month plus benefits.

Only recently, Marcie and her fiancé, Nelson, started breathing a little easier. For years, they have lived in fear that someone would report them and she would lose her benefits. Although they are not married, the VA could investigate them if it believed she was "holding out" to be married.

Because of the work of survivors and TAPS, that stipulation was removed from the policy, effective as of early 2025.[118] Previously, if a surviving unmarried spouse purported to be married or introduced themselves as a married couple to others (despite not being married on paper), they could lose their benefits.[119]

Because the average age of a surviving spouse is twenty-five years[120]—thirty years from fifty-five—it is likely that many survivors held themselves out to be married. It is estimated that only 5 percent of surviving spouses under the age of fifty-five officially remarry; the remaining don't because

---

[117] U.S. Department of Veterans Affairs, "§ 3.50 Spouse and Surviving Spouse," *Electronic Code of Federal Regulations*, accessed August 26, 2025, https://www.ecfr.gov/current/title-38/chapter-I/part-3/subpart-A/subject-group-ECFR2f2f66751230c72/section-3.50.

[118] H.R. 8371, *Senator Elizabeth Dole 21st Century Veterans Healthcare and Benefits Improvement Act*, 118th Cong., 2d sess., § 303, introduced May 14, 2024, https://www.congress.gov/bill/118th-congress/house-bill/8371/text.

[119] U.S. Department of Veterans Affairs, "§ 3.50 Spouse and Surviving Spouse," *Electronic Code of Federal Regulations*, accessed August 26, 2025, https://www.ecfr.gov/current/title-38/chapter-I/part-3/subpart-A/subject-group-ECFR2f2f66751230c72/section-3.50.

[120] TAPS, "TAPS Advocates for Survivors: October 20, 2021," *Tragedy Assistance Program for Survivors*, accessed August 26, 2025, https://www.taps.org/advocacy/2021/oct20.

of the financial losses.[121] However, for many, remarriage provides support that goes beyond finances. They are looking to find the emotional stability that the loss of a loved one takes away.

"My kids deserve that security. My kids deserve a father figure," said Marcie. "My [late] husband told me to get them one." Many military families have similar conversations, often before deployments to prepare for a worst-case scenario. Yet, she and others are waiting to get married, while at the same time weighing the loss of finances against knowing they do not have legal rights to be there for their partner or their partner's children in an emergency.

This policy was drafted at a time when women did not work outside the home. Daughters were taken care of by their fathers and wives by their husbands. They could not hold credit cards or take out a loan without a male sponsor. If a widow decided to remarry, the new husband would assume the responsibility to provide for them, essentially making death benefits unnecessary.

However, this gendered policy no longer aligns with societal norms, even within the military community. But again, Congress doesn't want to pay to correct it.

"As someone who just voted for the aid to Taiwan and to Israel and to Ukraine, or $95 billion worth of support overseas, it's very hard for me to reconcile voting for that and then somehow not having the resources to take care of families that have made the ultimate sacrifice. That disappoints me," said Congressman Dean Phillips in a 2024 interview.

Phillips, a Democrat from Minnesota, is a Gold Star child. Like Theresa's youngest son, who was born while her husband was deployed, Phillips never knew his father, who was killed during the Vietnam War.

---

[121] Candace Wheeler, "April 10, 2024 – TAPS Statement for the Record Before the Committee on Veterans' Affairs, United States House of Representatives, Disability Assistance and Memorial Affairs Subcommittee," *Tragedy Assistance Program for Survivors*, accessed August 26, 2025, https://www.taps.org/advocacy/2024/apr10#:~:text=According%20to%20the%20Department%20of,remarry%20due%20to%20these%20penalties.

Phillips' personal connection to the Gold Star community has led him to advocate for survivors in Congress.

"The reason that we find ourselves in these predicaments is there are highly mobilized, well-organized, well-resourced lobbying firms and industries that are very adept at making their case to Congress," he said.

The narrative that promises to protect military families if a service member dies doesn't say how it will honor this promise. It doesn't say when or if the promise will expire. It is a promise to the service member who is no longer alive. Military families are made to feel like they are taking money away from someone else when they stand up for themselves.

For spouses like Theresa Jones and Marcie Robertson, the narrative also shames them for wanting to remarry. It whispers a lie: "If you were a good spouse, you wouldn't seek remarriage."

The narrative that promises to look after surviving family members doesn't consider other messages that persist within the military community, namely the narrative that says military families are unissued baggage. This narrative minimizes family contributions and says we are nonessential members of the community. When someone is not seen as essential, they are forgotten and shamed into silence.

When the unimaginable happens, surviving spouses like Theresa and Marcie instantly go from unemployed or being a secondary breadwinner to being the only income. Their income is slashed in an instant. They scramble to care for children and plan for a future they didn't want. They suffer unimaginable tragedy and then have to find themselves within their new circumstances. They have had to prove to peers, reporters, Congress, and themselves that they are not looking for a handout but the earned benefits their spouse was promised.

Survivors are just looking to the military community to help them survive.

LEARNING A BETTER NARRATIVE FROM THE FRONT LINES

Stacy Correa was not expecting to get a phone call on October 1, 2016. It was a Sunday. Her husband never flew on Sundays. But the call still came. When she picked up, she found herself speaking to the wife of the squadron's executive officer.

During our interview, Stacy recalled how that conversation went.

"Stacy, are you home?"

"Yes."

"Are you by yourself?"

"Yes."

"Are you sitting down?"

"No."

"Why don't you sit down? There's been a crash." Then there was a pause.

"I knew something was really wrong," Stacy said.

What the executive officer's wife was able to share was minimal, but what she did say was the only information she needed to hear. "She said, 'I can't give any details, but I can tell you personally that if your spouse were involved in the crash, you wouldn't be getting a phone call; somebody would be coming to your door.'"

Stacy tried to reassure herself that she had gotten a call, not a knock. But she couldn't call anyone without causing panic or spreading misinformation. She eventually got a text from her husband that simply said, "I love you." She asked for more information, but he could not share anything else without breaking protocol.

Eventually, her husband did come home, unharmed. But because of reporting requirements, he could not confirm if anyone had died in the crash. She still held out hope that there were survivors. The reality was that Lieutenant Patrick Ruth and Lieutenant Junior Grade Wallace Burch were killed when their T-45C Goshawk crashed in the Cherokee National

Forest in Tennessee that Sunday evening.[122] Stacy constantly checked the news to see if the Navy had made an announcement; she ultimately received a text that the Navy had pronounced them dead.

Stacy may have found out via text message, but she was not the next of kin. As Training Squadron SEVEN's casualty assistance officer prepared to deliver official notifications, others within the squadron knew that neither Ruth's fiancée nor Burch's girlfriend were officially connected to their service members in the Navy's eyes. But Burch's friends didn't see it that way.

"These men got their dress blues on at 10 at night," Stacy said, on the verge of tears. "They found a duty driver and they loaded up a van and drove four hours to Mobile, Alabama, to knock on her door to give her proper notification because she wasn't going to get one officially from the Navy. If they wouldn't have done that, she wouldn't have received that officiality and that respect."

"They definitely didn't have to," Burch's girlfriend, Amber, told me in an interview. "It would have been much harder with my grief, especially not getting any notification had his friends not shown up."

"I watched my friend become a widow," Dana Dunne told me during a different interview. Dana has been a Marine Corps spouse since 1993 and has had numerous encounters with the ups and downs of military life. "I watched the Marine Corps fill his job the next day and life go on . . . Everyone is replaceable, and the machine will replace you and keep going."

Dana's husband flew the AV-8B Harriers, also known as a Marine Corps' widowmaker, for thirty years. According to Dana, she and her husband have said goodbye to fifty-six friends who have died in military-related accidents; only one died in combat. The most personal loss they experienced was when her husband's wingman, Marine Lieutenant

---

[122] Hope Hodge Seck, "Navy Identifies Two Pilots Killed in T-45 Crash," *Military.com*, October 3, 2017, https://www.military.com/daily-news/2017/10/03/navy-identifies-two-pilots-killed-t45-crash.html.

Colonel Christopher K. Raible, who he referred to as his son, was killed by the Taliban in 2012.[123]

"People don't want anything," said Dana. "They don't need anything. They're not worried about a cute tchotchke or a little memorial or something sweet that you bought at Hallmark. It's the people that show up, the people that sit there and hold her when she cries or that run defense for her . . . Don't ask them, 'Oh, how are you?' How do you think they are? Her husband just died. What do you want her to say, 'I'm fine' a million times? No, they're not fine."

Dana has had to confront death so many times that she jokingly referred to herself as a "death doula." That statement struck me because it was said with pride. She was happy to have been able to be there for survivors, even if she was struggling internally.

"The packs are heavy that I carry, and the scars are deep," Dana said of her experiences supporting families through their toughest days. Instead of describing how each loss may have affected her feelings about her husband's service, she continued to focus on how the lessons she learned can be passed on to others.

"There are scars, and people should know it's going to affect you for the rest of your life. You're always going to think about it and you always need to say their name," she said.

While individuals like Dana get better at dealing with loss, despite all its practice, the military institution isn't good at dealing with death. This is why a better narrative is needed if we are to truly remember the families of the fallen. We write the narrative by calling out what we think we know about this promise.

If the American public assumes this promise is the responsibility of the military community, they would be wrong. If the military community assumes this promise is the responsibility of the person's family, they would

---

[123] Dan Lamothe, "Marine Lt. Col. Christopher K. Raible," *The Fallen: Military Times*, accessed August 26, 2025, https://thefallen.militarytimes.com/marine-lt-col-christopher-k-raible/6568338.

be wrong. If the person's family assumes this promise is the responsibility of institutions like Congress and the military, they would be wrong.

When we tell survivors we are praying for them, we mean it. But the effort on its own doesn't get the job done. Furthermore, it is not that leaders who heard about the widow's tax didn't care about survivors. They likely did care. They just didn't care enough to prioritize the care of the families of the fallen above louder and more powerful voices.

That is why veterans corrected the Social Security offset long before the widow's tax offset was corrected. Veterans were loud and they were united. Surviving family members were not united until individuals like Kathy Prout and Edie Smith unified them. When Doug Jones and organizations like TAPS handed survivors a megaphone, it amplified their unified message.

We are all responsible for ensuring that the families of the fallen are not forgotten. Before meeting Theresa Jones, I repeatedly broke this promise because honoring it made me feel uncomfortable.

But it is not just military and political leaders and systems that failed survivors. All of us failed them.

HOW WE MUST CHANGE THE NARRATIVE
AS INDIVIDUALS

Human beings suck at sitting with sadness. As we approach these uncomfortable conversations, most of us do so with our own fear of death at the back of our minds. It is the one constant I have observed by talking to survivors and those who have sat with survivors on their worst day. We have a choice as bystanders to put ourselves first or to put survivors first.

Well-meaning phrases like "What can I do for you?" or "I am praying for you" can feel hollow when they're not accompanied by actions. These phrases are said for us, not for the survivors. After we say them, we get to tell ourselves, *I did my part. I reached out and showed love and concern. They are going through something hard. I certainly can't make it better, and talking about it again and again will probably make it worse.* This internal narrative lets us off the hook but leaves those we think we helped no better off than when we found them.

What if "What can I do for you?" is replaced with showing up with a bucket and mop to clean the house? Or a text saying you're picking up the kids for an impromptu play date to distract grieving children?

Thoughts and prayers mean the world when said but can turn into a cacophony of silence when not accompanied by a sustained and thoughtful effort. It's hard to know what a survivor needs. *They* may not even know. It takes a thoughtful survey of the person's situation, researching the nature of grief, and seeking the advice of others who have been in their shoes but who may have had more time to process their loss.

Putting survivors first requires more and goes much further than the proverbial thoughts and prayers.

AS AN INSTITUTION

The military largely avoids public discussions on death. Officially, this is out of respect for the fallen; practically, addressing every loss in depth is unfeasible. But silence is also strategic. Acknowledging military weaknesses, especially deaths, disrupts the illusion of invincibility that the DoD carefully maintains. The institution is not impervious, but it will never say so.

By contrast, the VA has been forced to acknowledge its institutional liabilities. In 2014, the VA was called out for excessive waitlists that resulted in poor care, with some veterans dying as they waited to be seen.[124] The VA couldn't hide from its very public failures. Instead, it adopted a

---

[124] U.S. Department of Veterans Affairs, Office of Inspector General, *Review of Alleged Patient Deaths, Patient Wait Times, and Scheduling Practices, Phoenix VA Medical Center* (Washington, DC: VA OIG, 2020), https://www.vaoig.gov/reports/audit/review-alleged-patient-deaths-patient-wait-times-and-scheduling-practices-phoenix-va.

more vulnerable narrative that acknowledged past mistakes and asked for Congressional support to correct them.

The DoD's job is to fight and win wars. The military doesn't wish to make death personal, because if it were personal, the public might start to weigh the cost. Instead, it examines the cause of the accident, keeping things clinical, with an abundance of detail or hardly any.

Theresa Jones ultimately learned that her husband's death was not the result of his own error, as was originally speculated. He did his job and was a good pilot. The Navy laid the fault at the feet of the skipper in command of the ship, who chose to travel at a fast speed through rough waters, conditions that the aviation community had previously warned the Navy were risky. While the skipper did not violate official Navy regulations, she made a dangerous choice and people died.[125]

While Theresa did receive an apology from individual Navy leaders for finding out about her husband's death on Facebook, the Navy never publicly owned the mistake.

The DoD's public narrative ignores the families of the fallen because it doesn't want to focus on the fact that the greatest fighting force on Earth is made up of mere mortals.

And its silence betrays the promise. The DoD narrative says it will care for the families of the fallen, but the reality very clearly shows that the survivors themselves have had to fight for this promise to be honored. While untrained individuals from within the community often step up and support their peers, the institution has to be strong-armed to get it to do its part. On Capitol Hill, elected officials talk about helping people in public but prioritize defense budgets and essential weapons systems behind closed doors. They too must be forced to honor this promise, or the machine will keep going without the family long after the service member dies.

---

[125] Sam LaGrone, "Fatal Knighthawk Crash Partially Blamed on Destroyer Skipper, Crew," *USNI News*, May 20, 2014, https://news.usni.org/2014/05/20/fatal-knighthawk-crash-partially-blamed-destroyer-skipper-crew.

AS A NATION

Our nation can no longer allow this narrative to be a silent promise. It needs to follow the lead of President Lincoln. It needs to be etched on the walls of the buildings we walk through, and talked about in the halls of Congress. Our news channels need to feature the stories of survivors. Just as the media has stopped glorifying terrorists by featuring their names above the names of their victims, we cannot focus only on the spectacle of death at the expense of those who survive. We cannot shy away from caring for the families of the fallen because it makes *us* more comfortable.

How *you* can change this narrative: Seasoned military families and civilian supporters, put aside your own fears and talk about death. Learn how to sit with sadness. Show up for those who are grieving. Don't wait to be asked.

New military families: In addition to the above, I encourage you to find a way to belong to this community. It is easy to look at a seasoned or senior military family member and think they have it all together, but the reality is they do not; they need you just as much as you need them.

How the DoD can change this narrative: Do not remain silent. Own the narrative that you will take care of families. You train and equip individuals for service. They know the risks. The nation knows the risks. Step up to take care of those who are left behind. Talk about their sacrifice and go to bat for them. This can start by endorsing the removal of the remarriage penalty that says a survivor will lose their benefits if they marry before the age of fifty-five. Stop trying to save money by adhering to dated and gendered assumptions. If service members die for their country, take care of their families. Regularly evaluate the notification processes to ensure families are prioritized on the worst day of their lives. Embrace the role military families and families of origin play. Support their efforts, remove red tape and administrative obstacles, and train all service members on how to treat families, especially Gold Star families.

These are just a few suggestions, but the reality is we owe survivors far more.

The Military Takes Care of Its Own

When Marine Corps veteran Kate Hendricks Thomas left the service in 2008, she did not have any idea she was about to fight another war.

During an interview with *CBS News*, Hendricks Thomas recalled how she told her son: "Mommy has a terminal condition that is going to kill her, but she'll always be with you."

"The radiologist said it looked like I'd been dipped in something," she told the interviewers.[126] When she attempted to get care through Veterans Affairs, she was initially denied. It took her three years to eventually get approval. This bureaucratic delay inspired her to fight not only for her own care but to improve access for other veterans.

Hendricks Thomas was diagnosed with stage four breast cancer in 2018, more than a decade after returning from Iraq. She was just thirty-eight years old. She was surprised that her doctor recommended an early mammogram because she'd read her file and knew "where [she] had been

[126] CBS News, "Veterans Exposed to Burn Pits Battle Breast Cancer and the VA," video, accessed August 26, 2025, https://www.cbsnews.com/video/veterans-exposed-to-burn-pits-battle-breast-cancer-and-the-va/.

stationed." She had no symptoms or family history, but the test results showed she had three different types of cancer.

She died in 2022, after fighting to raise awareness around burn pit exposure and improve access to care for others.

Hendricks Thomas is just one of the estimated 3.5 million service members who had been exposed to toxic burn pits while serving in Iraq and Afghanistan. Burn pits are large fires produced to dispose of trash. For the military, this waste includes food, plastics, vehicle parts, confidential materials, and medical and human waste. This waste must be disposed of, and in the absence of an incinerator in the field, the military has historically had to make do.

While burn pits had become commonplace in combat zones, they were not in the news until reporter and military veteran Kelly Kennedy broke the story in 2008.[127]

"It was no secret," Dan Clare told me during an interview. "Everyone knew it was awful." Clare is a Marine Corps veteran and chief communications and outreach officer for the nonprofit Disabled American Veterans (DAV).

Clare is not just another service member who was exposed to burn pits—he's the one who leaked the burn pits story to Kennedy. After serving on active duty, Clare joined the Air National Guard in 2001 and was deployed to Balad Air Base in 2007. His civilian job was with DAV, where he worked with Vietnam veterans exposed to Agent Orange. He knew burn pits were more than just an inconvenience.

"There's also the sense that you're going to get in trouble if you take pictures of the burn pit," Clare said. "You're supposed to look away."

And many did.

According to Clare, concerns about burn pits came up frequently, and leaders knew it was bad. "Burt Field was the general in charge of the 332nd

---

127 Kelly Kennedy, "Harmless or Hazardous? Troops Say Chemicals and Medical Waste Burned at Balad Are Making Them Sick, but Officials Deny Risk," *Military Times*, November 3, 2008, https://www.militarytimes.com/news/burn-pits/2022/03/07/harmless-or-hazardous-troops-say-chemicals-and-medical-waste-burned-at-balad-are-making-them-sick-but-officials-deny-risk/.

at the time, and he said that every time he would do those town hall meetings with the troops, every time [burn pits] came up," said Clare. "He knew."

According to Clare, leadership had other priorities. The base was routinely mortared, and those in charge were trained for battle, not running a small city. War had a way of making toxic things seem normal.

But when Clare finally saw Air Force Bioenvironmental Engineering Flight Commander Lieutenant Colonel Darrin Curtis' memo detailing his concerns,[128] it confirmed his fears. Leadership knew the burn pits presented "both an acute and a chronic health hazard" to troops. It further stated that "it is amazing that the burn pit has been able to operate without restrictions over the past few years." By the time Clare saw the memo, it was a year old. He knew leaders were aware yet had not shut down the pits.

So he decided to take care of his own.

"You just know something's such the right thing to do that [it] overwhelms the thought of getting in trouble," Clare said. But what came next was not easy.

"We got the story out about burn pits, and not a single burn pit changed that day. Not a single burn pit quit burning," he said. Ultimately, Clare, DAV, and countless others got to work to raise awareness, get the burn pits shut down, and get those exposed to toxins the help they needed.

In 2022, fourteen years after Kennedy and Clare broke the story, and the same year Hendricks Thomas died, the PACT Act was passed.[129] Before the PACT Act, if a service member was diagnosed with a burn pit–related illness like cancer, the burden of proof lay with them. They had to be able to connect their presence near a burn pit with their illness to be eligible to receive care from the VA.

---

[128] Darrin L. Curtis, Lt. Col., "Memorandum for 332 EAMD/SGP, Subject: Burn Pit Health Hazards," December 20, 2006, Department of the Air Force, accessed August 26, 2025, https://cswab.org/wp-content/uploads/2015/10/Burn-Pit-Memo-for-Record-20-Dec-06-LtColCurtis.pdf.

[129] The full name of the PACT Act is Sergeant First Class Heath Robinson Honoring our Promise to Address Comprehensive Toxins Act of 2022.

The PACT Act allowed veterans to be treated for their medical conditions without also having to prove their military service had caused them to need care. The PACT Act would also allow eligible veterans to collect disability benefits because of their exposure.

Clare, Kennedy, veteran service organizations, and countless individual veterans did the work to ensure the VA would finally get the funding and support to help take care of its own.

But it was Jon Stewart who shamed Congress into action.

"This may be one of the lowest-hanging fruits of the American legislative agenda. Those that took up arms in defense of this country and its Constitution suffered grievous harm in that defense," said comedian and activist Jon Stewart at a rally where he was raising awareness about burn pits. "And when they came home, we put them on trial. 'You got cancer? Prove it was us.'"[130]

The military allowed the burn pits to stay open despite known health risks. It covered up the risks and did not shut them down for years. Once the story broke in 2008, Congress held hearings. News media covered the story. Small advances were made to help those who sought treatment at the VA for lung issues, but proving a cancer diagnosis was service-connected remained a battle. Taking care of one's own comes with a high price tag that has to be approved by Congress, and admitting it had failed to take care of its own wasn't something the DoD was willing to do.

And Jon Stewart can't be everywhere.

Dominant narrative: The military takes care of its own.

A better narrative: The military can't take care of its own on its own. Taking care of service members and families is the job of every American, but few actually step up.

---

[130] PBS NewsHour. "WATCH: Jon Stewart Advocates for Veterans Affected by Burn Pits at the 'Pass the PACT Act Rally.'" *YouTube*, March 2, 2022. https://www.youtube.com/watch?v=9NHoC3FDKvQ.

WHERE THERE IS (TOXIC) FIRE, THERE IS (TOXIC) WATER

The weekend after Thanksgiving of 2021, Mary Monrose's two-year-old son began throwing up. She assumed he had caught a stomach bug before the holiday break and it was just catching up to him.

She was wrong.

Soon, she started noticing changes in her vision that were accompanied by painful headaches. She drank more water to ensure she was hydrated, but her symptoms persisted.

"I began to break out with a rash on my back, and I didn't know what it was from," said Mary. "The following week when I went to brush my teeth, I remember there was an extreme smell of gas." When she got in the shower, her skin began to burn.

A post in Mary's local military Facebook group asked if anyone had been noticing a sheen in their water. Mary has been a Navy spouse for over fourteen years and has experienced the ups and downs of the lifestyle. She knew that if she was going to get answers, she would likely get them from her peers. The community quickly put two and two together. This was not an isolated illness; the community had been exposed to an environmental hazard and the military had not yet told them.

The Monrose family and 90,000 other residents in and around Joint Base Pearl Harbor–Hickam on Hawaiian island Oʻahu had been exposed to toxic chemicals after a federal employee at the Red Hill Bulk Fuel Storage Facility accidentally hit a pipe and sent roughly 19,000 gallons of jet fuel into the local aquifer, contaminating the water supply.

While this November 20, 2021, accident caused the leak into the aquifer, it may have been made worse due to previous negligence. Months earlier, in May 2021, federal employees tasked with transferring jet fuel "took a shortcut."[131] Their actions resulted in what was estimated to be

---

[131] Jaclyn Hughes, et al., "Complaint for Civil Action Under the Federal Tort Claims Act," Case No. 1:24-cv-00059, filed February 5, 2024.

1,618 gallons of toxic jet fuel and additives spilling into the environment. The Navy was only fined $325,000 for the incident.[132]

The Navy's response to the May incident was later labeled "insufficient" by the secretary of the Navy, and was later seen as a missed opportunity to correct further failures.[133] The fuel from the May spill had been sucked up by an automatic sump pump system, but ended up lodged in retention lines intended to contain used firefighting foam. Some of the fuel went unaccounted for until the November accident, when all the lost fuel, plus additional fuel, found its way into the environment and drinking water. An investigation into the May incident did not result in swift action, and this delay contributed to the November spill.[134] The May spill was far worse than estimated, totaling 20,957 gallons, not the 1,618 previously estimated. And the total fuel that remains unrecovered is 5,542 gallons.[135]

The cost of this failure was paid not by military leaders but by the families under their care. Roughly 87 percent of residents reported experiencing at least one symptom of exposure, including neurological issues (headache, dizziness, etc.) and gastrointestinal trouble (diarrhea and nausea), while others reported anxiety and other mental health problems.[136] However, the cascade of poor decisions did not end there.

Although the Red Hill facility is run by the Navy, Joint Base Pearl Harbor–Hickam is a joint base that houses personnel from all service branches. As a result, how each branch saw fit to "take care of its own" differed greatly.

---

[132] Audrey Mcavoy, "Hawaii fines Navy $325K for fuel storage facility violations," *Associated Press, November 27*, 2021 https://apnews.com/article/hawaii-honolulu-us-navy-0b7d7dfa3348924eb767cd5c8ea86c12.

[133] Carlos Del Toro, "Memo: Secretarial Letter of Censure," *The Secretary of the Navy*, September 28, 2023, https://media.defense.gov/2023/Sep/28/2003310573/-1/-1/0/RH%20SLOC_SIGNED.PDF.

[134] According to reports, the Navy should have used a metal pipe; instead, contractors were approved to install PVC pipes, which is believed to have contributed to the scope of the accident.

[135] W. K. Lescher, "Memo: Command Investigation into the 6 May 2021 and 20 November 2021 Incidents at Red Hill Bulk Fuel Storage Facility," *Department of the Navy*, June 13, 2022, https://www.secnav.navy.mil/foia/readingroom/HotTopics/RED%20HILL%20INVESTIGATION/FOIA%20Release-Red%20Hill%20CI%20(June%202022).pdf.

[136] Hawaiʻi Department of Health and Centers for Disease Control and Prevention/Agency for Toxic Substances and Disease Registry, *Navy Water Contamination Survey Results*, May 26, 2022, https://health.hawaii.gov/about/files/2022/05/JBPHH-Water-Contamination-Survey-Results.pdf.

On November 29, the Navy put out a statement saying, "There is no immediate indication that the water is not safe. The Navy continues to investigate reports and is testing the water."[137]

On November 30, just days after Mary's son started showing symptoms that he had been exposed to contaminated drinking water, the Hawaiian Department of Health put out a notice contradicting the Navy's message, warning "Navy water system consumers not to drink, consume tap water."[138] After receiving 175 complaints, the Hawaii Department of Health (DOH) conducted preliminary tests a day later, on December 1st, and found a "petroleum product" in samples from Red Hill Elementary School.[139]

On November 28—two days before the Department of Health issued its statement, and the same weekend Mary noticed a change in her water—a small nonprofit organization, Armed Forces Housing Advocates (AFHA), issued a warning not to drink the water after hearing from 456 families.[140]

"I remember the first town hall meeting and [the Navy was] saying the water was still safe to drink," Mary recalled. "By this time, the Army had already come down with loads of trucks and set up literally like a camp in our big community area. They had portable showers. They had cases of water that they started to deliver to each house." The Army also began providing vouchers for families to get relocated to local hotels.

---

[137] U.S. Pacific Fleet, "Navy Investigating, Testing Water at JBPHH Family Housing," *U.S. Pacific Fleet News*, November 29, 2021, https://www.cpf.navy.mil/newsroom/news/article/2993562/navy-investigating-testing-water-at-jbphh-family-housing/.

[138] Hawai'i Department of Health, "Hawai'i Department of Health Advises Navy Water System Consumers Not to Drink, Consume Tap Water," *Hawai'i Department of Health Newsroom*, November 30, 2021, https://health.hawaii.gov/news/newsroom/hawaii-department-of-health-advises-navy-water-system-consumers-not-to-drink-consume-tap-water/.

[139] Hawai'i Department of Health, "Preliminary Results Detect Petroleum Product in Navy Water System," *Hawai'i Department of Health Newsroom*, December 1, 2021, https://health.hawaii.gov/news/newsroom/preliminary-results-detect-petroleum-product-in-navy-water-system/.

[140] Patricia Kime, "'Smells Like Gasoline:' Military Families in Hawaii Say They Are Being Sickened by Their Tap Water," *Military.com*, December 1, 2021, https://www.military.com/daily-news/2021/12/01/smells-gasoline-military-families-hawaii-say-they-are-being-sickened-their-tap-water.html.

The Navy's response was not as swift. While the Navy set up water distribution centers and requested logistical support, the Army brought water to the doors of residents and issued evacuation orders within days of the first reports.[141] Navy personnel watched how their neighbors of a different service branch were taken care of while they felt abandoned.

By the time the Navy finally confirmed the water was contaminated on December 2, Army families had already been told to get out.

The side-by-side comparison of how the military takes care of its own was striking.

Like the narrative that says "we will not forget the families of the fallen," the "we take care of our own" narrative highlights unofficial, unspoken promises to care for people made by institutions. When these narratives and promises are not institutionalized or standardized, they are just a burn pit or a fuel leak away from very public failure.

While the burn pits had Jon Stewart and Dan Clare, Red Hill families had Mary Monrose.

"Speaking up and advocating for people, that's always been a passion of mine," she said. Because jobs in Hawaii were hard to find, she began volunteering. In 2021, she was selected to serve as an advisory board member for the Military Family Advisory Network (MFAN), a nonprofit that creates programming based on data collected from the active-duty community.

Each board member is carefully selected to create a representative sample of the overall military community, including officer and enlisted families, different genders, various branches of service, and different regions of the country. Members serve a two-year term in which they are instructed to have their ears to the ground and report back to help inform MFAN research and programming. It was this role that would prove instrumental to the Red Hill water crisis.

---

[141] W. K. Lescher, "Memo: Command Investigation into the 6 May 2021 and 20 November 2021 Incidents at Red Hill Bulk Fuel Storage Facility," *Department of the Navy*, June 13, 2022, https://www.secnav.navy.mil/foia/readingroom/HotTopics/RED%20HILL%20INVESTIGATION/FOIA%20Release-Red%20Hill%20CI%20(June%202022).pdf.

As part of its operations, MFAN held a meeting with then–Deputy Assistant Secretary of Defense for Military Community and Family Policy Patricia Barron, a veteran Army spouse.

Barron asked in a virtual meeting if anybody had heard about what was going on in Hawaii with the jet fuel, Mary recalled. "It was crazy because . . . we're all on Zoom and they're secretly chatting me, 'Speak up!'" said Mary. And she did. She panned her camera around and showed Barron the hotel room, a room that she had to share with her three children and sometimes her husband for nearly six months.

Barron asked Mary to reach out to her community via Facebook groups and ask them what the DoD could do for them (in addition to cleaning up the jet fuel).

After she shared her story with Barron, Mary said things changed for the better. But this change was bittersweet. She was happy to feel like she could trust the information she was receiving, but she wondered what would have happened had she not spoken to Barron.

"I knew what I had done to make that happen," Mary said. "It was still hard to take in. Why did it take this long? It shouldn't have taken this long." Mary was in the right place at the right time, but what if she had not been?

In the military "taking care of one's own" is a sentiment often shared by leaders, political and military. But these leaders hid evidence of burn pits and protected the Navy's reputation over its people during the Red Hill incident. Taking care of one's own is more likely to be the nitty gritty business of the Jon Stewarts, Kate Hendricks Thomases, Dan Clares, and Mary Monroses of the world, individuals who see a broken system and are not afraid to stand up and say, "This is not working."

While the Balad burn pits were closed in 2009,[142] Red Hill is an ongoing issue, with concerns about the safety of the water supply and unknowns about how residents' long-term health may be impacted.[143]

THE MILITARY WELFARE STATE AND BIRTH OF MILITARY NONPROFITS

While individuals like Dan Clare, Jon Stewart, and Mary Monrose worked to take care of their own, they did not act alone. For decades, nonprofits staffed by veterans and military spouses have been taking care of military service members, veterans, and families.

The concept of taking care of our own was first seen in writing during World War II, when it became the slogan of the Army Emergency Relief (AER), an organization established in 1942 by the Secretary of War. This program was formed to remove the dependence of service members on nonprofit agencies like the Red Cross. When soldiers were conscripted into the Army, they were promised to be cared for because "the Army takes care of its own."[144] The Army wanted to control the narrative and did not want soldiers to have to turn to outside entities for help.

After the military converted to an all-volunteer force in 1973, the DoD needed to rethink who it recruited and how it recruited service members. No longer were service members single men. Male and female service members were married and had children who needed support while their service members were deployed.

---

[142] National Academies of Sciences, Engineering, and Medicine; Health and Medicine Division; Board on Population Health and Public Health Practice; Board on the Health of Select Populations; Committee on the Assessment of the Department of Veterans Affairs Airborne Hazards and Open Burn Pit Registry; David A. Butler, Anne N. Styka, and David A. Savitz, eds., *Assessment of the Department of Veterans Affairs Airborne Hazards and Open Burn Pit Registry* (Washington, DC: National Academies Press, 2017), https://www.ncbi.nlm.nih.gov/books/NBK436096/.

[143] Christina Jedra, "Report: Navy Mismanagement Led to Red Hill Water Contamination Disaster," *Civil Beat*, November 14, 2024, https://www.civilbeat.org/2024/11/report-navy-mismanagement-led-to-red-hill-water-contamination-disaster/.

[144] Office of the Chief of Staff of the United States Army, *White Paper 1983: The Army Family*, 1983, https://apps.dtic.mil/sti/pdfs/ADA143245.pdf.

The DoD tried to find ways to make service more palatable for families who had to move every two to three years and who were separated from family and friends. The military created programming to support families, including family housing, child care, health care, counseling, and more. Jennifer Mittelstadt, professor of history at Rutgers University and chair of military history at the U.S. Army War College, wrote in her book *The Rise of the Military Welfare State*, "These programs were far more generous than any offered in the civilian public sector."[145]

In the 1980s, the Reagan administration focused on reducing the size of the federal government and building up the size of the military. Later, the Clinton administration took aim at welfare. During his 1992 presidential campaign, Clinton vowed to "end welfare as we know it."[146] He ultimately cut program enrollment by roughly 60 percent.[147]

At the time, the narrative surrounding welfare was quite negative. Phrases like "welfare queen"[148] were used to describe those who were seen as wanting to take advantage of the system, allegedly stealing hard-earned taxpayer dollars. The government had been hollowed out and leaders forced Americans to lean into bootstrap-pulling behaviors by removing safety net programs. Politicians and government leaders were reminding Americans, the military community included, that they needed to take care of themselves.

According to Mittelstadt's book, the military did not wish to sustain what could have been considered a military welfare state in that political climate. It similarly began to cut military family programming and embraced messages of self-support and resilience.

---

[145] Jennifer Mittelstadt, How the Culture of "Welfare Reform" Changed the US Army," *Historians.org*, August 15, 2016, https://www.historians.org/research-and-publications/perspectives-on-history/summer-2016/how-the-culture-of-welfare-reform-changed-the-us-army.

[146] *Bill Clinton in 1992 Ad: "A Plan to End Welfare as We Know It"*, Washington Post, August 30, 2016, https://www.washingtonpost.com/video/politics/bill-clinton-in-1992-ad-a-plan-to-end-welfare-as-we-know-it/2016/08/30/9e6350f8-6ee0-11e6-993f-73c693a89820_video.html.

[147] *Clinton-Gore Administration A Record of Progress: Reforming Welfare*, The White House, https://clintonwhitehouse2.archives.gov/WH/Welfare/Accomp.html.

[148] Wahneema Lubiano, "Black Ladies, Welfare Queens, and State Minstrels: Ideological War by Narrative Means," in *Race-ing Justice, En-gender-ing Power: Essays on Anita Hill, Clarence Thomas, and the Construction of Social Reality*, ed. Toni Morrison (New York: Pantheon Books, 1992), 323–62.

Then 9/11 happened.

After 9/11, the military population grew and deployments surged.[149] While many single service members could respond to an increase in operational tempo with minimal disruption to their personal lives, half of all service members were married at the time.[150] The DoD was not tracking the second-order effect of a military population that had more dependents than service members. As fighting increased, so did the need for the military to take care of its own. But its attention was elsewhere.

A surge in military deployments combined with a diminished support network meant the military could not honor its 1942 promise to take care of our own. But no one said a word. Families didn't complain. They were too busy getting through deployments and supporting each other.

This public silence reinforced what America already thought about the all-volunteer force. It was a band of brothers, a community that did whatever it was asked to do to protect our nation. And, certainly, if it was in charge of protecting our nation, it was fully capable of taking care of its own. *If* and *how* the military took care of its own was no longer part of the public narrative. It was assumed.

This lack of programming, coupled with an increased demand for support, opened the door to a new model of military family readiness, one that the DoD had previously distanced itself from: nonprofits. In the 1940s, the military did not want soldiers asking the Red Cross for help, so it took care of its own. In the 2000s, the military flipped the script and pushed soldiers and families towards those same nonprofits.

---

149 Pew Research Center, "The American Veteran Experience and the Post-9/11 Generation," September 10, 2019, https://www.pewresearch.org/social-trends/2019/09/10/the-american-veteran-experience-and-the-post-9-11-generation/#:~:text=Roughly%20three%2Dquarters%20of%20post,served%20in%20a%20combat%20zone.

150 Center for Naval Analyses, *Population Representation in the Military Services Fiscal Year 2001*, March 2003, https://www.cna.org/pop-rep/2001/pdf/intro2001.pdf.

WHAT HAPPENS WHEN THE PROGRAMS THAT EXIST FAIL?

Dealing with disasters like the burn pits and the Red Hill incident is not the job of nonprofits or individuals like Dan Clare and Mary Monrose. There are government agencies tasked with caring for the health of service members and protecting the safety of military families. These incidents are examples of something called "sector failure." Sector failure is when a for-profit, nonprofit, or the government offers a solution to a problem that fails to meet the need.

Unlike civilian nonprofits, military-focused nonprofits are formed both when there is a gap in services and to help when funded DoD programs fail to meet the need; in short, they correct sector failure. When the military fails to take care of its own, it will not go out of business because it doesn't rely upon profit to keep its doors open. The only way it can know if it is meeting the need is if it stops to ask families whether the solutions it is offering are working. It must evaluate programs.

In 2013, the Military Family Readiness Council held a meeting to discuss a point-in-time survey of internal program evaluation practices. They found that only 30 percent of military family programs collected useful data that could be used to evaluate the effectiveness of the program.[151]

As a result, the Office of the Secretary of Defense (OSD) established a Common Services Task Force headed by Charles Milam. He and the task force authored a report that was never publicly released, so I emailed OSD asking for a copy. Because my request went unanswered, I submitted a Freedom of Information Act (FOIA) request for the report in February 2023. In June, they emailed me, but did not send the report. "We are currently reviewing this document for public release, but it will take a few

---

[151] Department of Defense Military Family Readiness Council, *Minutes of the January 22, 2013 Meeting*, January 22, 2013,
https://download.militaryonesource.mil/12038/MOS/MFRC/DODMFRCMeeting22January2013Minutes.pdf.

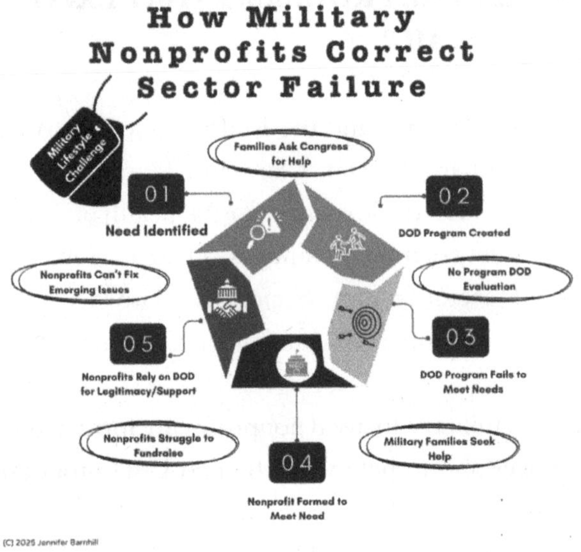

months, as the documents are voluminous," they said. They never did send the report.

When I finally obtained a copy from an anonymous source in 2024, I realized why the DoD had been sitting on the report. Its thirty-four pages were not voluminous, but what it did say spoke volumes.

According to the report, "The majority of programs do not report performance measures to OSD and may not capture cross-Service measures, leaving programs unable to discern if they are successful."[152]

Despite having oversight over military family readiness programming, the Pentagon has no idea how effective each service branch is at taking care of military personnel and their families.

Because the DoD does not regularly conduct program evaluations that might highlight its failure to meet needs, it can publicly say, "Hey, look, we're taking care of our own," while simultaneously failing to do so. And the American public has no idea because the DoD is controlling the data and, therefore, the narrative. When military families share that they are not being served by DoD programs, they are seen as squeaky wheels or

---

[152] Military Community & Family Policy Task Force on Common Services for Service Member and Family Support Programs, *Final Report V2.1*, May 14, 2014, 31.

complainers,[153] rather than whistleblowers.[154] Instead of informing needed change within the DoD, they are forced to go outside the system—to Congress—to get help.

When enough complaints are received by Congress, it may choose to force the services to change a program, or it may conduct its own program evaluation via the Government Accountability Office (GAO). Even when GAO reports inform policy change, it can take years to adopt their suggestions, resulting in the need to outsource support to the nonprofit sector.

Unlike civilian problems that become evident to a local community, military problems are kept quiet because it supposedly takes care of its own. When programs that are designed to take care of military families fail to meet the need, the only people who are aware of this failure are the individuals the programs are supposed to serve.

Because civilians don't know there is a need, military families themselves form nonprofits to solve the problems they themselves have experienced. Because they can come to the aid of families quicker, they are an essential way the military takes care of its own. Unable to offer this speed or flexibility, the DoD knowingly accepts sector failure as a limitation of bureaucracy and relies upon the existence of nonprofits to fill programming gaps.

This is where the "taking care of our own" narrative gets dicey. The DoD relies upon the military family readiness ecosystem, composed of government and nonprofit organizations and military family volunteers. Because it relies on a system it can't directly control, it doubles down on indirect control.

---

[153] Military families report being fearful to report issues with DOD services and programming for fear of retaliation from the military and/or military contractors.
Sasha Ingber, "Military Families in Privatized Housing Afraid to Come Forward, Survey Says," February 13, 2019, https://www.npr.org/2019/02/13/694366838/military-families-in-privatized-housing-afraid-to-come-forward-survey-says.
[154] Government Accountability Project, "Whistleblowers Tell U.S. Senate About Continuing Mistreatment of Military Families in Privatized Housing," April 18, 2023, https://whistleblower.org/press-release/whistleblowers-tell-u-s-senate-about-continuing-mistreatment-of-military-families-in-privatized-housing/.

Regulations stipulate that the government can't publicly support any non-federal entity (NFE). NFEs must be vetted before they can be endorsed by the DoD. To be approved, nonprofits can't compete with existing government programs.[155] If an NFE isn't approved, military personnel can't tell families about the resource, even if it is a better resource or the only available resource.

These regulations also limit what these nonprofits can say if they want to partner with the DoD. Regulations state that partner organizations "shall not in any way prejudice or discredit the DoD Components or other Federal Government agencies."[156] In other words, you can partner with the DoD as long as you don't contradict them.

The military lifestyle creates a problem, offers its own program, tells nonprofits they cannot compete with that solution, all while not measuring the effectiveness of their program in addition to using regulations to silence those who are in a position to speak out. This policy, rather than being an extension of taking care of one's own, actually does the opposite. What was intended to ensure the military doesn't play favorites has actually created a nonprofit monopoly that funnels financial resources toward those who are willing to adhere to the DoD's chosen narrative.

HOW THIS NARRATIVE CREATES NEW PROBLEMS

Clearly, the DoD and military personnel rely on nonprofits. And these nonprofits rely upon the American public to donate money to support their efforts. Since COVID-19, nonprofits have struggled, as charitable giving has been on the decline.[157] And of the roughly 1.49 million 501(c)(3)

---

155 Electronic Code of Federal Regulations (eCFR), "32 CFR 212.6—Procedures," accessed August 26, 2025, https://www.ecfr.gov/current/title-32/part-212#p-212.6(d.

156 Ibid.

157 Amy Silver O'Leary and Tim Delaney, "It's Real: Charitable Giving Plummeted Last Year," *National Council of Nonprofits*, June 26, 2023, https://www.councilofnonprofits.org/articles/its-real-charitable-giving-plummeted-last-year.

organizations in America,[158] 92 percent make less than $1 million annually.[159] What was already a competitive fundraising environment is even more so when the problem they are trying to solve impacts just 1 percent of the nation.

Military Service Organization/Veteran Service Organization Roundup

Organization	*Year Founded*	*Founding Story/Mission**	*2021 Annual Revenue*	*2021 Paid Staff vs. Volunteers***
Disabled American Veterans (DAV)	1920	"Made up exclusively of men and women disabled in our nation's defense, the [DAV] is dedicated to one single purpose: building better lives for all of our nation's disabled veterans and their families."	$170,633,533	661 staff; 14,161 volunteers
Navy-Marine Corps Relief Society (NMCRS)	1904	"Several Naval officers, wives of Naval officers, and civilian friends saw a need for organized assistance."	$29,210,374	204 staff; 4,000 volunteers
Blue Star Families (BSF)	2009	"Founded by military spouses in 2009 to empower families to thrive as they serve."	$11,402,884	78 staff; 457 volunteers
The National Military Family Association (NMFA)	1969	"Founded by a handful of military wives who wanted to make sure their widowed friends were properly taken care of."	$9,411,080	39 staff; 484 volunteers

[158] "Nonprofit Organizations in the U.S. – Statistics & Facts," *Statista*, accessed August 26, 2025, https://www.statista.com/topics/1390/nonprofit-organizations-in-the-us/#topicOverview.
[159] "Common Myths About Nonprofits," *National Council of Nonprofits*, accessed August 26, 2025, https://www.councilofnonprofits.org/about-americas-nonprofits/myths-about-nonprofits.

Military Family Advisory Network (MFAN)	2013	"Was created in 2013 to connect military families with the resources they need to thrive."	$4,165,176	14 staff; 1,114 volunteers
Armed Forces Housing Advocates (AFHA)	2021	"Our founders began individually advocating for their neighbors and friends in [military] housing."	Under the $50,000 IRS reporting requirement	0 staff; 100% volunteer

*Pulled from organization websites.
**The actual number of volunteers may not be accurately reported as the IRS 990 form only requires an estimated number.

A 2015 Center for a New American Security (CNAS) report, "Charting the Sea of Goodwill," confirmed military-focused nonprofits were struggling to fundraise. The report looked at pre- and post-9/11 military and veteran nonprofits and measured their overall success by tracking annual revenue. It found that military-focused organizations were worse off financially than civilian nonprofits.

According to the report, "The overwhelming majority—29,109, or 69 percent of the total—reported less than $100,000 in revenue,"[160] compared to 40 percent of civilian nonprofits that made that amount. In other words, the majority of military nonprofits struggle to keep their doors open, despite being an essential component of military readiness.

While veterans impacted by burn pits had large, established organizations like DAV with hundreds of millions of dollars in revenue and Jon Stewart to turn to, families impacted by the Red Hill incident turned to smaller organizations like Military Family Advisory Network (MFAN) and Armed Forces Housing Advocates (AFHA).

---

160 Phillip Carter and Katherine Kidder, *Charting the Sea of Goodwill: A Landscape Analysis of Philanthropy for the Military and Veteran Community*, Center for a New American Security, December 2015, https://s3.amazonaws.com/files.cnas.org/documents/VeteransPhilanthropy_151207_rev.pdf?mtime=20160906082558.

AFHA, a small nonprofit founded and run 100 percent by military spouse volunteers, was dedicated to helping military families living in privatized military housing.[161] For years, DoD-contracted housing companies refused to respond to military families who were forced to live in mold-infested government housing.[162] Because privatized housing was run by contractors, the DoD would throw up its hands when faced with family complaints, saying it could do nothing to change contracts or force the contractors to act.

AFHA was founded to serve families when the housing companies and DoD did not. They sent mold-test kits to families, taught them what to look for, and helped them navigate the system. However, their work was threatened when a privatized housing agency served them with a subpoena, asking them to reveal client data.[163]

The founders were the proverbial David to the government contractor's Goliath. And this Goliath had a stone up its sleeve. Its subpoena required AFHA to fund its own legal counsel, forcing the founders of an all-volunteer, military spouse-run 501(c)(3) organization to risk paying out of pocket to solve a problem the DoD should have fixed in the first place. These military spouses were fighting companies with billions of dollars of revenue to maintain their ability to take care of their own. While the DoD ultimately worked to improve its privatized housing challenges, it did not step in to help AFHA because it had signed contracts with Goliath.

When I first learned about AFHA's situation, I wondered why families hadn't turned to larger military family nonprofits. They had more revenue. They cared about the impacted military families. The big organizations were not prepared to provide this type of niche housing support.

---

[161] "AFHA | Facebook," accessed August 26, 2025, https://www.facebook.com/AFHAorg/.
[162] U.S. Congress, Senate Armed Services Committee, *The Current Condition of the Military Housing Privatization Initiative*, hearing before the Subcommittee on Personnel and Subcommittee on Readiness and Management Support, 116th Cong., 1st sess., February 13, 2019, https://www.govinfo.gov/content/pkg/CHRG-116shrg54809/html/CHRG-116shrg54809.htm.
[163] Patricia Kime, "Private Base Housing Firm Tried to Get All Communications Records from a Military Family Advocacy Group," *Military.com*, May 11, 2023, https://www.military.com/daily-news/2023/05/11/nonprofit-gets-caught-crossfire-of-military-housing-lawsuits.html.

This is considered a good nonprofit business practice. Mission creep—straying from an established mission—is discouraged. As nonprofits grow larger, they have to be careful not to spread themselves too thin, and may hesitate to respond to emerging needs without an obvious funding source.

In other words, DAV was positioned to help veterans poisoned by burn pits, but it would not likely send out mold-test kits to active-duty families or put Red Hill families up in a hotel. This is why small military nonprofits are needed. The big ones avoid straying from their primary mission or being publicly seen as doing the DoD's job for them. They know they have to wait for the DoD to acknowledge there is a problem that it needs help solving.

Furthermore, research performed by the Center for a New American Security (CNAS) shows that military nonprofit organizations are becoming increasingly dependent on government grants.[164] According to Doug McCormick, co-author of "Changing Tides in the Sea of Goodwill," this funding, while not substantial enough to sustain veteran nonprofits, served as a stamp of approval, opening the door for private funders.[165] However, small nonprofits generally can't meet grant application requirements and are not established enough to get a Memorandum of Understanding (MOU) with the DoD.

The primary funding source available to small, newly formed nonprofits is often individual donors. However, if the DoD already has a program in place, that sends a message to would-be-donors: "Don't worry, we take care of our own." This narrative subtly hints that no funding is needed, because the DoD has a solution.

The public is left to assume that if the program the military offers is failing, the DoD will fix it or ask for help. When the DoD does neither,

---

164 Phillip Carter and Katherine Kidder, *Charting the Sea of Goodwill: A Landscape Analysis of Philanthropy for the Military and Veteran Community*, Center for a New American Security, December 2015, https://s3.amazonaws.com/files.cnas.org/documents/VeteransPhilanthropy_151207_rev.pdf?mtime=20160906082558.

165 Douglas McCormick, Emma Moore, and Andrew Swick, *Changing Tides in the Sea of Goodwill: A Financial Analysis of Veteran-Serving Nonprofits*, Center for a New American Security, October 2018, https://s3.amazonaws.com/files.cnas.org/documents/Changing-Tides-Working-Paper-Final.pdf?mtime=20181018132021.

organizations like AFHA provide services to military families without an official DoD agreement or financial support. They stand up all-volunteer organizations and operate without pay for years. Some even pay out of pocket to ensure services are provided to families. Sure, there are larger nonprofits that could raise the alarm, but because they have agreements with the DoD that limit what they can do and say, they remain silent until the DoD officially recognizes the issue.

HOW DID WE GET HERE? ADDRESSING CONFLICTING NARRATIVES

The way the military takes care of its own is complex. It offers programs but fails to evaluate them. It outsources the work to nonprofits, but only established nonprofits that agree not to violate the narrative the DoD crafts. While outsourcing the taking care of one's own to nonprofits is a good model of support, the policies the DoD has in place limit nonprofit effectiveness and keep the military community stuck in a broken cycle.

This model wasn't always how the military honored the promise. The way the military takes care of its own has evolved over the years, responding to changing social norms and political climates.

FAMILY FIRST

"The Army is an institution not an occupation . . . Our goal is to increase the bonding between the family unit and the Army community—create a sense of interdependence."

—U.S. Army Chief of Staff General John A. Wickham
on the Army Family in 1983[166]

[166] Office of the Chief of Staff of the United States Army, *White Paper 1983: The Army Family*, 1983, https://apps.dtic.mil/sti/pdfs/ADA143245.pdf.

Before the DoD began to push against the military welfare state narrative, it openly embraced military families. The idea of the "Army family" was based on a patriarchal system, with the Army itself serving as the grandfather of the family, the service member as the dad who depended on the Army, and the wife and children who depended on both the Army and the service member.

This family-first model was dated even in the 1980s, as women were increasingly entering the workforce, undermining this military strategy of interdependence. According to the American Psychological Association, interdependence is a relationship in which "one cannot change without affecting the other."[167]

The Army anticipated how this may be perceived, but rather than distance itself from this narrative, it doubled down. "In fostering interdependence between the family and the Army, we are again looking at the Army as an institution," wrote Army Chief of Staff General John A. Wickham. "The Army has a responsibility to its members and the members have a responsibility to the Army and each other."[168]

The Army family was intended to unify soldiers, family, and the institution in a "sense of common identity—a shared purpose and commitment to the overall mission. They come to view the Army as providing for their total basic needs in exchange for total commitment."[169]

Families were asked to accept hard truths. *You will move. It will be disruptive. You could die. This is part of serving. The military asks more of you and your family than a civilian job.*

But we will take care of our own. The "Army Family" white paper said, "[This plan] recognizes that ad hoc programs established on a piecemeal basis that treat the symptoms but not the causes of family stress are no longer sufficient."[170]

---

167 American Psychological Association, "Interdependence," *APA Dictionary of Psychology*, accessed August 26, 2025, https://dictionary.apa.org/interdependence

168 Office of the Chief of Staff of the United States Army, *White Paper 1983: The Army Family*, 1983, https://apps.dtic.mil/sti/pdfs/ADA143245.pdf.

169 Ibid.

170 Ibid.

As it turned out, the message that said the Army was a family could not survive the war against welfare, changing gender roles, and twenty years of war. The Army family narrative was dropped in the 1990s and a period of program austerity and self-reliance and resilience took its place.

After 9/11, service members and families were asked to take on even more to support the increased operational tempo. Families were holding up their end of the military family/interdependence bargain. They formed strong bonds through shared hardship. When programs, ad hoc support, or the DoD failed to meet the need, they founded nonprofits to take care of their own. But the military did not reciprocate. No longer bound to an Army family, the DoD distanced itself from soldiers and their families and started calling them "resilient."

Despite this shift, the narrative that the military takes care of its own persisted. Its silence did not signal to the American people that the Army was no longer taking care of its own, just that it was continuing as promised behind Pentagon walls.

GOODBYE FAMILY FIRST, HELLO PEOPLE FIRST

In 2020, the Army unveiled the new Army People Strategy in response to the disappearance and murder of Fort Hood Specialist Vanessa Guillén in April of that year.[171] Guillén's sexual assault and murder by her military supervisor sparked outrage in both the civilian and military communities.

The Army hoped its people-first campaign would "confront unhealthy behavior in the ranks (e.g., sexual assault or harassment and violent extremism), build cohesion and understanding in the ranks (including diversity, inclusion, and equity), manage Army talent differently, and

---

[171] Michael E. Linick et al., *Addressing the Friction Between the Army's People First Initiatives and Its Readiness Generation Process*, RAND Corporation, RR-A2006-1, 2023, https://www.rand.org/pubs/research_reports/RRA2006-1.html.

provide support to soldiers and their families in dealing with unique aspects of Army life."[172]

In the years following, DoD memos from senior leaders also touted people-first[173] initiatives across all branches. In 2023, the congressional House Armed Services Committee joined in, establishing a quality-of-life panel designed "to ensure we are prioritizing people over hardware."[174] Both the DoD and Congress listed quality-of-life efforts they wanted to prioritize.

Leaders wanted to change the narrative; they wanted to take care of their own. They signaled to Americans that the military was putting its people first. The Army had a strategy, and it was willing to evaluate it. But it didn't evaluate it because it wanted to ensure the program's success. It studied it because it knew "the imperatives of the People First initiatives and programs are at odds with the successful achievement of units' [mission readiness]."[175]

Research conducted by the nonprofit think tank and research institute, RAND, found that "in addition to inconsistent messaging, the units perceived that there were no discernible rewards for doing well at People First. There were, however, clear incentives to achieve [operational] goals (and disincentives to failing to achieve them)."[176] It turned out that People First, like the Army Family before it, was a well-intended message designed to reassure the military community and the American public that the military can keep its own house in order. But it couldn't.

---

[172] Ibid., v.

[173] U.S. Department of Defense, *Resilient and Healthy Defense Communities Strategy*, OSD008028-23, February 14, 2024, https://media.defense.gov/2024/Feb/15/2003394891/-1/-1/1/RESILIENT_AND_HEALTHY_DEFENSE_COMMUNITIES_OSD008028_23_RES_FINAL%20.PDF.

[174] U.S. House of Representatives, Committee on Armed Services, "HASC Announces Creation of Quality of Life Panel," press release, June 14, 2023, https://armedservices.house.gov/news/documentsingle.aspx?DocumentID=1715.

[175] Michael E. Linick et al., *Addressing the Friction Between the Army's People First Initiatives and Its Readiness Generation Process*, RAND Corporation, RR-A2006-1, 2023, https://www.rand.org/pubs/research_reports/RRA2006-1.html, v.

[176] Ibid.

People-focused programs don't work because most aren't prioritized or measured. What isn't measured doesn't count. What isn't counted doesn't get funding. When a program fails but is allowed to operate, it stands in the way of nonprofit or for-profit solutions. And it is the people in the military community who feel the failure. When people feel the failure, trust in the institution wanes.

The DoD allows this to happen because it is tasked with too much as it is. It hopes that nonprofits will spring up to fill the void it has created. It then is morally free to talk a good people-first game because it believes the military nonprofit ecosystem will fill the gaps. To a large extent, this works; these nonprofits do great work, until they don't. If the military's public narrative denies there is a problem, no one will show up to donate to the effort.

This is why Dan Clare's supervisor did not want him to leak the burn pit story until he had moved on to a different position. This is why Mary Monrose and Facebook group communication helped protect Red Hill families when the Navy failed to do so. "People first" and "family first" are just iterations of "we take care of our own," a narrative that is destined to fail because it relies upon the military to either fully succeed in honoring the promise or tell the nation it failed. Because under the current narrative, a problem is not a problem until someone at the Pentagon says it is.

A MORE HONEST NARRATIVE

Despite being part of a system that is set up to fail, individual military leaders do get it right. I have seen it. When my friend Esther received a devastating cancer diagnosis, her husband was given liberal leave to take care of things at home. The command did everything it could to help make this tragic time easier on their family. They drew up plans to change his deployment schedule and stood by to take care of their own in the only way they could.

This example is just one of many. If the military constantly and routinely failed its people, this narrative would have died out a long time ago. Individuals try to change the system and fail because it is so daunting. So the system continues to fail its people.

It is time we break the cycle.

This starts with changing the narrative. Systems can't be repaired if we don't admit they are broken. This begins with embracing program evaluation. We shouldn't wait for whistleblowers like Dan Clare to raise concerns about burn pits. Military leaders should have taken care of their own by asking Congress via the Pentagon for financial resources to set up an incinerator. The VA should have been asking exposed veterans how they were doing and monitoring their health, rather than waiting for nonprofits like DAV to connect the dots for them.

While the military should do more to solicit feedback from its people, nonprofits like DAV will always be essential. They are able to respond to emerging issues more quickly than the DoD or the VA. And they need to be allowed to do so.

When the DoD places restrictions on who it partners with and what they are allowed to say, it limits nonprofits' ability to effectively help the military take care of its own. When it fails to publicly acknowledge emerging issues faced by service members and families, it threatens the livelihoods of small nonprofits that step up to meet the need, like AFHA.

If the American public thinks that the military is caring for its own, then why would they need to donate money to an organization that is seen as duplicating that effort? This results in military service members, veterans, and their families relying on nonprofit organizations that could close their doors tomorrow. These policies must be changed to allow this military nonprofit ecosystem to flourish. However, this will require a mindset shift from the DoD.

The DoD cannot take care of its own on its own.

It needs to say this to itself over and over until it sticks. Admitting this reality is not admitting weakness. The DoD needs to be focused on its primary mission of protecting our nation. While taking care of its own is an essential part of that mission, the DoD is not a school or a childcare facility or a landlord, although it operates as all three. It can't be expected to do any or all these things properly when regular program evaluation is not budgeted for or reported to the public.

Because of its size, the DoD can't be trusted to evaluate itself. The Common Services Task Force is just one example of how the DoD's lack of objectivity and siloed power structures stifle its own evaluation efforts and waste taxpayer dollars. Regular evaluations are required. Ineffective programs must be allowed to fail. And the DoD can't stay silent about these failures, or it will signal to the American public that help and resources aren't needed.

Despite all this, you won't hear many military families complain. We pride ourselves on being able to push through hardship. When we do ask for help, we really need it. The DoD must stop perpetuating the narrative that we take care of our own on our own. This narrative tells the American public that they can rest easy. It says your money isn't needed. It says we know what is best for our people, so go about your business. But when the DoD and VA fail to meet the needs of their people, this narrative pushes away the very network of support that is needed to fulfill the promise.

A better narrative combines the Army family interdependence model and a new form of nonprofit support. If the military can't be a benevolent patriarch, it still needs to be honest about the realities of military service, its benefits and its drawbacks. In doing so, it opens the doors to nonprofit support. This narrative will require the DoD to step away from the perception that strength means never admitting fault and decide to see transparency as an asset, not a liability.

The reality is the military can't take care of its own on its own. And that is okay. The all-volunteer force experiment is not just about the few who sign up to fight. It is an experiment that relies upon the participation of the entire nation. America wants to find ways to thank service members for their service. Letting go of the notion that the military takes care of its own will open the door for them to do just that.

How *you* can change this narrative: Support military families and nonprofits by sharing your time, talent, and treasure. Do not simply thank someone for their service; ask them how you, too, can serve by supporting the military.

How the DoD can change this narrative: Publicly recognize that it will take the entire nation to step up and take care of our own. Update DoD instructions[177] to make it easier for nonprofits to take care of military service members and families, with a primary goal to grow public-private partnerships with both small and large organizations. Conduct regular program evaluation. Use this information to improve or sunset foundering programs. Tell the American public when military families need help. This will foster healthy competition and allow smaller nonprofits to fundraise more effectively. Do not discuss quality-of-life policies without including them in DoD budgets. Create a pathway to measure how effective leadership is at implementing new initiatives. Let those who take care of military families take care of families. Don't let paperwork or policy get in the way.

[177] Both DODI 1342.22 and DODI 1000.15 are just two examples of instructions that, if updated, could make it easier for entities other than the DOD to help care for military service members and families.

Military Families Are Resilient

Kaitlin Erkkila's one-year-old son William was losing weight to the point of starvation. She knew life with her son would be hard after he was diagnosed with Down syndrome at birth, but her gut kept telling her this was something more. She went to the doctor seventeen times, with her two-year-old son Jonathan in tow, in search of an answer. Her husband was deployed, and Kaitlin was doing the best she could. She was highly educated, more than capable, and used to taking whatever life and the military threw at her. She was the picture of a resilient military spouse.

"He was back down to nine-month-old, six-month-old clothes and he was truly starving," Kaitlin said. "I could not figure out why feeding him wasn't working." Ultimately, it took her husband coming home from a deployment, putting on a uniform, and demanding the referral.

William had leukemia.

Two years later, his brother Jonathan was diagnosed with a genetically unrelated, malignant brain tumor.

Kaitlin became a full-time caregiver. While her husband was deployed, Kaitlin wiped tears (including her own), learned medical terminology, and attended 258 medical appointments over the course of one year. She became exceptionally good at acting like a resilient military spouse who fields all the hardships thrown her way.

However, Kaitlin learned that her resilience was being held against her during a phone call she received from a military treatment facility (MTF) case manager. "You haven't been selected for my case list, but I had to give you a call," the case manager said.

The case manager proceeded to recount her supervisor's reasoning: "This is a mom who came in and presented as clean, dressed. She's educated. She has a master's degree. That is, she knows how to navigate this system. We have so many other mothers who need more help. She's going to be fine. She doesn't need your services."

Limited resources are a reality within military treatment facilities. For years, the DoD planned to reduce nearly 18,000 uniformed medical positions,[178] a concern for military families since 2019.[179] COVID-19 further exacerbated the military provider shortage. The Erkkila family knew there were not enough case managers to go around, and so did administrators. Having two children with cancer is a lot to handle for anyone, surely qualifying her as someone in need of assistance.

She asked one of her children's doctors, "'If I came in pajamas with dirty hair and no makeup, looking exhausted, screaming for help, would you say that my kid wasn't okay? Or would you flag me as someone who needed help with caregiving who wasn't capable of doing what was necessary?' And she looked me dead in the face and goes, 'You know what, that's exactly what would happen.'"

Caseworkers saw the Erkkilas' brave faces and labeled them resilient. The family was left to navigate the medical, financial, educational, and emotional impacts of childhood cancer—times two—alone. If you were to

---

[178] Tom Philpott, "More Than 17,000 Uniformed Medical Jobs Eyed for Elimination," *Military.com*, January 10, 2019, https://www.military.com/daily-news/2019/01/10/more-17000-uniformed-medical-jobs-eyed-elimination.html.

[179] Jennifer Barnhill, "Looming Changes to Military Medical Care Cause Uncertainty," *Military Spouse*, accessed August 26, 2025, https://www.militaryspouse.com/news/looming-changes-to-military-medical-care-cause-uncertainty/.

meet Kaitlin, it would be clear she is good at putting on a brave face despite having to navigate situations that would bring most people to their breaking point. She routinely spent hours on the phone with medical and insurance providers, navigating bureaucracy, including fifty-eight hours resolving just three bills that weren't coded properly. But she remained resilient in the face of her circumstances.

"It isn't hard because you're doing it wrong or because you're not doing enough," Kaitlin said she shares with anyone who asks. "It's hard because it's hard."[180]

I couldn't help but ask myself two questions: Why had Kaitlin's resilience been used against her? And is the way the military uses the term "resilient" inaccurate . . . or even dangerous?

Dominant narrative: Military families are resilient.

A better narrative: Don't focus on resilience in its current form, which says resilience is the measure of the speed of our recovery. Admitting weakness will not cause the military or our nation harm. To admit weakness is a strength because by listening to each other and our needs, we can truly understand and support each other.

IS RESILIENCE A SKILL OR A LABEL?

We may be familiar with the term "resilience" from psychology. In this context, resilience is "an ability to recover from or adjust easily to misfortune or change."[181]

This use of the word in this way is relatively new. "Resilience" was

---

[180] Jennifer Barnhill, "Should Military Families Be Forced to Embrace the Suck?," Military.com, October 17, 2022, https://www.military.com/daily-news/2022/10/17/should-military-families-be-forced-embrace-suck.html.

[181] "Resilience." Merriam-Webster Dictionary, Merriam-Webster.com. https://www.merriam-webster.com/dictionary/resilience. Accessed July 24, 2024.

first used as an engineering term that assessed the physical strength of a given material. Merriam-Webster says it is "the ability of an elastic material (such as rubber or animal tissue) to absorb energy (such as from a blow) and release that energy as it springs back to its original shape." In humans, it is bouncing back after "a jarring setback."[182] This is not how the military defines resilience.

> "Dealing with frequent moves, long deployments, and major transitions requires stamina and strength. Some families seem to handle the ups and downs better than others. Building resilience—the ability to withstand, recover, and grow from stress—can help your family deal with the demands of military life."
> —Military OneSource[183-184]

By contrast, the clinical definitions of resilience focus on short-term reactions to strain, rather than prolonged strains on a material or person. One's ability to recover from a *single* incident is resilience. Just as metal will break if it is continually bent, so will people.

While Kaitlin and her family displayed resilience after William's leukemia diagnosis, it would be understandably more difficult to bounce back after hearing their other son also had cancer. She may have appeared to have bounced back, but denying her family care assumed (intentionally or otherwise) that she was inherently a resilient person, ready to take on a new challenge and incapable of breaking.

Military resilience has been reduced to a verbal pat on the back for military families to earn—a label that is awarded, not a skill they develop.

The DoD was warned that this could happen. In 2011, the Office of the Secretary of Defense sponsored a research report with the RAND Corporation, "Promoting Psychological Resilience in the U.S. Military."

---

[182] Ibid.
[183] U.S. Department of Defense, *Keeping Your Family Strong*, Military OneSource, accessed August 26, 2025, https://www.militaryonesource.mil/resources/millife-guides/keeping-your-family-strong/.
[184] Sarah O. Meadows et al., "Family Resilience in the Military: Definitions, Models, and Policies," *RAND Health Quarterly* 5, no. 3 (2016): 12, https://www.rand.org/pubs/periodicals/health-quarterly/issues/v5/n3/12.html.

RAND conducted a deliberate literature review on behalf of the DoD in order to help it in its program design.

In this literature review, RAND clearly stated that clinicians "recommended that the term 'resilience' be reserved to describe the process of adjustment after experiencing significant adversity. This recommendation is based on the concern that labeling an individual as having or lacking the personality trait of resilience carries the risk that some people will feel that they have inadequate resources for coping." In other words, resilience is a skill to be developed, not a label to award those who rise to the occasion. The RAND report continued, "We also consider resilience to be a process because if it were a trait, it would not be malleable; therefore, training to improve resilience would be futile."[185]

While the DoD may have wished to better understand how it could help military families by tapping into the latest psychological research, it did so reactively, not proactively. By this point, it had already deeply invested in the narrative that military service members and families are and should be resilient.

The RAND report evaluated over seventy military and civilian programs that focused on building and developing resilience among service members and civilians. The report revealed that these efforts were not evidence-based, and it debunked the theory that resilience could be trained. RAND reported, "Although there are many programs available to the military and civilian communities, there is very little empirical evidence that these programs effectively build resilience. Similarly, there are a number of factors related to resilience, but there is almost no evidence that resilience can be taught or produced."[186]

If there is little to no evidence that programs result in actual resilience—and if resilience cannot be trained—then what is the point of the military's focus on resilience? [Cost] control.

---

[185] Lisa S. Meredith et al., *Promoting Psychological Resilience in the U.S. Military*, RAND Corporation, MG-996-OSD, 2011,
https://www.rand.org/content/dam/rand/pubs/monographs/2011/RAND_MG996.pdf.
[186] Ibid., 75.

ALL IN ON THE RESILIENCE EXPERIMENT

I don't remember the first time I walked through a dark parking lot with my keys strategically placed between my fingers. As a young woman, I just knew that I needed to take out one of my car keys and hold the plastic part in my palm and the metal part out like a small weapon. I also knew that I needed to yell *fire*, not *help*, because I was told that the average stranger is more likely to get involved if it is a fire rather than an assault.

Women are trained to be prepared for sexual assault at a too-young age because it is easier to solve a hard problem by training victims to be on high alert than solve the underlying problem.

Resilience as policy is a similar strategy.[187]

After the military became an all-volunteer force, it struggled to meet recruitment numbers and used benefits to entice would-be service members. Programming sprang up around the military family, with missions that seemingly understood their important role. They offered services that supported families, and families began to rely on the programs.

However, this came at a time when our nation was pushing against the idea of public welfare programs. The military also felt the pressure to reduce military families' dependence on programming. The Army "enjoined soldiers to 'take care of themselves.'"[188]

The field of psychology offered the military a clinical justification for its reduction in support programming. While teaching a girl how to protect herself in a dark parking garage has been studied and proven to help improve the outcomes of an attack or even prevent it,[189] the DoD's

---

187 Brianna Suslovic and Elle Lett, "Resilience is an Adverse Event: A Critical Discussion of Resilience Theory in Health Services Research and Public Health," *Community Health Equity Research & Policy* 44, no. 3 (2023): 339–343, https://doi.org/10.1177/2752535X231159721.

188 Jennifer Mittelstadt, *The Rise of the Military Welfare State* (Cambridge, MA: Harvard University Press, 2015), 12.

189 U.S. Department of Justice, "Fighting Back: Neighborhood Antidrug Strategies," National Criminal Justice Reference Service, 1996, https://www.ojp.gov/ncjrs/virtual-library/abstracts/fighting-back.

overarching policy of resilience is not based on tested evidence but rather a new field of study: positive psychology.

Positive psychology is the study of what goes right in life, with a focus on strengths-based training.[190] Although the concept of highlighting positive outcomes and experiences has long been part of psychology, this concept was first pioneered by Dr. Martin Seligman, then president of the American Psychological Association (APA), in 1998.

It could not have come at a better time for the U.S. military. Prior to Seligman's coining of the term "positive psychology," the psychology industry focused on the disease model, which examined perceived deficiencies. This new field of study and its positive outlook held promise, especially for the military. Facing PTSD and suicide crises, the Army turned to Seligman for help in 2008. They awarded the University of Pennsylvania's Positive Psychology Center, run by Seligman, a $31 million single-source government contract.[191]

One early military resilience program informed by Seligman's work was the Army's Battlemind training program. Battlemind training was developed at the Walter Reed Army Institute of Research (WRAIR) as an early intervention program for reintegration following combat. It began piloting programming in 2005.[192] The Battlemind strategy "positively reframes traditional post-deployment transition difficulties such as PTSD, depression, and sleep problems as being a natural consequence of having developed effective occupational coping skills related to combat."[193]

---

190 Christopher Peterson, *A Primer in Positive Psychology* (Oxford: Oxford University Press, 2006).

191 Martin Seligman, "The Hoffman Report, the Central Intelligence Agency, and the Defense of the Nation: A Personal View," *Health Psychology Open* 5, no. 2 (2018): 2055102918796192, https://doi.org/10.1177/2055102918796192.

192 Charles W. Hoge, MD, et al.. "Walter Reed Army Institute of Research Contributions During Operations Iraqi Freedom and Enduring Freedom: From Research to Public Health Policy." In *Combat and Operational Behavioral Health*, chapter 5. Walter Reed Army Institute of Research, U.S. Department of Defense, 2011. https://medcoeckapwstorprd01.blob.core.usgovcloudapi.net/pfw-images/borden/combat-operational/CBM-ch5-final.pdf

193 Amy B. Adler et al., "Battlemind Debriefing and Battlemind Training as Early Interventions with Soldiers Returning from Iraq: Randomization by Platoon," *Journal of Consulting and Clinical Psychology* 77, no. 5 (2009): 928–940, https://doi.org/10.1037/a0016877.

Its effectiveness was studied in 2009. Researchers examined different types of post-deployment/combat training programs aimed at helping soldiers reacclimate to normal life. Battlemind did this by helping soldiers to "adapt combat skills for the home environment."[194]

In the combat environment, soldiers developed close bonds with unit members to cope. Historically, they would continue to rely on these relationships on the home front, resulting in negative behaviors and alienating their families. Battlemind training encouraged soldiers to establish similar bonds with their families, which minimized negative family impacts.

The research suggested Battlemind training was moderately successful, particularly for those with high levels of combat exposure, but its effectiveness was not universal. It was unclear if behavioral changes were maintained over the long term because the study did not address how well participants retained these skills over time.

The Army also began work to develop the Comprehensive Soldier Fitness' (CSF) Master Resilience Training (MRT) program, which launched in 2009. CSF would come to be known as "one of the largest mental-health interventions geared at a single population in the history of humanity."[195]

This training sought to improve resilience and psychological health (R/PH) along four dimensions: emotional, family, social, and spiritual fitness. The program "purposely distances itself from the Army medical community"[196] to minimize the stigma of seeking behavioral health care.

Instead, CSF training was managed and led by unit leadership to send a message that leadership supports mental health. This intentional decision to destigmatize the training by moving it out of clinical offices became

---

194 Ibid.

195 Tom Bartlett, "Positive Psychology Goes to War," *The Chronicle of Higher Education*, June 7, 2011, https://www.chronicle.com/article/positive-psychology-goes-to-war.

196 CPT Paul B. Lester, Ph.D, et al., *The Comprehensive Soldier Fitness Program Evaluation - Report #3*, University of Pennsylvania Positive Psychology Center, December 2011, https://ppc.sas.upenn.edu/sites/default/files/csftechreport3mrt.pdf.

standard practice and a practice that was also replicated by the Navy's Families OverComing Under Stress (FOCUS) resilience training.[197]

The CSF program and its findings made headlines. Although the findings pointed to program success, the data collected were self-reported. Soldiers' feedback was not anonymous, and their resiliency scores followed them. If someone wanted to fake resilience, they could easily skew their own scores.

The Army researchers knew it. "A central limitation to the program and this evaluation must be acknowledged. That is, it is impossible to determine the mechanisms through which the presence of MRT training impacts the self-reported R/PH of Soldiers," an evaluation of the program detailed.[198] However, positive self-reported data was better than no data or negative data, so the program continued.

Other military units looked into how this new field could help service members in a clinical setting. Studies were conducted within the VA that asked veterans enrolled in the psychiatric recovery program to identify their own strengths, asking them to evaluate statements like, "I always allow others to leave their mistakes in the past and make a fresh start."

"Most report that their mood improves after receiving their results and they think more positively about themselves," researchers reported in an evaluation of the program. "We have less information about the long-term benefits, but we have been impressed by how quickly and enthusiastically this community of veterans has adopted the language of strengths."[199]

While early research only provided a snapshot of the program's success, the military felt it was promising enough for it to inform military family programming and public messaging.

---

[197] William R. Saltzman, et al.. "Mechanisms of Risk and Resilience in Military Families: Theoretical and Empirical Basis of a Family-Focused Resilience Enhancement Program." *Clinical Child and Family Psychology Review* (2011). https://doi.org/10.1007/s10567-011-0096-1.

[198] CPT Paul B. Lester, Ph.D, et al., *The Comprehensive Soldier Fitness Program Evaluation - Report #3*, University of Pennsylvania Positive Psychology Center, December 2011, https://ppc.sas.upenn.edu/sites/default/files/csftechreport3mrt.pdf.

[199] Sandra G. Resnick and Robert A. Rosenheck, "Recovery and Positive Psychology: Parallel Themes and Potential Synergies," *Psychiatric Services* 57, no. 1 (2006): 120–122, https://doi.org/10.1176/appi.ps.57.1.120.

The military went all in by continuing to build up its clinical support offerings. The Military and Family Life Counseling (MFLC) program started as a pilot program out of Germany that offered counseling to families. It expanded to all services and locations in 2004, offering confidential, non-medical counseling to military families.

The MFLC program surged in the following years to support the additional strain placed on families as a result of the Global War on Terror. Counselors provided support for issues such as stress, relationships, and parenting, contributing to overall family resilience. The military's policy of resilience seemed to be going well. But the scientific theories MFLC was built on were about to be put to the test by two decades of war.

"Generations within that cohort were experiencing the limits of being asked to be vulnerable," Corie Weathers told me in an interview describing the themes of her book *Military Culture Shift*, which examines how two decades of war have impacted the military community and how different generations respond to these circumstances. "In previous generations, there were moments of wartime, peacetime, wartime, peacetime. Now we have two decades of war where we have a constant message of 'Don't be vulnerable. Don't show cracks. Be resilient.'"

What the military narrative doesn't mention is that resilience without relief isn't resilience. It's toxic positivity.

Toxic positivity is the "excessive and ineffective overgeneralization of a happy, optimistic state across all situations. The process of toxic positivity results in the denial, minimization, and invalidation of the authentic human emotional experience."[200] Positivity is great, but when it's overdone, positivity can be used to intentionally cover up hardship.

The problem with the policy of resilience is not that the individual studies were flawed or that positive psychology and resilience are not great concepts. Resilience didn't get corrupted because it wasn't thought through or didn't provide resources to equip the military community with

---

200 The Psychology Group, "Toxic Positivity: The Dark Side of Positive Vibes," 2018, https://thepsychologygroup.com/toxic-positivity/.

the skills needed to develop resiliency. The DoD offered resilience training and earnestly attempted to ramp up the availability of trained psychologists who could offer clinically trained support. But the train-the-trainer model slowly got away from them.

The problem with resilience as policy is that it found its way into the hands and mouths of those who are not trained clinicians. Without a clear understanding of psychology, resilience can be weaponized. When resilience became policy and entered the military culture, it became self-policing in the worst possible way. It reduced the valuable skill of resilience to an accolade to be earned or denied.

ROUTINE RESILIENCE

I first saw how expectations of resiliency weighed on service members in 2008, while living in Atsugi, Japan. My husband and I moved to the country just shy of our second wedding anniversary. We had a few weeks to settle into the new culture, arrange housing, buy a "base beater" (read: car), make friends, and attempt to find excitement before sending him on his first deployment aboard the *USS Kitty Hawk.*

Early into our time in Japan, one of my closest friends, Dawn Limmer, shared with me that she had experienced a first-trimester miscarriage. She and her husband had been trying to get pregnant for years after having conceived their first child without difficulty. When she finally got pregnant, their family was ecstatic.

When she lost the baby on Mother's Day, she was understandably devastated. Her husband was deployed, so she was processing much of this alone while caring for her four-year-old daughter. She was given medicine to help her "resolve" the pregnancy and was sent home to wait for the baby to pass. She did what we were all expected to do: she reached out to her community. While a few were supportive, many were more misguided.

Dawn heard comments anywhere from "we've all been through that" and "miscarriages are so common" to "you just have to pick yourself up by the bootstraps and carry on."

Although these comments came from positive intentions, they felt like an accusation. At a time when she should have been processing her grief, she also worried about falling short of expectations by not behaving as a resilient military spouse would.

Ultimately, she returned to the U.S. to see a civilian counselor and work through the situation. "The civilian counselor said, 'It's okay, you can grieve,'" she recalled. Instead of being resilient, she needed to be allowed to sit with her sadness, and she needed her community to allow her to grieve.

This example of routine resilience highlights another flaw in the resilience-as-policy narrative. It asks families to adopt an ideology or personality of resilience. This is why people wear it with pride. They want to be seen as resilient because it makes them feel part of the larger military community. They receive praise from their spouse or their neighbor after lending a hand. These instances of reciprocation and pats on the back feel good. The problem with the military version of resilience is that it subconsciously asks military families to enter into a relationship with the DoD.

Corie Weathers equates this relationship to that of a married couple having an argument. One member of the couple presents a problem. Perhaps that person gets a little heated. Their voice increases in volume and becomes frantic. Often, their partner will say something like, "Calm down." In that moment, the person who has been experiencing a legitimate problem is now focused on addressing this new perceived attack. We have all been there. We know what it feels like to be told to calm down when we are trying to have an entirely different conversation.

The DoD uses the term "resilience" in a similar manner. When presented with a legitimate concern, like a lack of caseworkers who could have helped the Erkkila family, DoD officials rely upon families to "be resilient." This takes the focus away from the underlying problem and focuses on the person experiencing the problem. Their resilience, or lack thereof, is on display, and the DoD is allowed to shirk its responsibility to address the problem it caused in the first place.

In Dawn's case, the problem was that she was forced to cope with a pregnancy loss without her husband, who was deployed. She turned to the military community for support and was told to calm down. Her problem was minimized. No accolades were given. She was not resilient. In the resilience narrative, Dawn was unable to cope, and this deployment was no harder than another. Deployments are supposed to be hard.

"I work with veterans from the Vietnam era," Chris McGhee told me in an interview. Chris is a twenty-year Air Force veteran who hosts the *20 Years Done* podcast, which looks at military life and focuses on challenging its status-quo culture. "When they were currently serving, there was not widespread information available for the global service member experience. They might have thought their platoon had issues or was very difficult, but they didn't know it was a widespread, policy-driven thing."

According to Chris, this ignorance made resiliency easier. This makes sense. The American people had access to images of war because Vietnam was televised, so they became disillusioned. They could see what was being asked of their brothers, sons, and friends. When you see what is broken in front of you, faith in the cause wanes. "It's easier to have hope when you don't know how widespread the problem is," said Chris.

Modern-day service members have access to the bigger picture. And this access forces them to confront yet another unsettling narrative: The military is the source of their harm. Others around them are experiencing similar frustrations. And rather than addressing the root cause of the problem, the military's solution is to tell them to "calm down."

IS MILITARY RESILIENCE JUST TOXIC POSITIVITY?

There is a perception within the military family community that grief and negative emotions are contagious. We focus on positivity because we are afraid of what could happen if we let ourselves acknowledge the hardships. We stiff-arm pain and rush through our negative emotions quickly to keep up morale so we can get through the deployment, move, fight, job loss, etc. When we take on these hardships, we fall into one of four categories:

	Outwardly Positive	*Outwardly Negative*
Inwardly Positive	Real Resilience	Real Resilience
Inwardly Negative	Faked Resilience	Rejects Resilience

Based on my observations this can result in a few outcomes:

- *Inwardly + outwardly positive = real resilience*: Individuals actually build psychological resilience and learn more about themselves in order to cope with their circumstances in a healthy way.
- *Inwardly + outwardly negative = rejects resilience*: Some begin to resent the military and desensitize themselves to the hardships they face by always assuming the worst and embracing an overwhelmingly negative attitude.
- *Outwardly positive + inwardly negative = faked resilience*: Individuals display outward resilience and hold in their emotions, creating stress.
- *Outwardly negative + inwardly positive = real resilience*: Individuals may talk about what is broken, which allows them to heal, but they may seem negative to outsiders. Resilience does not have to appear positive to be resilience.

REAL RESILIENCE

For some, resilience is a badge of honor they are happy to wear. When we are repeatedly asked to rise to the occasion and then do, this achievement can become part of our identity.

Heather Kline retired from the Navy after twenty-two years and is still an Army spouse who volunteers her time in support of her husband's command and larger military community. "I want to help and learn as much as I can because it's my duty—the expectation I put on myself," Heather told me in an interview. "Where's that resilience come from? Well, from a nautical naval perspective, it's never giving up the ship." For Heather, being a positive contributor to the mission of the military and the military community has become part of her identity.

"I feel like I am the cheerleader for armed forces strength—resilience—whatever you want to call that buzzword," Heather said. "I feel as though it's my duty, my vow, like I was talking about the family I'm sworn into. How I was conditioned via the Navy is to continue remaining positive."

To be very honest, I cringed when she mentioned she was conditioned to remain positive. But then I checked myself and my biases. What makes me cringe can be a genuinely positive experience and outcome for another. As Heather continued to share her perspective on the importance of remaining positive, she said something that changed the way I viewed the impact of the DoD's policy on resilience.

"My head always goes back to this high suicide rate. I can't get it off my mind," she said. "Are we really resilient?" It was a stark change of tone, going from calling herself a cheerleader to the brink of tears. She was a sailor brought up on the DoD's policy of resilience, trained to never give up the ship, to take care of her shipmates, and to be resilient.

Heather is the picture of what the military intended when it began its resilience programming. She absorbed the clinical message as the DoD intended. But she, like others raised on this policy, was confused why, if it worked for her, it wasn't working for others.

The defect is not an individual's lack of resilience. The defect is in the resilience narrative. This narrative *tells* the community that it is resilient but doesn't equip them to be. If individuals fail to rise to the occasion, they may fake it until they make it—or fake it but never make it. And when resilience or positivity is faked, it can mask underlying conditions.

Despite displaying genuine resilience, Heather showed signs of burnout in between positive statements. "I want to be able to contribute more," she said, despite her active support of the community, she worries there's still something more she should be doing.

I wanted to jump through the computer screen and hug Heather, whose story made me worry about the pressure so many have put on themselves to care for those around them, to take on the unending responsibility to take care of our own. It is Heather's passion, love, and concern for the institution that makes future generations want to join the military. But does the policy of resilience come at a price?

THE COST OF (FAKING) RESILIENCE

In 2016, Kristin Martin was serving in the Key Spouse Program, the Air Force's spouse support program, when she first heard the word "resilient."

"It became almost taboo to talk about your real feelings or your real experience," she told me when I asked about her resilience training. The military community is expected to put on a brave face. She was there to receive training to support other spouses and was left with the impression that being comfortable talking about hardship was not welcome. "Everything needed to be shiny and happy and perfect." If positivity is built into the training program without room for negativity, even expressed in a healthy manner, it can become negative. Whether by accident or design, the military's view of strength becomes binary, with only positive outlooks appearing to be resilient and, therefore, strong.

Instead of trying to mitigate the negative aspects of military life by finding solutions to our very real problems, the DoD's resilience narrative asks us to "embrace the suck." We are told to accept our circumstances, however unreasonable, making true resilience less and less of an achievable reality. Military families learn to let go of hope to avoid disappointment. Because they can't control deployment dates, they control themselves. They pretend to be strong, hoping to even fool themselves. Some settle for unfulfilling jobs, while others start to resent the military—or their spouse.

When the resilience narrative doubled down on positive psychology while not actively trying to reduce the underlying causes of the hardships experienced by military families, it did not foster resilience. It denied their reality. And this denial comes at a high cost.

On the surface, the community seems resilient, but underneath many are in pain. While they may be able to hold onto resilience throughout their time in the military, what about those who make it to retirement and are finally ready to stop faking it? Just as the body stores stress hormones, forced "resilience" may store up negative emotions, which are finally released at retirement. If things don't improve after they put down their packs, depression can set in.

"We're talking about the allostatic load, which is the cumulative effects of chronic stress and life events on mental and physical health," said Kristin, who is also a nationally board-certified health and wellness coach and registered nurse. "That's something that's really being missed among leaders for both service members and for our families." Faked resilience has a cost.

Researchers from Columbia University confirm this, writing, "Emotion theorists have increasingly argued that whether one expresses or suppresses emotional expression is not as important for adjustment as is the ability to flexibly express or suppress emotional expression as demanded by the situational context."[201]

Put simply, it is just as valuable *to be able* to express your emotional response as it is to repress it. Harm is not experienced during the release or holding back of emotions, but when the individual doesn't get to choose how they display emotions.[202] And there is no way to know if those who are faking resilience will finally reach a breaking point or if they will find the resources and support they need to adjust in a healthy way upon leaving the military.

WHAT HAPPENS WHEN YOU STOP FAKING RESILIENCE?

When I first interviewed Navy Lieutenant Christa Gunsauley for an article that I was writing for *Military.com*, I was overwhelmed by the sheer volume of documentation she had: emails, medical reports, screenshots of text messages. She had accumulated a mountain of paperwork during her two-year battle with the Navy, fighting not because she was told she did anything wrong, but because she, the alleged victim of sexual harassment, had to prove that she wasn't crazy.

After filing a claim, she said she was stripped of duties, ones that, if performed, would help her get a promotion. As the investigation progressed, Christa says a Navy doctor who was not her regular provider erroneously told investigators she had been diagnosed with a personality disorder, a diagnosis that lawmakers have argued has been used to discredit service members and deny them medical retirement benefits.

According to Christa, the charged work environment began to impact her mental health. She attempted to overdose on medication but reached

---

[201] George A. Bonanno, et al., "The Importance of Being Flexible: The Ability to Both Enhance and Suppress Emotional Expression Predicts Long-Term Adjustment," *Psychological Science* 15, no. 7 (2004): 482–487, https://doi.org/10.1111/j.0956-7976.2004.00705.x.
[202] Ibid.

out to her therapist, who called an ambulance, saving her life. During our conversations, which took place years after the initial incident, Christa felt as though she were reliving her darkest days.

"My medication dosage was increased, and my therapy sessions are now being conducted every week rather than biweekly," she said in an email. "Why am I telling you this? First, I would like to emphasize how the constant search for justice is extremely burdensome to the victim."[203]

The military asks a lot of service members, even those who have not experienced what Christa did. They spend months away from loved ones in austere environments and within communities that ask them to minimize their emotions. They routinely put their lives in harm's way and see the unimaginable. These responsibilities take a toll, resilience training or not.

THE RESILIENCE NARRATIVE & MILITARY SUICIDE

Active-duty suicide rates have gradually increased since 2011. Veteran suicides are consistently and significantly higher than civilian suicide rates. It is estimated that seventeen veterans die by suicide each day, making it a tragic and urgent problem for the VA and military community.

Although there are countless theories, papers, and strategies aimed at analyzing and reducing service member suicide, what the community can agree on is that the transition from active duty to civilian life is a deadly time.

Even though resilience is studied, resilience as policy is not yet up for public debate, despite research hinting at its questionable results.[204] While

---

[203] Jennifer Barnhill, "Burying Victims in Paperwork?" *Military.com*, November 6, 2023, https://www.military.com/daily-news/opinions/2023/11/06/burying-victims-paperwork.html.
[204] Marc Vincent Jones et al., "A Systematic Review of Resilient Performance in Defence and Security Settings," *PLoS ONE* 17, no. 10 (2022): e0273015, https://doi.org/10.1371/journal.pone.0273015.

we may never know the true impact the resilience narrative has had on the military and veteran communities, it is worth examining.

New approaches to understanding suicide may offer a better way to evaluate resilience.

Historically, researchers have focused on conducting post-mortems, focusing their research only on those who attempted or died by suicide, but neglecting to examine those who experienced similar stressors and environments but did not act. But this is changing.

In his book *Rethinking Suicide: Why Prevention Fails, and How We Can Do Better*, author Craig J. Bryan says today's suicide treatment strategies are similar to early infectious disease treatment strategies. In the mid-19th century, Hungarian doctor Ignaz Semmelweis noted that mothers who had just given birth in the obstetrics clinic were dying of infections at an alarming rate as compared to those who were treated in the separate midwife clinic. The rate was so high that "the death rate in the obstetrical clinic was actually higher than the death rate among women who gave birth on the street outside the hospital."[205]

Doctor Semmelweis ultimately stumbled onto a discovery that would help inform early germ theory. The medical students in the obstetrics clinic were in contact with both new mothers *and* cadavers. They would go back and forth between the autopsy room and the delivery room, unknowingly transferring "cadaverous particles" and causing infection. He ordered everyone to wash their hands in a lye solution, and the obstetric mortality rate dropped to the same as those treated by midwives.

Despite being aware of a relatively successful strategy for mitigating infection, clinicians continued to resist hand washing. They defaulted to the status quo. Despite having evidence that it could reduce mortality, they held tight to their previously held medical best practices because they could not see germs. They were focused on proof, not outcomes.

---

[205] Craig J. Bryan, *Rethinking Suicide: Why Prevention Fails, and How We Can Do Better* (Oxford: Oxford University Press, 2021), 134.

Bryan writes that suicide prevention needs to find its handwashing equivalent by observing the conditions of those who live and those who die, not just those who die. Researchers also need to debunk previously held best practices, ones that may actually be doing more harm than good. In suicide prevention, the status quo relies on the post-mortem model and highlighting an individual's faults—adverse childhood experiences, mental illness, etc.—rather than reflecting on damage caused by a misunderstood cure: resilience.

Those who currently embrace the status-quo resilience narrative are similarly resistant to handwashing. Resilience is a lifesaving skill when done properly. But when it is not properly messaged, it is a toxic cure.

For instance, during the COVID-19 pandemic, we were told we needed to wash our hands for twenty seconds with soap and water in a particular pattern to fully remove germs and receive the benefit of handwashing. When resilience is performative, it is like quickly running your hands under the faucet without soap. You tell everyone you washed your hands and make a show of drying them. But all the while you are unprotected and at risk of infection.

When resilience training left the clinician's office and entered the culture, teaching military families *how* to wash their hands became the business of the DoD. The military told the community *to* wash their hands, but it didn't teach them *how*. It said, "wash your hands," but didn't provide soap. And it limited access to sinks and punished or shamed those who asked for instructions or help.

Without a clear resilience strategy, service members and families turned to their peers, many of whom outwardly appeared resilient. But inwardly, for many, it was an unsustainable, faked resilience. According to researchers, when foisted on minority or oppressed populations, resilience is a very effective method of control.[206]

---

[206] Brianna Suslovic and Elle Lett, "Resilience Is an Adverse Event: A Critical Discussion of Resilience Theory in Health Services Research and Public Health," *Community Health Equity Research & Policy* 44, no. 3 (2023): 339–43, https://doi.org/10.1177/2752535X231159721.

The military's resilience narrative was successful. It told families what they needed to do to get through the challenges of military life, but it didn't help them get through. It conditioned them to police each other, to rush each other through hardship, like the loss of a child, too quickly. The resilience narrative did not require the military institution to change. It had successfully conditioned an entire community to minimize their physical and mental health needs, patted them on the head, and called them resilient. Just as mid-19th-century doctors didn't want to admit it was their cures that had caused the deaths of new moms, the DoD doesn't want to admit that its cure has turned toxic.

Instead, when faced with military community suicide, it focuses on "lethal means safety" as a way to reduce military death by suicide by reducing access to firearms via gun locks and safes. Lethal means safety, like handwashing, offers a proven cure, but doesn't answer why some service members and families die by suicide and others do not.

I don't dare assume that improved studies into the narrative of resilience will prove to be the germ theory of military mental health, but we can't ignore the possibility. And we can't wait for the institution that controls the resilience narrative to begin this research. Just as obstetric doctors did not want to look inward, the DoD doesn't always dig deep enough to find the root cause of the problems its personnel are facing.

HOW RESILIENCE GOT CORRUPTED AND HOW WE CAN FIX IT

After the military doubled down on resilience after 9/11, it began to build programs based on the research currently available[207]—research it told

---

[207] John M. Orsingher et al., "Battlemind Training System: Armor for Your Mind," *U.S. Army Medical Department*, 2008, https://stimson.contentdm.oclc.org/digital/api/collection/p15290coll3/id/725/download.

people could not fully be relied upon because it was self-reported and, therefore, not objective data.

That did not stop Army leaders from moving forward. A 2012 article put out by the Army read, "Study concludes Master Resilience Training effective".[208] It went on to tout the success of resilience training.

"I think in the future, even under this budget, we're going to fund [MRT]. We believe this will save us money through prevention [because] it helps our soldiers, family members, and Department of the Army civilians deal with adversity in their life and more importantly thrive," Brigadier General Jim Pasquarette, CSF program director, said in the article.[209]

Did resilience training help many people? I'm certain it did. Because resilience, taught correctly, is lifesaving. But self-reported data that captures effectiveness over the short term doesn't apply to conditions that require sustained resilience—without relief—over the course of a multi-year military career. Data could not predict what would happen when this training was offered by laypeople. This distance from medical professionals may have served to destigmatize mental health, but it inadvertently bred a new form of toxic resilience.

"It took on a life of its own," said Kristin Saboe, who previously worked as the Chief of Science & Research at the Army Resiliency Directorate for the Deputy Chief of Staff of the Army for Personnel in D.C. Saboe was referring to how resilience messaging and programming went from the drawing board to relatively successful programming to military messaging and finally to the community. The Army at large never intended the resilience narrative to focus on being happy or sad, she noted; it was a nuanced message focused on building the skill of resilience.

Resilience training's early message spread. It was adopted by other branches, and implemented locally by individuals with varying levels of training. Even the surrounding community picked up on these resilience

---

[208] U.S. Army, "Study Concludes Master Resilience Training Effective," *Army.mil,* January 19, 2012, https://www.army.mil/article/72431/study_concludes_master_resilience_training_effective.
[209] Ibid.

messages, with nonprofits calling military families and children resilient often and loudly, inadvertently reinforcing the toxic message.

The military saw the spread and attempted to correct course in the late 2010s. "There was a shift in Army messaging so we could align with what research was telling us," said Saboe, recalling the military's reaction to how the resilience narrative had begun to get away from its original context. This was evidenced by the Army shifting from abstract images portraying a flat picture of soldiers to images featuring real soldiers and families, which helped humanize service and reinforced the important resilience messages it had originally crafted.

However, the second the resilience narrative entered the military culture, it was destined to fail. It was too nuanced. So as it spread across the institution, it was simplified. Unlike simplifications that can be good and help disseminate an important message to a wide audience, simplifying resilience actually undermined its message. No longer was resilience a skill that takes time to develop, a skill that requires moments of reprieve to be effective; leaders, service members, and families came to see resilience as being happy or sad. If individuals were outwardly happy, they were resilient. If they were outwardly sad, they were not. This simplification conditioned service members and families to fake it. Some were able to fake it until they made it, but others could not.

By this measure, even those who have developed real resilience skills can't live up to the resilience narrative because it requires perfection. When they are stretched and stretched without reprieve, they are more likely to come to a breaking point. Some have protective factors surrounding them and skills to fall back on to continue the fight. Others do not. Some collect their praise, and others look on, wishing they were stronger.

We need a new narrative, one that embraces the hardship inherent in the lifestyle. Resilience does not do this. It softens our struggles and minimizes our strength. Telling people to be resilient as you harm them does not foster resilience. It denies their reality.

A NEW NARRATIVE

Resilience training seeks to mitigate the trauma inflicted upon military service members and their families as a result of their service. It does this by strengthening the victim, not lessening the harm done by the system. In some cases, trauma can be avoided by building better systems. If systems fail military families, the DoD cannot shrug its shoulders and assume *that's just the way it is*. It must follow the admonition of Craig Bryan who is leading the way in suicide prevention: "If a thing is harming people or poses a threat to people, the best method for protecting people is to get rid of that thing."[210]

The DoD asks service members and families to do hard things. That's what military service is. That is not going to change. But resilience cannot be the solution to the military's people problems. It must attempt to lessen the need for service members and families to be resilient in the areas over which it has full control.

When people are pushed to their breaking point, it is not because they are called resilient but because they regularly encounter military systems that fail them, noted Saboe.

When Kaitlin Erkkila asked for a caseworker to help her get through the complexity of raising two children with cancer, she expected to receive help. She did not expect the system to tell her she was too put together to qualify. Surely, childhood cancer times two would be a qualifier. She also thought that dealing with military insurance provider Tricare would be straightforward. Instead, Kaitlin spent hours each week dealing with paperwork and waiting on hold for hours. Navigating the system felt like a full-time job and tested the resilience she had already built up.

"What is the trauma that people are experiencing, primary and secondary, from the system that has failed them and, therefore, actually set them back more?" Saboe asked. "[When] the system is broken and

---

[210] Craig J. Bryan, *Rethinking Suicide: Why Prevention Fails, and How We Can Do Better* (Oxford: Oxford University Press, 2021), 159.

continues to break, it breaks the person when they're trying to not be broken."

Saboe says that when families like the Erkkilas run into system problems but are met with resilience messaging, it makes them feel forgotten and causes system trauma. It is hard to stop people from feeling like they are failing at resilience. This narrative is too ingrained in the community to go anywhere any time soon.

But hope is not lost. There is a way to reclaim resilience. The military community can focus on fixing the root causes of the problem and fix the fixable. When families report waiting on hold with insurance providers, examine why. Don't accept a system failure as status quo. If the DoD offers a service, it must be a good service. A good service conducts program evaluation, and asks its customers about their experience. Being stuck in a restrictive government contract does not absolve the DoD of its responsibility to its personnel.

While service members and families need to be mentally fit, we also need the system to stop inflicting harm unnecessarily. This will create periods of reprieve, allow us to meet the conditions of resilience, and spring back to our original state.

A better narrative acknowledges the role the word "resilience" has played in this community. What started as a positive method of supporting the military community has morphed into a method of control. This will require the DoD to fix the systems harming military service members and families. If it is not willing or able to do so, it must be prepared to face the consequences of people who are no longer comfortable with faking resilience.

A new narrative would not focus on a military family's ability to endure hardship but our ability to endure hardship honestly. When service members and families fake resilience, they inadvertently absolve the DoD from having to focus on the ways it can make an actually strong force, not just a superficially strong force.

Real resilience isn't staying silent; it's speaking up.

Real resilience isn't denying your reality; it's acknowledging the hardships of your reality.

How *you* can change this narrative: The military community should stop calling each other resilient and curtail the abuse of the clinical term. Rather, we should create an environment that encourages honest disclosure of hardships. Civilians should call out instances when resilience is similarly misused.

How the DoD can change this narrative: Follow the advice given by RAND in 2011. Collect data that is not self-reported to see if "resilience programming" is actually effective. If it is not, improve or sunset the program. Research the effect resilience training and DoD messaging has had on the community at large. Stop calling service members and families resilient and praising resilience without addressing system failures. Proactively seek out ways to minimize the need for families to rise to the occasion in the first place. Reduce bureaucracy and study ways to improve quality of life efforts. Evaluate the relationship between operational tempo, burnout, and suicide over the lifecycle of a service member. Stop using research to serve political purposes and instead use it to make the service member experience more tolerable. In the end, a more tolerable experience will serve your purposes.

How *researchers* can change this narrative: Don't wait for the DoD to fund research on the negative effects of its resilience training. Just as the military nonprofits leverage DoD support to generate private funds, the field of positive psychology looks to the DoD. However, it does so with incomplete data, and it bases its nationwide strategies on an incomplete narrative. Additional research is required to write a better narrative on resilience as policy.

The Military is Woke

During the Vietnam War, the Navy was facing both a recruiting and retention crisis. Young Americans were disillusioned with the military and did not sign up to serve. Many were drafted. Because Vietnam was the first televised war, young people saw firsthand what would be asked of them, and many wanted nothing to do with it. This disillusionment was not limited to civilians; many service members were also disillusioned with the war and the military institution.

According to a 1976 article published in *Proceedings* magazine, there were "four riotous, mutinous episodes" that took place aboard Navy ships in 1972. On the *USS Kitty Hawk*, "bands of marauding blacks, charging racist practices, rampaged through the ship," according to the article. Four days later, aboard the *USS Hassayampa* oiler, "dissident blacks assaulted white crewmen." On the *USS Saratoga* two days later, "a group of truculent men . . . refused to disperse when ordered to do so."[211] During the final incident, a group of approximately sixty Black sailors aboard the *USS*

[211] Captain Paul B. Ryan, Retired, "USS Constellation Flare-up: Was It Mutiny?" *Proceedings*, U.S. Naval Institute, January 1976. https://www.usni.org/magazines/proceedings/1976/january/uss-constellation-flare-was-it-mutiny.

Constellation, a Navy aircraft carrier, "refused to leave the mess deck and threatened to 'tear up the ship.'"[212]

Now known as the Constellation Incident, the event stemmed from growing racial tensions, dissatisfaction with living conditions, and perceived injustices in the treatment of sailors, particularly Black crew members. Sailors refused to report for duty while the ship was docked in San Diego, California, preparing to deploy to Vietnam; instead, they staged a sit-in on the pier and refused to return to the ship.

The tone of these accounts implies that the Navy's knee-jerk reaction was discipline. Mutiny would not be tolerated.

Z-GRAMS, RETENTION STUDY GROUPS, AND FRATERNIZATION—OH MY!

Just two years earlier, in 1970, Admiral Elmo R. Zumwalt Jr. had become the youngest chief of naval operations (CNO) at the age of forty-nine. He received an early promotion, endorsed by two Republican leaders: Secretary of Defense Melvin Laird and Secretary of the Navy John Chafee, who served in the Nixon administration.

Chafee had a vision of a Navy administered by younger officers who would help modernize the ranks. Zumwalt's appointment was one of the steps Chafee took to make his vision a reality. Critics believed Chafee's desire to modernize the Navy was a primary cause of the mutinies of 1970.[213]

Zumwalt took command during a period of significant change, with the military fighting against communism in Vietnam and civilians peacefully protesting in America as part of the Civil Rights Movement.

---

[212] Ibid.
[213] Ibid.

Zumwalt was a young, modern, and controversial pick for the CNO role. Rather than telling his subordinates what he wanted them to do, he sent very public instructions he called "Z-grams" to the entire Navy.[214]

His first Z-gram message was related to his taking over as CNO. His second Z-gram was the establishment of retention study groups, focus groups tasked with directly advising Navy leadership on policies affecting morale and retention to help reverse declining reenlistment rates and improve Navy life. This Z-gram set both Zumwalt and the Navy on course to improve quality-of-life efforts by getting to know the fleet, with the study groups as the vehicle. Rather than insisting senior leaders steer the ship, retention study group leadership was "composed exclusively of young officers and enlisted men"[215], in line with Chafee's vision for the Navy.

Zumwalt did not want to rely on filtered messages delivered by senior officers; he wanted to hear directly from the people he was trying to help. And he did so publicly. The Navy's previous course of action sought to fix problems quietly, often based on the personal experiences of senior leaders alone. This did not work, and Zumwalt wanted to try something new.

In his memoir, *On Watch*, Zumwalt writes that his public, if not theatrical, approach to naval reforms was intentional. He knew that others did not approve, but he was convinced his public strategy was the only way to get the job done. He believed the Navy had to change and change fast if it was going to shed the perception that it was a "humorless, tradition-bound, starchy institution owned by and operated for the benefit of white males."[216]

Despite becoming a racially integrated military in 1948, ignored racial tensions were still felt twenty years later. Zumwalt met the tensions head-on. He put forth a new public narrative that put sailors and their families

---

[214] Elmo R. Zumwalt Jr., "List of Z-Grams," Naval History and Heritage Command, *Online Reading Room*, accessed August 26, 2025, https://www.history.navy.mil/research/library/online-reading-room/title-list-alphabetically/z/list-z-grams.html.
[215] Elmo R. Zumwalt Jr., "Z-Gram 2," Naval History and Heritage Command, *Online Reading Room*, accessed August 26, 2025, https://www.history.navy.mil/research/library/online-reading-room/title-list-alphabetically/z/list-z-grams/z-gram-2.html.
[216] Elmo R. Zumwalt Jr., *On Watch: A Memoir* (New York: The New York Times, 1977), 178.

front and center. He formed what would be known as the Navy's Mod Squad, made up of young officers who were promoted earlier than anticipated to disrupt the old-guard way of thinking.

Zumwalt could have easily joined the old guard and settled into the status quo. But he knew he and his peers were part of the Navy's problem, and he was finally in a position to do something about it. Rather than squashing the mutinies, he elected to address the racist actions that inspired these protests. After the 1972 Constellation Incident, Zumwalt published Z-gram #117, entitled "Good Order and Discipline," stating: "There must be no substitution of one prejudice for another. That the prejudice against good order and discipline is as bad as the prejudice of race."[217]

Zumwalt affirmed the old guard's desire for good order while addressing the flaws he observed in the Navy that led to these incidents. He did not sweep inconvenient truths under the rug. But he wasn't doing this because he had a political agenda. He saw racial tension as a threat to the good order of the military. It had a proven negative impact on morale and negatively impacted retention and recruitment. His efforts are credited with setting the Navy on a new course and humanizing its leadership.

"The interesting thing about Dad being in the military and rising in the ranks as he always did, he regarded his current job as though it was going to be the last job he ever had," Zumwalt's daughter, Ann, told me during an interview. "By doing so, he could then make controversial decisions and not worry about it." When he set out to correct the issue of recruitment and racial tension, he did not worry about what he would unearth because, according to his daughter, he wasn't being political about his decisions. He was likely just listening to his wisest counselor—his wife, Mouza.

---

[217] Elmo R. Zumwalt Jr., "Z-Gram 117," Naval History and Heritage Command, *Online Reading Room*, accessed August 26, 2025, https://www.history.navy.mil/research/library/online-reading-room/title-list-alphabetically/z/list-z-grams/z-gram-117.html.

Dominant narrative: The military is woke.

Better narrative: The military is neither woke nor conservative. It is a diverse group of people who want and need policies that serve this diversity.

UN-WOKE WAYS THE MILITARY CREATES POLICIES TO SERVE ITS PEOPLE

Mouza Coutelais-du-Roche Zumwalt was born to a French father and Russian mother, and was raised in Manchuria, China, having fled there after the 1917 Russian Revolution. She met then-Lieutenant Elmo Zumwalt in Shanghai after the Japanese surrendered, bringing World War II to a close.

Zumwalt writes of their first encounter, at a dinner party in Shanghai, in *On Watch*, recalling his "heart stood still."[218] Mouza stood out from the other women he encountered in his social circles. She was described as having a dark complexion and dark hair. He soon proposed to Mouza, and they were married within five weeks of their first encounter.

What drew Zumwalt to Mouza had the opposite effect on American women, especially her fellow naval officer wives. Her accent confused them. Their adherence to Navy customs and traditional courtesies confused her. Instead of trying to fit in where she felt like an outsider, in her early days as a Navy spouse she found belonging in unlikely—if not taboo—friendships with the wives of enlisted sailors.

In befriending the wives of her husband's subordinates, Mouza, too, bucked a long-established military tradition of avoiding "fraternization," or the mixing of officers and enlisted personnel. Officers are college graduates commissioned to lead and make strategic decisions, while enlisted personnel are trained to carry out those orders. The military

[218] Elmo R. Zumwalt Jr., *On Watch: A Memoir* (New York: The New York Times, 1977), 17.

maintains that fraternization can undermine authority and discipline by blurring the boundaries essential to the chain of command. Mouza rightly saw that neither she nor the wives of enlisted or junior officers were actually part of the military and could let go of these dated traditions. She made it clear that officer wives did not have to follow the same rules that applied to their husbands.

This was just one of the stances Mouza took that would positively impact the Navy forever.

Segregation was still common in Virginia in the early 1970s. "Even in the places of worship . . . black members were sent to the back rows of the church or up to the balcony. Mouza had heard of this, and was determined to do her own personal sit-ins," wrote Admiral David Oliver in his autobiography, *A Navy Admiral's Bronze Rules: Managing Risk and Leadership.*[219]

Before Oliver reached the rank of admiral himself, he served as an aide to Zumwalt from 1970 to 1974. "Every Wednesday, Mouza would collect [my wife] Linda, and the two of them would attend services in a different Virginia church. Once inside, they would sit with black parishioners," he wrote. After the services, a fired-up Mouza would share her experiences with her husband and demand he press forward with his work to improve race relations within the Navy. Oliver dreaded these sit-ins because of the action items he would be tasked with afterward.

Zumwalt could have dismissed Mouza's insistence that he consider people of color and Navy families in his decision-making. His predecessors had not wanted to push the needle on either front. But he examined the retention and recruitment crisis and saw it for what it was: The Navy was out of touch with the American people, and holding closely to Navy traditions would only widen the gap.

Mouza gathered intelligence by building relationships with individuals within her sphere of influence and intentionally trying to widen that

---

219 David R. Oliver, *A Navy Admiral's Bronze Rules: Managing Risk and Leadership* (Annapolis: Naval Institute Press, 2021).

sphere. Her personal experience as an outsider and what she saw at area churches was not gossip. She researched the problems she observed.

(In the photo on the left: Mouza Coutelais-du-Roche Zumwalt appears on the cover of *Navy WifeLine* in 1973—Photo courtesy of Naval Services FamilyLine.)

Other spouses noticed her intentionality and influence. She was referred to as the N.O.W. (Naval Officers' Wives) Club's First Lady.[220] In 1971 she was asked to join the board of *Ladycom*, a military wife–focused magazine, because of her "unique position to understand and assist the wives and families of our military, diplomatic and government service career men around the world as well as the thousands of women directly employed in those areas."

Mouza received a note from Admiral Horace B. Robertson Jr., who served as special counsel to CNO Zumwalt. She needed to turn down the request because it "might be construed as an endorsement of this commercial enterprise."[221] Mouza was even asked by her Navy wife friends if she was responsible for the increased appreciation shown by the Navy under Zumwalt's leadership. Mouza's friend wrote: "Someone (meaning

[220] Naval History and Heritage Command Archives, *Zumwalt Papers*, Box 318, Correspondence 71, Folder 2.
[221] Ibid.

[Zumwalt]) is doing more than giving lip service to [the] stamina and devotion of Navy wives. Do I [detect] your fine hand in this area?"[222]

Even service members recognized Mouza's unofficial position of authority. In 1970, she received a letter from Steward Petty Officer 1st Class Jose V. Ignao. He wrote Mouza to let her know he had been robbed in Angeles, a city in the Philippines, and did not want to go back because "I'm too young to die." He also said his wife was about to undergo an operation to cure her infertility. After sharing his personal story, he asked Mouza to help him receive a "humanitarian" duty assignment so he could relocate to a more desirable station.

Mouza replied less than two weeks later with good news: "I spoke to my husband about the humanitarian transfer . . . the Bureau of Naval Personnel will take action as soon as they receive your request."[223] She operated within her sphere of influence and made her own mark on the Navy while Zumwalt worked to modernize the dated and gendered unofficial military tradition of relying on pillow talk to inform policy.

For a senior leader of a hierarchical organization, it would have been easy to not reach down the chain of command to get a handle on the issues faced by the Navy. But he knew he couldn't rely on what was reported to him. He and Mouza knew they needed to go straight to the source: sailors and their families.

Elected officials and military leaders are only as good as the people they listen to, and no doubt listening to someone who has a different perspective (like a spouse) adds value. Although Mouza was not the CNO, her position as his wife, like the role of First Lady, gave her significant influence. Her actions led to positive but largely unacknowledged change within the Navy.

As was common at that time, Zumwalt relied on his wife to spark ideas, but he knew he needed better data with which to make decisions impacting the world's most powerful Navy. Retention study groups were expensive

---

[222] Naval History and Heritage Command Archives, *Zumwalt Papers*, Box 318, Invites, Folder 2.
[223] Naval History and Heritage Command Archives, *Zumwalt Papers*, Box 318, Correspondence Jun 70-Mar 71 Folder 1.

and time-consuming. It would have been easier to roll over in bed and ask Mouza what she was hearing, and to spend money on direct operational missions, like shipbuilding, rather than the indirect operational mission of supporting the well-being of the force. Using pillow talk to inform policy and insisting the Navy was colorblind was what his predecessors did. Sadly, it was his challenging of the status quo that left many wondering if his legacy as CNO was positive.

When Zumwalt left office in 1974, his policies and legacy were highly contested. To senior officers and enlisted personnel, the changes he brought forced them to work harder to maintain order. In 1974 an anonymous Navy California-based Captain told the *San Diego Reader*, "To senior officers, he's a traitor to his class. He represents all that is bad to these people."[224] Even supporters questioned if his efforts were worth the racial unrest and overall upheaval.

With hindsight, it is clear racial tensions within the Navy were a ticking time bomb, one Zumwalt proactively tried to defuse. Society was changing, and the Navy needed someone like Zumwalt to see race relations as a Navy-wide problem, not a problem within the Black community. We can never know what might have happened had the bomb gone off with a different leader at the helm.

Zumwalt's efforts were called "mod," but today many of his initiatives, like the retention study groups, are not seen as progressive or woke at all. They are accepted as an extension of the progress society has made and an example of a leadership best practice. If history tells us anything, what was seen as mod yesterday may be normal today, and what is seen as woke today will be seen as normal tomorrow.

---

[224] Willard Hamilton, "Polishing Navy Brass," *San Diego Reader*, May 2, 1974, https://www.sandiegoreader.com/news/1974/may/02/cover-polishing-navy-brass/.

IS WOKE JUST THE NEW MOD?

The term "woke" is generally attributed to singer Huddie Leadbetter, known as Lead Belly. When talking about his 1938 song "Scottsboro Boys," Lead Belly encouraged people to "stay woke" to avoid conflict with white authority.

Other uses of the word "woke" are aimed at the Black community. In his 1962 *New York Times* article "If You're Woke You Dig It," novelist William Melvin Kelley talks about the appropriation of Black language but only mentions the word "woke" in the article's headline.[225]

At that time, Black Americans were widely encouraged to "stay woke" and "wake up." Waking up to the behavior of those in power is not a new concept, and "woke" is not a new term.

To be woke was to be aware.

Today, the word "woke" has been appropriated by the very individuals it had originally warned Black Americans about: white men in power. A function of the new woke narrative is to wake up white people to policies that protect minority populations and/or undermine conservative-leaning agendas.

THE WAR ON WOKENESS

Politicians are masters of rhetoric. They use carefully crafted narratives to gain political advantage. And although the use of the term "woke" is a tool of the modern-day Republican Party, Democrats are equally guilty of manipulating the public narratives surrounding the military. Recent Democratic Presidents Barack Obama and Joe Biden haven't hesitated to take photos with troops on Veterans Day and the Fourth of July. Like

---

225 William Melvin Kelley, "'If You're Woke, You Dig It': No Mickey Mouse Can Be Expected to Follow," *The New York Times*, May 20, 1962, https://www.nytimes.com/1962/05/20/archives/if-youre-woke-you-dig-it-no-mickey-mouse-can-be-expected-to-follow.html.

Republican presidents, they influence government contracts and steer policy to win political favor with their base.

Obama pushed forward social change while serving as the commander in chief. During his time in office, he ended the military's "Don't ask, don't tell" ban on gay service members. He also supported removing the ban that prevented women from serving in all military occupations. These were political wins for Obama (and Biden). In 2008, 70 percent of LGBTQ+ voters and 56 percent of female voters chose Obama.[226] When Obama won the 2012 election, exit polling revealed 76 percent of LGBTQ voters[227] and 55 percent of female voters[228] chose Obama, helping him win again.

Biden too got political with the military during the COVID-19 pandemic, when Secretary of Defense Lloyd Austin sent a memo mandating troops be vaccinated or face early discharge.[229] At the time, vaccinations were seen by many as the primary path to a post-COVID world and a way to ensure the readiness and lethality of the force.

But not everyone agreed. Many Republicans were vocally anti-vaccine,[230] making the decision to mandate vaccinations unpopular among some conservatives. While mandatory vaccinations are not new within the

---

226 Roper Center for Public Opinion Research, "How Groups Voted in 2008," accessed August 26, 2025, https://ropercenter.cornell.edu/how-groups-voted-2008.

227 Micah Cohen, "Gay Vote Proved a Boon for Obama," The New York Times, November 15, 2012, https://www.nytimes.com/2012/11/16/us/politics/gay-vote-seen-as-crucial-in-obamas-victory.html.

228 Margie Omero and Tara McGuinness, "How Women Changed the Outcome of the Election," *Center for American Progress*, December 12, 2012, https://www.americanprogress.org/article/how-women-changed-the-outcome-of-the-election.

229 Department of Defense, "Memorandum for Mandatory Coronavirus Disease 2019 Vaccination of Department of Defense Service Members," August 24, 2021, https://media.defense.gov/2021/Aug/25/2002838826/-1/-1/0/Memorandum-for-mandatory-coronavirus-disease-2019-vaccination-of-department-of-defense-service-members.pdf.

230 Grace Sparks, Lunna Lopes, and Ashley Kirzinger, "KFF COVID-19 Vaccine Monitor: MAGA Republicans' Relationship With COVID-19 Vaccines," *KFF*, December 14, 2023, https://www.kff.org/health-information-and-trust/poll-finding/kff-covid-19-vaccine-monitor-maga-republicans-relationship-with-covid-19-vaccines.

military,[231] many claimed they were denied the opportunity to seek a religious exemption[232] as part of the military's medical waiver process.

The mandate was seen as a political move on Biden's part, slamming home his message that vaccines were the only path forward if we wanted to restart the American economy. While the Biden administration did open the door for additional waivers in 2023,[233] his message had been received, and his decisions were seen as political.

TRUMP REBRANDS "WOKE"

In December 2018, President Trump announced the nomination of Army General Mark Milley for chairman of the Joint Chiefs of Staff, the highest-ranking position within the DoD. While the secretary of defense is usually a civilian with military experience, the position of Joint Chiefs chairman is reserved for active-duty uniformed officers. Milley had previously served as chief of staff of the Army and was more than qualified to hold this prestigious position. It took a little over a year for Milley and Trump's relationship to sour.

Shortly after the death of George Floyd at the start of the COVID-19 pandemic, the country was in a state of upheaval. Protests were springing up across the country. In Washington, DC, Trump ordered law enforcement to clear a peaceful protest using riot techniques like tear gas so he and senior administration officials, including Milley, could walk from the White House to St. John's Episcopal Church, where an individual had

---

231 Institute of Medicine (U.S.) Committee on a Strategy for Minimizing the Impact of Naturally Occurring Infectious Diseases of Military Importance: Vaccine Issues in the U.S. Military, Stephen M. Lemon, Susan Thaul, Selamawit Fisseha, et al., eds., *Protecting Our Forces: Improving Vaccine Acquisition and Availability in the U.S. Military* (Washington, DC: National Academies Press, 2002). https://www.ncbi.nlm.nih.gov/books/NBK220954/.

232 Meghann Myers, "Services May Be Improperly Denying Vaccine Religious Waivers, IG Says," *Military Times*, September 21, 2022, https://www.militarytimes.com/news/your-military/2022/09/21/services-may-be-improperly-denying-vaccine-religious-waivers-ig-says/.

233 Karen Jowers, "Troops Discharged After Refusing COVID Vaccine Can Now Rejoin," *Military Times*, February 28, 2023, https://www.militarytimes.com/news/your-military/2023/02/28/troops-discharged-after-refusing-covid-vaccine-can-now-rejoin/.

started a fire in the basement during a Black Lives Matter protest the night before.[234]

When a photo of the walk was published, Milley found himself in an awkward situation. He appeared in uniform with Trump at a time when Trump was trying to control a political narrative. It was believed that Trump staged the event to show the world he would use the military to put down protestors. While the military supports law enforcement in times of crisis, the military's mission is to defend the country against outside threats, not to police its citizens. Milley's presence being used in Trump's political narrative set a dangerous precedent.[235]

Milley acknowledged that the photograph of him with Trump sparked a national debate about the role of the military in civil society.

> "I should not have been there. My presence in that moment and then that environment created a perception of the military involved in domestic politics. As a commissioned uniformed officer, it was a mistake that I've learned from and I sincerely hope we all can learn from. We wear the cloth of our nation, come from the people of our nation. And we must hold dear the principle of an apolitical military that is so deeply rooted in the very essence of our Republic."[236]

This response seemed to anger Trump, who responded by crafting a new narrative: Military leaders and policies have become weak and woke.

After he left office, Trump began calling military leaders—some of whom he had nominated—"woke" as often as he could. By labeling Milley woke and associating wokeness with weakness, Trump implied the decisions Milley made as a military leader of more than forty years were

---

[234] Tom Gjelten, "Peaceful Protesters Tear-Gassed to Clear Way for Trump Church Photo-Op," *NPR*, June 1, 2020, https://www.npr.org/2020/06/01/867532070/trumps-unannounced-church-visit-angers-church-officials.

[235] CBS News, "Trump says he's 'president of law and order,' declares aggressive action on violent protests," *CBS News*, June 2, 2020, https://www.cbsnews.com/news/trump-protest-president-law-and-order.

[236] Luis Martinez, "Milley Apologizes for Taking Part in Trump Church Walk: 'I Should Not Have Been There'" *ABC News*, June 11, 2020, https://abcnews.go.com/Politics/milley-apologizes-taking-part-trump-church-walk/story?id=71195023.

not to be trusted. When Milley responded to Trump's accusations, he entered the political arena, proving Trump's point. While Milley may have been providing guidance and orders to service members, as is his job, the damage had been done. The military had become politicized.

This is why the woke military narrative is more dangerous than the mod narrative. Critics of Zumwalt undercut his specific policies and approach, but their aim was not at him as a person. He tried it his way and they tried it theirs and let the results speak for themselves. By focusing the narrative on wokeness itself—whether of a person or a policy—the conversation does not have to be about the facts or outcomes.

Calling military leaders "liberal" or "woke" intentionally undermines their fitness as leaders by bringing their apolitical status into question. They can't defend themselves without getting political, and if they do, it proves the point of those who wield the word "woke." This political approach ignores the underlying reason for a policy or strategy and drags the military into the political fray.

A DANGEROUS PRECEDENT OR MORE OF THE SAME?

In February 2023, Senator Tommy Tuberville launched a campaign to hold up the promotions of senior military leaders, promotions that required congressional approval. He did so as a peripheral protest against the military's reaction to the repeal of *Roe v. Wade* in June 2022. The *Roe* repeal did not prohibit abortion, but removed federal protection for it. Laws reverted back to the states, with conservative states like Texas instituting full abortion bans,[237] making life for service members and families stationed in those states complicated.

While voters based in these more conservative communities may have supported these changes, female service members and military spouses and

---

[237] Allison McCann and Amy Schoenfeld Walker, "Tracking Abortion Laws Across the Country," *The New York Times*, Updated July 7, 2025, https://www.nytimes.com/interactive/2024/us/abortion-laws-roe-v-wade.html.

children were subject to state laws in communities in which they did not have a vote. Military personnel and families do not vote in the communities in which they live. They live where the military sends them, and do not have the ability to vote with their feet, by leaving a community.

Because female service members and families lost access to reproductive care overnight, the DoD wanted to ensure every member of the community had access to the same medical care, regardless of their location. It adopted policies that would allow military hospitals to continue to perform medically necessary procedures, regardless of state law. Other policies supported service members and families who needed to travel out of state to receive necessary medical treatment.

Tuberville's promotion holds were labeled a "blockade"[238] intended to end the DoD policy that covered leave and travel costs for abortions for personnel who could no longer access them in their assigned duty station. The holds caused a backlog of retirements and delayed and extended orders, which eroded morale. The military promotion holds became increasingly unpopular.

"His argument did change," Tom Porter, vice president of government affairs for Blue Star Families, told me in a conversation about how the woke narrative has evolved over the past few years. "It was abortion in the beginning, and then they started talking about woke-ism later." By August of 2023, the conversation started to shift away from abortion and to a more generic focus, the overall wokeness of military and DoD leadership.[239]

---

[238] Reuters Staff, "Senator Tuberville Lifts Abortion-Related Blockade on Some U.S. Military Promotions," *Reuters*, December 5, 2023, https://www.reuters.com/world/us/republican-senator-tuberville-says-he-will-release-some-military-holds-us-media-2023-12-05/.

[239] Jamie McIntyre, "Tuberville May Never Agree to Military Promotions by Unanimous Consent," *Washington Examiner*, August 24, 2023, https://www.washingtonexaminer.com/news/senate/2572880/tuberville-may-never-agree-to-military-promotions-by-unanimous-consent/.

"I don't want our military to turn into a woke political military," Tuberville told News Nation. "They're making laws from the White House and the Pentagon."[240]

Tuberville dropped the holds on promotions in December 2023, after receiving pushback from both Republicans and Democrats who worried about the impact they were having on military readiness.[241] But the damage had been done: The military and its policies had been labeled "woke" and no longer were about the people the policies were serving.

Because civilians don't know much about the military, Tuberville could tell Americans the military had been corrupted by liberals pushing woke policies.

The message sent: These "woke" policies must be a result of the ones at the top corrupting the boots on the ground.

IS WOKENESS ACTUALLY WEAKENING THE MILITARY?

"It sounds unbelievable, but I once attended a lecture in a building I wasn't familiar with. During a break, I asked where the women's restroom was. I was told there wasn't one," active-duty Marine Corps Officer Abigail Seitz wrote in a 2022 essay about women in the military. "For the duration of the lecture, they cleared out one of the men's rooms and had someone guard the door while all the women used it. We had to do this every time any woman used the bathroom during the all-day lecture. When we asked why there was no women's restroom, the explanation given was 'It's an old building.' Somehow, this was justification for not retrofitting one of the *four* men's bathrooms into a women's room in the decades since it was built. And by 'retrofitting,' I mean changing the sign on the door to read

---

[240] News Nation. "Sen. Tuberville Fighting 'Woke, Political Military,' Defends Military Block." *YouTube*, July 25, 2023. https://www.youtube.com/watch?v=SRSfIG2J3Zw.

[241] Eric McDaniel, "Sen. Tuberville Drops Remaining Holds on Senior Military Promotions," *NPR*, December 19, 2023, https://www.npr.org/2023/12/19/1220492250/tuberville-drops-blockade-military-promotions.

WOMEN instead of MEN. Because the bathroom itself was perfectly functional for women."[242]

Although women have served in some capacity since the Revolutionary War, women were only officially permitted to serve in the armed forces starting in 1901, when Congress established the U.S. Army Nurse Corps. Other branches soon followed the Army's lead and officially welcomed women into the ranks. The jobs they could perform were initially limited to clerical positions, and women only made up 1.1 percent of uniformed personnel.[243]

It was not until the feminist movement of the 1970s that women began to enter the civilian workforce—and ultimately the military—en mass. This cultural shift just happened to coincide with the establishment of the all-volunteer force of a highly traditional, highly masculine military.

Despite the military's masculine image, women were undeterred. The result was a striking increase in the rate of females joining the armed forces from 1973 to 1978. According to a 1979 review of the all-volunteer force, "It can be argued that without the greater number of women in the labor force generally, the relative success of the initial phase of the all-volunteer force would not have taken place."[244] Fast forward forty years and women would be able to serve in all areas of the military.

However, the rate of females joining has stagnated. As of 2023, females only represented 17.5 percent of uniformed personnel, despite making up roughly 50 percent of the U.S. population. Because, as Abigail Seitz discovered in her search for a female restroom, the DoD is highly resistant to change.

In the years leading up to women being eligible to serve in all military occupational specialties, including combat jobs, there was a nationwide debate about their fitness. Some said women would be a distraction if they

---

[242] Amy McPhie Allebest, host. "Episode 1: Down Patriarchy in the US Marines – Abby's Story." *Breaking Down Patriarchy*, https://breakingdownpatriarchy.com/episode-1-abby/.
[243] Morris Janowitz and Charles C. Moskos Jr., "Five Years of the All-Volunteer Force: 1973–1978," *Armed Forces & Society* 5, no. 2 (Winter 1979): 171–218, https://www.jstor.org/stable/45346127.
[244]Ibid., 181.

were allowed to serve in special operations combat units. Not only would their presence increase the likelihood of consensual sex, but also sexual assault, which results in unit disruption.[245] This is particularly interesting because sex seems to be a perennial distraction for male service members. This was the same argument against allowing gay service members to openly serve, which did not prove to be as problematic as "Don't ask, don't tell" proponents argued. It was also similar to the arguments presented by those who protested racial integration.

Less than one hundred years ago, the Army War College declared African Americans "inferior mentally"[246] to white people. Women were not allowed to serve in combat until 2015 because they were not considered to be "physically, mentally and emotionally qualified."[247]

In 1977, Congressman Robin Beard testified before the Subcommittee on Manpower and Personnel as to the status of the all-volunteer force. He reported that when the draft ended, a "new composition in the Army was begun. More women, more blacks, lower-income groups, and lower mental group personnel are joining the services."[248]

According to researcher Jennifer Mittelstadt, "Beard cast new recruits almost as members of an underclass, a term that would gain wide usage in the early 1980s."[249] However, just a year later, Charles C. Moskos Jr., a professor of sociology at Northwestern University, presented congressional testimony that contested the notion that Black service members were in any way inferior to white service members, saying:

---

245 Anna Simons, "Here's Why Women in Combat Units Is a Bad Idea," *War on the Rocks*, November 18, 2014, https://warontherocks.com/2014/11/heres-why-women-in-combat-units-is-a-bad-idea/.
246 Tuskegee Airmen Inc., "Negro Manpower in War," 1925, https://tuskegeeairmen.org/wp-content/uploads/2020/11/TAI_Resources_Negro-Manpower-In-War.pdf.
247 Debra Bell, "Arguing for and Against Women in Combat, in 1978," *U.S. News & World Report Press Past*, May 15, 2013, https://www.usnews.com/news/blogs/press-past/2013/05/15/arguing-for-and-against-women-in-combat-in-1978.
248 U.S. Senate, *Status of the All-Volunteer Armed Force: Hearing Before the Subcommittee on Manpower and Personnel of the Committee on Armed Services*, 95th Cong., 1st sess., 1977, https://www.govinfo.gov/app/details/CHRG-95shrg29845O/context.
249 Jennifer Mittelstadt, *The Rise of the Military Welfare State* (Cambridge, MA: Harvard University Press, 2015), 74.

> "It is important to stress that the decline in educational levels of NPS [non-prior service] male recruits is not correlated with the rising number of black servicemen. Since the end of the draft, the proportion of black high school graduates entering the Army has exceeded that of whites, and this is a trend that is becoming more pronounced. In point of fact, today's Army is the only major arena in American Society where black educational levels surpass that of whites, and by quite a significant margin."[250]

Yesterday's narratives: Black people are "inferior mentally."[251] Women are "physically unable to do the work."[252] Gay service members will "damage unit cohesion."[253]

Today's narrative: Military leaders are "woke."

The narrative that says certain groups are unfit to serve has often been based on opinion, not facts. When the narrative discusses a lowering of military standards, it is actually a dog whistle; history has repeatedly proven this to be true. Black, female, and gay military members serve with distinction and heroism. And our nation needs all of them to serve if it wants to avoid a draft.

However, what neither politicians nor the military want to admit is that military fitness standards are not static. Services regularly adjust standards to ensure they meet recruiting goals. It is political manipulation to blame certain groups as the cause of changing these standards. Rather than admitting this is a reality of the all-volunteer force, updates to policies are cast as a *lowering* of standards, not a *changing* of standards.

"I'm straight up just saying we should not have women in combat roles. It hasn't made us more effective. Hasn't made us more lethal. Has

---

[250] U.S. Senate, *Status of the All-Volunteer Armed Force: Hearing Before the Subcommittee on Manpower and Personnel of the Committee on Armed Services*, 95th Cong., 1st sess., 1977, https://www.govinfo.gov/app/details/CHRG-95shrg29845O/context.

[251] Tuskegee Airmen Inc., "Negro Manpower in War," 1925, https://tuskegeeairmen.org/wp-content/uploads/2020/11/TAI_Resources_Negro-Manpower-In-War.pdf.

[252] U.S. Senate, *Status of the All-Volunteer Armed Force: Hearing Before the Subcommittee on Manpower and Personnel of the Committee on Armed Services*, 95th Cong., 1st sess., 1977, https://www.govinfo.gov/app/details/CHRG-95shrg29845O/CHRG-95shrg29845O.

[253] U.S. Senate, *Testimony Relating to the "Don't Ask, Don't Tell" Policy: Hearing Before the Committee on Armed Services*, 111th Cong., 2nd sess., 2010, https://www.govinfo.gov/content/pkg/CHRG-111shrg57495/html/CHRG-111shrg57495.htm.

made fighting more complicated,"[254] veteran and Fox News host Pete Hegseth told the *Shawn Ryan Show* podcast host Shawn Ryan in November 2024. Hegseth reignited the question of whether women should serve in combat roles after he was selected as Trump's nominee for Secretary of Defense. When his nomination was put to a vote, Congress was split 50-50. Vice President JD Vance broke the tie, confirming Hegseth on January 24, 2025.[255] Unlike Zumwalt, whose public stances were based on anecdote and tested with data, Hegseth's comments were largely based on anecdotes alone. He asserted that standards had been unofficially lowered *in response to* external pressure from woke leaders who wanted more women in the military.

It is hard for Hegseth to cite facts because there is not enough data on women in combat roles. Some studies measure success in combat by looking at a candidate's rate of staying in service, a measure that is impacted by a multitude of variables that have nothing to do with the candidate's performance.[256] What the narrative doesn't admit is, while generic physical fitness tests are different based on age and gender, women who want to join the elite combat units most Americans think of when they hear "women in combat" have to meet the specifications of those jobs and the same requirements as men.[257]

Hegseth's concerns are not new. In fact, the concern about how the presence of women would lead to lower standards was part of early debates against allowing women to serve at all. His statements show he believes woke politicians wanted to politicize the military by pushing women into

---

[254] Lolita C. Baldor, "Should Women Serve in Combat? Trump's Defense Pick Reignites Debate," *Military Times*, November 18, 2024, https://www.militarytimes.com/news/pentagon-congress/2024/11/18/should-women-serve-in-combat-trumps-defense-pick-reignites-debate/.
[255] Lisa Mascaro, Mary Clare Jalonick and Farnoush Amiri, "Pete Hegseth Confirmed as Defense Secretary in Tie-Breaking Vote," *AP News*, December 15, 2024, https://apnews.com/article/pete-hegseth-defense-secretary-trump-cabinet-confirmation-12491935023692bce0a04d149663e784.
[256] Emma Moore, "Women in Combat: Five-Year Status Update," *Center for a New American Security*, November 2020, https://www.cnas.org/publications/commentary/women-in-combat-five-year-status-update.
[257] Meghann Myers "Navy SEALs Won't Change Standards for Women, Admiral Says," *Navy Times*, December 17, 2015, https://www.navytimes.com/news/your-navy/2015/12/17/navy-seals-won-t-change-standards-for-women-admiral-says/

roles they are not capable of holding. While he may be right that some politicians want to use the conversation for political gain, the result of their efforts is opening up the military to more people. The subsequent question of fitness and lowered combat effectiveness is an essential question we must answer, but answers require facts.

One fact that is often overlooked is that in the late 1970s, the Army *did* lower some standards for women to make them comparable to the lower standards men were held to. In a June 1978 congressional hearing on the status of the all-volunteer armed forces, John P. White, assistant secretary of defense overseeing manpower, testified:

> "The Army has had much higher standards for women than for men. The average Army [Armed Forces Qualification Test] score for women is 75, while it is 50 for Army men. The cutoff score for men is 16. For women, it recently has been reduced from 59 to 50. The floor for women is still above the average for Army male accessions."[258]

Allowing women to serve in all roles does not equal a lowering of standards. "Frankly, the people who really do not want the standards to be lowered are women," said Senator Claire McCaskill in a 2016 hearing regarding opening ground combat units to women. "The last thing in the world a woman needs is to join a unit with everyone looking over their shoulder saying, 'Well, you are not the same as we are.'"[259]

Many on the left have publicly stated that if the standards for both shouldn't be lowered, then don't lower them. And at a minimum, don't say they were lowered without proof.

But women in combat is not the only gender-based military policy that the woke narrative has politicized.

---

[258] U.S. Senate, *Status of the All-Volunteer Armed Force: Hearing Before the Subcommittee on Manpower and Personnel of the Committee on Armed Services*, 95th Cong., 1st sess., 1977, 99, https://www.govinfo.gov/app/details/CHRG-95shrg29845O/context.
[259] U.S. Senate, *The Implementation of the Decision to Open All Ground Combat Units to Women: Hearing Before the Committee on Armed Services*, 114th Cong., 2nd sess., February 2, 2016, 64, https://www.govinfo.gov/content/pkg/CHRG-114shrg24850/pdf/CHRG-114shrg24850.pdf.

A NEW "UNFIT" GROUP

On July 26, 2017, during his first term, Trump posted a flurry of tweets: "After consultation with my Generals and military experts, please be advised that the United States Government will not accept or allow[260] . . . transgender individuals to serve in any capacity in the U.S. Military. Our military must be focused on decisive and overwhelming[261] . . . victory and cannot be burdened with the tremendous medical costs and disruption that transgender in the military would entail. Thank you."[262]

This announcement was formalized in an August 2017 memorandum that ordered a halt to new enlistments and gender-affirming medical treatment for active-duty service members. However, the policy quickly faced multiple legal challenges, and several federal courts issued injunctions that temporarily blocked its enforcement.

In March 2018, then-Defense Secretary Jim Mattis released a revised policy, framing the ban around the medical diagnosis of gender dysphoria. Under this revision, individuals with a history or diagnosis of gender dysphoria were largely barred from serving unless they agreed to serve under their sex assigned at birth. On April 12, 2019, the DoD officially implemented the policy, restricting the ability of most transgender people to join or remain in the military.

President Biden reversed the ban shortly after taking office in 2021.

Upon returning to office in January 2025, Trump signed two executive orders, one titled "Defending Women from Gender Ideology Extremism and Restoring Biological Truth to the Federal Government" and "Prioritizing Military Excellence and Readiness." The first took aim at

---

260 Donald J. Trump, "After consultation with my Generals and military experts, please be advised that the United States Government will not accept or allow……," *X (Formerly Twitter)*, July 26, 2017, https://x.com/realDonaldTrump/status/890193981585444864.

261 Donald J. Trump, "….Transgender individuals to serve in any capacity in the U.S. Military. Our military must be focused on decisive and overwhelming…..," *X (Formerly Twitter)*, July 26, 2017, https://x.com/realDonaldTrump/status/890196164313833472.

262 Donald J. Trump, "….victory and cannot be burdened with the tremendous medical costs and disruption that transgender in the military would entail. Thank you," *X (Formerly Twitter)*, July 26, 2017, https://x.com/realDonaldTrump/status/890197095151546369.

transgender Americans by saying there were only two genders, male and female. The second directed the DoD to revise policies to exclude transgender individuals, citing concerns over unit cohesion and military effectiveness. Just as before, the military would cite a medical diagnosis of gender dysphoria as the reason for their dismissal, allowing them to stay in the military if they could obtain a medical waiver.

The first executive order was widely criticized for being unscientific, as not all people are born with XX (female) or XY (male) chromosomes; some are born intersex, with both male and female reproductive organs and other possible chromosome combinations, including XXY or XO.

The second executive order was also criticized, as the argument against transgender service members was not well-founded. Not only do many serve with honor, but cisgender personnel also undergo costly elective procedures and take expensive medications, costing the DoD far more than transgender service members.

In fact, the military spends nearly eight times more on Viagra than it does on transgender care.[263] Both are gender-affirming care, but only one is considered woke.

The woke narrative says people-focused policy decisions are made for political reasons and ignores the fact that the military institutes policies that serve those on the front lines. Using terms like mod and woke pulls the focus from the actual policies in question and puts one's political opponents on the defense. In adopting this strategy, bad political actors have corrupted the apolitical nature of the military.

And military leaders can't publicly defend their people or policies because the military is supposed to be apolitical.

This type of political propaganda capitalizes on the fact that the average American knows next to nothing about the military. If Americans knew more about the military community, they would realize it is not woke, nor is it progressive. It is a cross-section of American society, full of

---

[263] Sophie Clark, "US Military Spending on Viagra vs. Gender-Affirming Care," *Newsweek*, March 15, 2024, https://www.newsweek.com/us-military-spending-viagra-gender-affirming-care-2044114.

conservatives, liberals, and the apathetic. What the Republican woke narrative doesn't tell the American people is that the military mirrors the rest of society; it needs programs and policies to serve the people who serve. What the Democratic agenda neglects to share is that some of the policies it promotes impact very few members of the military and are seen by the DoD as another box to check. No matter what side of the political aisle you sit on, you will hear stories about the military that are only half true.

IS THE MILITARY A THERMOSTAT OR THERMOMETER?

"Stop using the Army as a test bed for social evolution. Misusing the Army in this way detracts from its core purpose while doing little to reshape the American social structure. The Army no longer reflects national demographics to the degree that it did before 1974 when the draft was eliminated."
—Project 2025[264]

This statement befuddled me when I first read it. The Army has never reflected our national demographics, ever. And it won't until the Army is 50 percent female.

In my experience, rather than being a groundbreakingly woke institution, the military is usually far behind the curve. The 1993 "Don't ask, don't tell" policy allowed gay service members to remain in and join the military, but it, along with its repeal in 2011, did not *drive* social change. Rather, it reflected change that had already occurred in American society. For instance, before we knew how HIV/AIDS was transmitted, people were fearful of touching people with the disease, travel bans were in place, and those with HIV, the majority being gay men, were criminalized.[265] As

[264] Project 2025 is the conservative policy blueprint published by The Heritage Foundation designed to reshape the federal government to align more closely with the values of its authors.
[265] J. Stan Lehman, et al., "Prevalence and Public Health Implications of State Laws that Criminalize Potential HIV Exposure in the United States," *Americans with Disabilities Act*, U.S. Department of Justice, 2011, https://archive.ada.gov/hiv/HIV-criminalization-paper.htm.

our scientific understanding grew, the way society responded to the sick changed and many (but not all) bans were lifted.[266]

Scientific discovery helped shape society's views. The military did not. Were these changes seen as political? Sure. However, reality and facts are just that: reality and facts. When politicians portray anecdotes and pillow talk as facts, which are then amplified by the media, they are using rhetoric to manipulate what the public thinks about the military.

The power the military has is its role in documenting the changes already present in our nation by updating its policies to keep up. The authors of Project 2025 may see the military as a thermostat, when in reality is supposed to be a thermometer.

In his 1963 letter from Birmingham City Jail, Martin Luther King Jr. described how the church used to be a thermostat that set the temperature for the rest of society, but he noted it had become more like a thermometer, responding to society.[267] Using his analogy, the military is intended to be a thermometer that reflects the temperature of society, not a thermostat that sets the temperature. It is unlikely that the military, whose service members represent less than 1 percent of the nation's population, could wield enough influence to set the temperature for the other 99 percent.

If the military is a thermometer, we can logically conclude that if the military is woke, so is America.

Ultimately, the analysis of this narrative highlights an uncomfortable truth: Some conservative policies make it harder for all Americans to serve. Whereas woke policies often expand service eligibility.

The proponents of the woke narrative and authors of Project 2025 want to reflect on a time when the military was strong. But no such time existed. The military and those who serve in the military have never been good enough for politicians. The all-volunteer force was a floundering

---

[266]Susanna E. Winston and Curt G. Beckwith, "The Impact of Removing the Immigration Ban on HIV-Infected Persons," *AIDS Patient Care and STDs*, December 2011, https://pmc.ncbi.nlm.nih.gov/articles/PMC3263303/#:~:text=The%20ramifications%20of%20the%20HIV,held%20in%20the%20United%20States.
[267] Martin Luther King Jr., "Letter from Birmingham Jail," August 19, 1963, https://www.csuchico.edu/iege/_assets/documents/susi-letter-from-birmingham-jail.pdf.

institution saved by an influx of Black and female service members, who were cast as lesser than but were not. It was further revived by woke policies that supported its new diversity.

This doesn't mean everyone in the military agrees with woke or mod policies; many do not. The military is liberal and conservative. And it must be allowed to remain so. It needs conservative policies just as much as it needs liberal ones.

However, policies that challenge the status quo will always seem harder to swallow, as this goes against our biological desire for stability. Growth requires overcoming hardship. The status quo is comfortable. This is why Abigail Seitz had to speak up when she was in a building without a women's restroom. This is why Elmo and Mouza Zumwalt had to push against race relations and the reliance on anecdotes. In both cases, it took a conscious effort and targeted policies to move this sluggish bureaucracy toward a more productive and ready force.

When we can distinguish between policies serving those who serve versus policies and narratives serving politicians, we can safeguard the apolitical nature of our military. Because military policies should not serve politics. They must serve the Americans who serve our country.

If our nation becomes too uncomfortable embracing woke policies, all Americans will need to get more comfortable with being drafted.

How *you* can change this narrative: When you see politicians on either side of the aisle labeling a military policy woke or outdated, take note. Unsure if what you're hearing is fact or fiction? Talk to the military community. Read military news. Don't take a politician's word for it. Ask questions.

How the DoD can change this narrative: Continue to do the policy work that serves the people who serve. Seek to overturn policies that limit who can serve.

Be All You Can Be

"Why is everybody saying Gen Z is going to get drafted? No, the fuck we're not," said a TikToker in 2023. "And you know how I know that? We are just going to say no. How are they going to actually get us to get up and go to war? We're also, like, really mentally ill. I have, like, six of these [medicine bottles]. What makes you think I'm qualified to have a gun?"[268]

This post prompted comments denouncing Gen Z, with others commenting, "Y'all saying what Millennials been thinking," as well as:

"I'll take jail time. This country is not worth laying down my life for."

"'You'll go to jail,' oh no free healthcare and rent. Yeah I'll take jail over dying for a war I don't support."

"Gov spent the last 3 decades ignoring the needs of the people but suddenly think we're able to go to war in our current physical/mental states?"

---

[268] Bill Maher, "New Rule: The Not-Working Class," *Real Time with Bill Maher* (HBO), April 18, 2025, https://www.youtube.com/watch?v=SbhJR0plGbs.

"You'll be a bullet sponge. But take heart women will be joining you The last commenter was referencing another thread created by TikToker Timothy James.

James also posted a video saying, "Ladies 18 to 26, I hope you're ready to get drafted!"

The video went viral, with over 55,000 comments from women clearly indicating they have no interest in being drafted or serving, including:

"Girl I use my period to get out of PE I'm not fighting in a war."

"My mom says I can't go if there will be boys."

"My therapist said I should stand my ground and say no to anything that makes me uncomfy."

"Has anyone created a 'going to war' Pinterest board yet?"

"Im a talker if I get captured Im spilling all the tea and drawing maps for them, leave me alone."

"Fine but they'll regret that decision when I start crying because the vibes are off and I forgot to take my meds."[269]

At the time, the war in Ukraine and conflicts between Israel and Palestine forced Americans to question U.S. military capabilities. Gen Z dominated this public narrative.

America is not ready for a draft. The military doesn't want one and, certainly, Gen Z doesn't either. While Gen Z briefly entered the military narrative, laughing at the notion that they would be considered fit—or unfit—to serve, the DoD was ready to regain control after social media stopped buzzing.

In recent years, the services have struggled to reach recruiting goals.[270] Military service academies' application rates have fallen[271] and the DoD

---

[269] What's Trending, "Behind Gen Z's Hilarious Spin on the Hypothetical Women's Draft," *YouTube*, October 19, 2023, https://www.youtube.com/watch?v=eJkK4zTBCAo.

[270] David Vergun, "DOD Addresses Recruiting Shortfall Challenges," *Department of Defense News*, December 13, 2023, https://www.defense.gov/News/News-Stories/Article/article/3616786/dod-addresses-recruiting-shortfall-challenges/.

[271] Steve Beynon, "Applications to Service Academies Plummet Amid Recruitment and Pandemic Woes," *Military.com*, August 19, 2022, https://www.military.com/daily-news/2022/08/19/applications-service-academies-plummet-amid-recruitment-and-pandemic-woes.html.

reports only 9 percent of youths ages sixteen through twenty-four are likely to serve—the lowest "propensity to serve" rates since the nation learned of Abu Ghraib and became disillusioned with the War on Terror in the mid-2000s.[272] Although recruiting numbers have improved since 2024,[273] with politicians on both sides of the political aisle wanting to claim credit,[274] recruiting an all-volunteer force is inherently difficult.

According to the Pew Research Center, the majority of adults under thirty (53 percent) don't think the military has a positive impact.[275] All in all, the majority of Americans are "ambivalent" toward military service, with 48 percent saying they would recommend young people join and 41 percent saying they would not.[276] And older generations have a more positive view of service.

Over the decades, DoD officials have cited a hard sell, but today's recruiting environment may be the hardest yet. When the services fail to meet recruiting goals, often the shortfall is attributed to both realistic factors (the economy or the fitness of the average American) and political factors (woke leadership or discriminatory policies).

Both Republicans and Democrats have their default stances on the root causes. Politicians have come up with many possible explanations: the sacrifices required of service, the offer of a better job, or because

---

[272]Office of People Analytics, *Youth Propensity to Serve in the U.S. Military: Fall 2021 Public Release Propensity Update*, accessed August 26, 2025, https://jamrs.defense.gov/Portals/20/Documents/YP51Fall2021PUBLICRELEASEPropensityUpdate.pdf?ver=FE5vDYeDzsgNRbEssX3Z4g%3d%3d.

[273] U.S. Department of Defense, "Military Met 2024 Recruit Contracting Goals, Plans for Repeat," August 22, 2024, https://www.defense.gov/News/News-Stories/Article/Article/4151948/military-met-2024-recruit-contracting-goals-plans-for-repeat/#:~:text=%22Fiscal%20year%202024%20saw%20improvements,nonmonetary%20authorities%20granted%20by%20Congress.%22.

[274] Melissa Goldin, "Fact Check: Trump credited with rising military recruitment. Growth started before his reelection," *AP News*, April 25, 2025, https://apnews.com/article/fact-check-military-recruitment-trump-hegseth-91700f0b688c3460458e467da95c8268#:~:text=U.S.%20military%20recruitment%20has%20made,have%20also%20played%20a%20role.

[275] Pew Research Center, "The U.S. Military," February 1, 2024, https://www.pewresearch.org/politics/2024/02/01/the-u-s-military/#:~:text=Adults%20under%2030%20are%20the,those%20ages%2030%20to%2049

[276] Pew Research Center, *Chapter 5: The Public and the Military*, October 5, 2011, https://www.pewresearch.org/social-trends/2011/10/05/chapter-5-the-public-and-the-military/.

Americans are unqualified, overweight, or drug users.[277] Unsatisfyingly, a multitude of variables influence recruiting; despite what is reported by mainstream media and politicians, there is no single determining factor.

While research examines why service members choose to serve and why the majority of people choose *not* to serve, we rarely evaluate military recruiting messages put forth by leaders and recruiting offices. We don't publicly question who those messages are most likely to attract. So let's take a look.

Dominant narrative: The military is an elite institution that can help all Americans be all they can be.

A better narrative: The military's elite status has distanced itself from the average American. As a result of this disconnect, recruiting relies upon positive word-of-mouth marketing provided by veterans and military families.

MILITARY MARKETING NARRATIVES

"I Want YOU for the U.S. Army."[278]

Everyone knows that poster. The one where Uncle Sam in his starred top hat sends a finger pointed in your direction. He is not bashful, and he knows what he wants. Military recruiting slogans like this have been key to the DoD's public-facing recruitment plan. In addition to supporting

---

277 Leo Shane III, "Sluggish Military Recruiting Worries Congress," *Military Times*, April 27, 2022, https://www.militarytimes.com/news/pentagon-congress/2022/04/27/sluggish-military-recruiting-worries-congress/.

278 U.S. Department of Defense, "WWII Posters Aimed to Inspire, Encourage Service," February 12, 2019, https://www.defense.gov/News/Feature-Stories/story/Article/1990131/wwii-posters-aimed-to-inspire-encourage-service/#:~:text=Perhaps%20the%20most%20iconic%20was%20the%20Uncle,captioned:%20%22I%20Want%20You%20for%20the%20U.S.

recruiting, it is one way the services tell the nation who it is and how individuals fit into that narrative.

While it may seem like the military would follow straightforward marketing practices, it does not. Typically, marketing starts with a product, idea, or person. You identify a target audience for that product and customize the marketing of that product to appeal to that audience. If it is unsuccessful, you would review the product and messaging to see if there is any improvement that can be made.

Military marketing in the all-volunteer era takes a different tack. Rather than marketing to its broad potential audience (Gen Z), the military targets its messages at those who are more likely to serve, and it hopes veterans will produce good word-of-mouth marketing.[279]

In many ways, this follows marketing best practices. Apple designs products with a people focus. It launches them and leverages its popularity with tech enthusiasts and early adopters. Those early purchasers create a buzz around the product that spreads via word of mouth to the majority of consumers. The product it creates has features that are appealing to a wide audience, and Apple reaps the benefits. By contrast, the military's product is not universally appealing. Military service costs lives. But it doesn't say so. It doesn't highlight the costs, just the *feelings* service can produce: courage, pride, toughness, belonging, and more.

Military recruiting units do not have the ability to make service more appealing (increasing pay and benefits, prioritizing the prevention of sexual assaults, etc.). Its marketing is targeted to attract Americans who are more likely to serve based on who has signed up in the past. Marketing has historically been focused on individuals who want to leave the normalcy of civilian life behind and challenge themselves while serving something greater than themselves. If that is what service sells, is Gen Z buying it?

---

[279] U.S. Department of Defense, Joint Advertising, Market Research & Studies (JAMRS), *Futures Survey*, Spring 2024,
https://jamrs.defense.gov/Portals/20/Documents/YP58Spring2024_PropensityUpdate_Briefing.pdf.

THE DOD DIGS THE MILITARY-CIVILIAN GAP

After the all-volunteer force began in 1973, the military faced a recruiting crisis. Those who enlisted were less educated and from poorer families than those who served under the draft.[280] Volunteers signed up precisely because of the opportunities military service afforded,[281] and the DoD was left to figure out what to do with a growing group of government and military leaders labeled an uneducated "underclass."[282]

The DoD wanted to attract a new type of volunteer and tried to change the military narrative. It did so by distancing itself from the general public. It branded the military as an elite "warrior class." The Reagan administration contributed to this narrative by demonizing and reducing the availability of welfare to civilians while publicly praising the military as an elite force that had earned its right to government support in the form of the GI Bill (aka the Servicemen's Readjustment Act of 1944).

"This helped the Army recast its soldiers, and it became a centerpiece for the upwardly mobile image of the Army in the 1980s," wrote Mittelstadt in *The Rise of the Military Welfare State*.[283]

The Reagan administration and the DoD had accomplished two things: They averted a recruiting crisis while appealing to Reagan's conservative base, who now saw the military as elite warriors rather than a group of people who accepted handouts via the GI Bill.

The military was portrayed as elite, a class worthy of respect. The few who pulled the many up by their bootstraps. At the time, and still today, respect for the sacrifices of our military is a good thing. But this view of the military was different. Under the draft, the average American likely knew someone who had served. They had gone to school together and shared

---

280 Morris Janowitz and Charles C. Moskos, "Five Years of the All-Volunteer Force: 1973–1978," *Armed Forces & Society* 5, no. 2 (1979): 171–218, accessed September 17, 2024, http://www.jstor.org/stable/45346127.
281 *Congressional Record, 127th Congress, 1st Session, 1981.* Accessed August 26, 2025. https://archive.org/stream/congressionalrec127aunit/congressionalrec127aunit_djvu.txt.
282 Jennifer Mittelstadt, *The Rise of the Military Welfare State* (Cambridge, MA: Harvard University Press, 2015), 85.
283 Ibid., 119.

similar life experiences. The civilian knew that service asked a lot, but also knew the average person could rise to the occasion because the boy next door had. But the elite warrior narrative came with unintended consequences.

The DoD's own narrative made the military lifestyle unapproachable to the average American. This nationwide lack of familiarity with military life is known as the military-civilian gap or the military-civilian divide.

The military had started digging, widening the military-civilian gap. At the same time, the DoD started to buy into its own marketing messages. It sees itself as an elite warrior class that relies upon deference to function.[284] This elite warrior class has withheld answers when questioned by Congress or reporters, won court cases other agencies would lose,[285] and is exempt from anti-discrimination laws. In its elite haze, it does not see how its own narrative has negatively impacted recruiting.

As recently as 2019, the DoD has come out officially stating that the military-civilian divide has been exacerbated by a "shrinking military footprint in the United States" and "a declining veteran population."[286] Even the acting undersecretary of defense for personnel and readiness, Anthony M. Kurta, blamed the "uninformed and often misguided" messages from organizations or media on the risks of military service. He went on to say, "Combined, these factors have led to a youth market which is less interested in the military and does not appreciate the social worth or intrinsically motivating elements of military service."[287]

---

[284] Polina Beliakova, "Erosion by Deference: Civilian Control and the Military in Policymaking," *Texas National Security Review* 4, no. 3 (Summer 2021): 55–75, https://tnsr.org/2021/06/erosion-by-deference-civilian-control-and-generals-in-policymaking/.

[285] Until 2024, the military benefitted from a policy of legal deference generally referred to as "the military deference doctrine." Under this precedent, courts would defer to the DoD's expertise rather than require them to prove their case in the same way other agencies or individuals would be required to do so.

Lindsay Lyon Rodman, "Doing Away with the Military Deference Doctrine: Applying Lessons from Civil-Military Relations Theory to the Supreme Court," *North Dakota Law Review* 99, no. 2 (2024): 327–376, https://law.und.edu/_files/docs/ndlr/pdf/issues/99/2/99ndlr327.pdf.

[286] Department of Defense, "DOD Official Cites Widening Military-Civilian Gap," *Defense.gov*, March 6, 2019, https://www.defense.gov/News/News-Stories/Article/Article/1850344/dod-official-cites-widening-military-civilian-gap/.

[287] Ibid.

Rather than trying to appeal to its audience, who is theoretically anyone aged eighteen to forty-two,[288] the military blames the messenger. When its intended audience does not pick up on the messages it puts out, it points fingers outward, not inward.

Its elite status prevents it from seeing its role as the designer of the military stories Americans are told. Instead of presenting Americans with the stories they need to hear about the military, it maintains the status quo. It continues to market to likely joiners without looking at ways to improve its "product," assumes younger generations are afraid or weak, and then wonders why Gen Z isn't signing up.

Military Recruiting Slogans

Branch	*1980s*	*1990s*	*2000s*	*2010s*	*2020–*
Army	"Be all you can be."	"Be all you can be."	"Army of One" (2001–2006); "Army Strong" (2006–2015)	"Army Strong" (2006–2015); "Warriors Wanted" (2015–present)	"Warriors Wanted"; "Be all you can be."
Navy	"You Are Tomorrow; You Are the Navy"	"Accelerate Your Life"; "You and the Navy, Full Speed Ahead" (1990–1996); "Let the Journey Begin" (1996–2001)	"Accelerate Your Life" (2001–2009)	"A Global Force for Good" (2009–2015); "America's Navy" (2014–2017); "Forged by the Sea" (2017–present)	"Forged by the Sea" (2017–present)
Marine Corps	"The Few, the Proud"	'The Few, the Proud"	"The Few, the Proud, the Marines"	"The Few, the Proud, the Marines"	"The Few, the Proud, the Marines"

[288]U.S. General Services Administration. "Requirements to Join the U.S. Military." *USAGov*, March 10, 2025. https://www.usa.gov/military-requirements.

Air Force	"Aim High"	"Aim High"	"Aim High"	"Aim High"; "Cross into the Blue" (2017–present)	"Aim High"; "Cross into the Blue" (2017–present)
Coast Guard	"Semper Paratus" (Always Ready)	"Semper Paratus" (Always Ready)	"Semper Paratus" (Always Ready)	"Semper Paratus" (Always Ready); "Born Ready" (2018– present)	"Semper Paratus" (Always Ready); "Born Ready" (2018–2023); "Protect. Defend. Save." (2023–present)
Space Force	n/a	n/a	n/a	n/a	"The Sky Is Not the Limit"

Despite being a large part of what the American public is told about the military, recruiting slogans are not tracked. According to a report put out by the Government Accountability Office (GAO), the research arm of Congress, the DoD "has not collected or tracked sufficient data to help support decisions related to its recruitment and retention efforts."[289] Additionally, it doesn't have plans for how it will recruit and retain female service members.[290] In other words, these slogans may be part of a recruiting plan, but the military may not be able to share how successful or unsuccessful they—or other efforts—actually are.

Military recruiting narratives focus on the individual and where they fit into the bigger picture. It is a winning marketing strategy and a powerful narrative tool. We all want to be marketed to, not at.

---

[289] U.S. Government Accountability Office. *National Security Snapshot: DOD Active-Duty Recruitment and Retention Challenges*. GAO-23-106551. Washington, D.C.: March 28, 2023. https://www.gao.gov/products/gao-23-106551.

[290] U.S. Government Accountability Office, *Female Active-Duty Personnel: Guidance and Plans Needed to Improve Recruitment and Retention*, GAO-20-61, January 2020, https://www.gao.gov/assets/gao-20-61.pdf

An example of this is Hillary Clinton's 2016 presidential campaign. One of her unofficial slogans was "I'm with her." During the campaign, Clinton struggled to relate to the average American and was described as cold. The "I'm with her" narrative focused on Clinton, not the American people. A better version of this slogan would have been "She's with us."

Trump, a master of narrative, called her out. "'Her campaign slogan is, 'I'm with her.' You know what my response to that is? I'm with you, the American people," he said.[291]

Military Slogan Narrative Review

<table>
<tr><th>Branch</th><th>1980s</th><th>1990s</th><th>2000s</th><th>2010s</th><th>2020–</th></tr>
<tr><td>Army</td><td colspan="2">Emphasized personal growth and achievement during a period of increased individualism in society.</td><td colspan="2">Highlighted the importance of individual soldiers in modern warfare, particularly relevant in the post-9/11 era</td><td>Embraced nostalgic campaign to go back to its early recruiting boom</td></tr>
<tr><td>Navy</td><td>Highlighted individualism</td><td colspan="2">Highlighted opportunities for personal and professional growth within the Navy</td><td>Highlighted the Navy's role in promoting stability and security worldwide</td><td>Emphasizes the Navy's maritime heritage and nostalgia</td></tr>
<tr><td>Marine Corps</td><td colspan="5">Emphasizes the elite nature and pride of being a Marine</td></tr>
<tr><td>Air Force</td><td colspan="4">Encouraged individual recruits to set ambitious goals and pursue excellence</td><td>Reflects the Air Force's expanded focus on space and cyberspace operations</td></tr>
<tr><td>Coast Guard</td><td colspan="5">Focuses on the service's motto vs. a recruit's place in the service</td></tr>
</table>

[291] Oliver Darcy, "Trump on Hillary Slogan: 'I'm With You'." *Business Insider*, June 22, 2016. https://www.businessinsider.com/trump-hillary-slogan-im-with-you-her-2016-6.

Military recruiting slogans are intentionally less inclusive. Two of the most familiar slogans, "Be All You Can Be" and "The Few, the Proud, the Marines," focus on idolizing a military elite or warrior class and challenging Americans to ask themselves if they could measure up to that ideal.

The Marines are very successful in their marketing, routinely hitting their recruiting goals. This is partially because they have a lower goal, only representing 13.4 percent of the armed forces.[292] In addition to selling exclusivity, they sell *belonging*, saying, "Once a Marine, always a Marine."

The Army, the largest service branch at 35.4 percent of the total military,[293] is less successful, despite being a boots-on-the-ground service branch like the Marines. The Army narrative promises to develop strength but not community. That is why its "Army of One" slogan was largely mocked.[294] This slogan was intended to highlight the fact that soldiers would retain their identity in the military.[295]

Meanwhile, other recruiting slogans make promises that are not always reflective of their reality. New airmen find themselves at the lowest rank and are told they should aim high. Sailors are told they are a "global force for good," but may spend their days landlocked and in an office. Some slogans are more realistic than others, focusing on the honor of being a part of a longstanding tradition.

These contradictory military narratives may be what caused TikTok posts from Gen Z to go viral. Military service is hard and asks people to put their identity to the side. The promise of feeling strong or courageous may not be enough. Gen Z is comfortable admitting what previous generations would not: all humans are flawed. The elite warrior doesn't exist.

---

[292] U.S. Department of Defense. *DOD's 2022 Demographics Profile of the Military Community*. 2022. https://download.militaryonesource.mil/12038/MOS/Reports/2022-demographics-report.pdf.
[293] Ibid.
[294] Brig. Gen. Jeffrey Phillips. "Commentary: Army of Ones." *Army.mil*, July 16, 2010. https://www.army.mil/article/42395/commentary_army_of_ones.
[295] Associated Press. "Army of One: The U.S. Military's Recruiting Slogan." *NBC News*, December 27, 2006. https://www.nbcnews.com/id/wbna15197720.

No military member—or human being—can ever live up to this mythology. This is why, when war heroes are fawned over, they often minimize their actions. They know what the rest of us suspect: Service members are not gods or demi-gods. They are people with weaknesses and flaws. Their choice to serve may be the most heroic action they take.

This choice to serve asks citizens to put their own needs to the side to protect our country. For some, military service is the ultimate test of courage. For the idealists, it is a way to give back to their nation. For those looking for belonging, the military offers bonding through shared adversity. For the realists, it is a way to develop leadership skills and get a free education.

The DoD makes marketing promises. But sometimes the product doesn't live up to the hype.

During recruiting, the military focuses on the individual and how they fit into the institution. Then it asks them to put away their individuality when they don the uniform. The initiation process (boot camp) and military training exercises are designed to minimize, if not remove, individuality. However, these military milestones do not take away individuality as much as they create moments of shared experience. When the military narrative pretends service member individuality no longer exists, we enter dangerous territory.

Recruiting a warrior elite is not a sign of unity. It is actively recruiting from an increasingly narrow group of Americans.

While this has conspiratorial implications—it risks the establishment of a military dictatorship—history proves that this narrative is actually destructive. It distances the military from the American people, which negatively impacts recruitment and retention.

MILITARY FAMILY RECRUITING NARRATIVES

Before the military transitioned into an all-volunteer force in 1973, the chances of being related to or knowing someone who served was high. The Vietnam War was still being fought by draftees. Today, our personal and family connections to the military are at a record low.

According to research, 77 percent of adults ages fifty and older said they had an immediate family member—a spouse, parent, sibling, or child—who had served in the military. This group likely knew someone who was drafted prior to 1973. Only 33 percent of young people aged eighteen to twenty-nine said the same.[296]

It is estimated that only 23 percent of Americans are eligible for service[297] due to fitness and moral policies, which prohibit recreational drug use, visible tattoos, and obesity. Recruiting requirements and the military-civilian gap have forced the services to double down on recruiting from an ever-shrinking pool of likely recruits. Recruits who more often than not come from military families.[298] As a result, the military relies upon military families and veterans to promote military service.

The rest of this chapter is dedicated to highlighting how military families impact military recruitment. Some military families, like the Pearsons, have a positive influence, recruiting future generations of military personnel from within. Others, like the Picchinis, recognize the benefits of service but encourage their children to pursue other opportunities. Still others, like the Ridgeways, fight the military to ensure their children have the right to serve.

---

[296] Pew Research Center. "The Military-Civilian Gap: Fewer Family Connections." *Pew Research Center*, November 23, 2011. https://www.pewresearch.org/social-trends/2011/11/23/the-military-civilian-gap-fewer-family-connections.

[297] U.S. Department of Defense. "After Tough Year, Military Recruiting Is Looking Up." *Defense.gov*, December 22, 2023. https://www.defense.gov/News/News-Stories/Article/article/3625464/after-tough-year-military-recruiting-is-looking-up.

[298] Pew Research Center. "The Military-Civilian Gap: Fewer Family Connections." *Pew Research Center*, November 23, 2011. https://www.pewresearch.org/social-trends/2011/11/23/the-military-civilian-gap-fewer-family-connections.

HAPPY TO SERVE: THE PEARSONS

Military recruiting often relies upon positive word-of-mouth marketing, and who better to tout the positive aspects of military service than veterans and their families? This can be an effective strategy. The Pearsons are an example of how good word of mouth has positively impacted military recruiting.

"As it turned out, the weekend that he came to get me in June of 1969, he got orders to Vietnam," recalled Anita Pearson of her earliest experiences as a military spouse. "That threw all of our plans [to set up their new home] out of whack. I returned home to be with my parents for that year, and he went to jungle training in Panama." And she was not alone; in the 1960s, the entire nation had been pulled into the war due to the draft. As a result, Anita's experiences were instantly familiar to those already closest to her: her childhood friends.

Anita's military spouse story is at the crossroads of many movements. As a Black woman who came of age in South Carolina in the 1960s, she was immersed in the Civil Rights Movement while also pulled into the war in Vietnam because of her marriage to a young Army officer.

"There were a number of us 'home' girls who decided to return home that year since our husbands were in Vietnam," said Anita. "We got this big map of Vietnam, and we learned where each of our husbands were going to be stationed. And we got pushpins in different colors to represent their locations. And each of us kind of kept track of what was happening in terms of the war and each of those areas."

Thankfully, the husbands of her 'home' girls all returned. But many of the battles that originated in Vietnam continued on the home front. "We had a number of persons from home who we lost and then some became ill [due] to addiction," she said with sadness, but almost in passing. She wasn't making light of the loss or addiction; she, like all Americans, knows not all battles end on the battlefield. What they are less familiar with is the impact family service has on military spouses like Anita.

"[My husband] got orders for Germany, and it was a challenge for me because I had just gotten a master's in speech pathology and I needed to work under the auspices of someone with that [degree], and that was just an impossibility," said Anita. "But it was okay. I loved the experience." Despite the initial professional setback, she persisted, as military spouses do, and made the best of her situation, soaking in cultural experiences, learning the language, and ultimately carving out a professional role at the installation, where she found personal and professional fulfillment.

"I think one of the biggest challenges is having an extended period of unemployment when you're used to being a working person," said Anita. "That was my toughest challenge."

Although her desire to work mirrors a modern military spouse's experience, it was not the norm for others within her community. "Most of the Black wives worked, and I guess it was just our expectation," recalled Anita. "And that wasn't necessarily true as a cultural thing [for the white wives]."

Her working status and race stood out within a predominantly white community. It was not just her perception; her working status became part of how others saw her. "I will never forget that I had gone to a tea and the general's wife introduced me as 'our one who works,'" she said.

While the Pearsons learned how to be part of a predominantly white military culture, they were also trying to stay connected to their Black peers. "Young Black kids would say, you guys need to make sure to be on the right side [of the war]," Anita shared. "That was kind of tough." She knew the war and military service were unpopular, but that did not stop her from getting involved in the Civil Rights Movement when she was just seventeen years old.

"We've all been to jail; all our kids, our friends have been to jail," said Anita. "We had trainers from all over the country teach us how to do peaceful marches and peaceful protests."

One of the protests was at a segregated bowling alley that was located in the middle of town. Black students from South Carolina State University marched on the bowling alley and were met with violence. "The highway patrolmen came, guns came out, and before we knew it, three folks had been murdered," she said. This event would later become known as the Orangeburg Massacre.[299]

The Pearsons' experiences coincided with the Vietnam War and Civil Rights Movement, a time of cultural churn. While there is a tendency to look back upon historical moments with nostalgia, labeling them "a different time," the 2000s, 2010s, and 2020s have similarly upended our nation.

The terrorist attacks of 9/11 and the COVID-19 pandemic have had a significant impact on American culture, which has shaped the modern military. The difference between these cultural moments is Vietnam and the Civil Rights Movement happened during the draft, and 9/11 and COVID happened to an all-volunteer force.

This distinction is important because the level of familiarity with military life was quite different before the establishment of the all-volunteer force.

Even though the war in Vietnam was not popular, the hardships of service were familiar to the average American because nearly everyone knew someone who had been drafted. They attended funerals and watched the war on television. This type of national suffering was felt by all Americans, even if it wasn't impacting everyone the same way.

The Pearsons' positivity through military hardships became part of their family narrative. They were used to overcoming struggles, both racial and logistical. They acknowledged that the military lifestyle required sacrifice, but they were surrounded by a community that was going through the same thing. To the Pearsons and many others, the experience was worth it. And it was this family narrative that influenced their daughter's desire to serve. Today, Major Alva Michelle Pearson Hicks is currently serving in the Army.

---

[299] History.com. "Orangeburg Massacre." *History.com*, April 6, 2018. https://www.history.com/articles/orangeburg-massacre.

The military relies upon stories like the Pearsons'. They had a positive experience that subsequent generations wanted to replicate. Their service brings their family pride and honor.

But it should not come as a surprise that post-9/11 military families are not as likely to recommend service. According to research, "post-9/11 veterans are more likely to have been deployed and to have served in combat."[300] Vietnam certainly asked Americans to go above and beyond, but this research says 9/11 asked more of fewer people. And families were impacted.

As anyone in customer service can tell you, you have no control over whether a product meets customer expectations. But you can control how you respond when it fails. That is why the military needs to be more proactive in addressing the needs of service members and their families. In providing good "customer service" by proactively improving the lived experiences of a diverse group of military families, the DoD ensures more and more military families will tell their positive stories of service across a wider pool of recruits. Because not everyone knows a family like the Pearsons.

IT'S YOUR CALL . . . TO SERVE: THE PICCHINIS

According to a 2024 Blue Star Family report, only one in three military families would recommend service to a young family member (a child, niece, nephew, etc.).[301] And there is a reason for it. Once they sign up to serve, to be all they can be, they see the promise of service not for what it

---

[300] Pew Research Center. "Key Findings About America's Military Veterans." *Pew Research Center*, November 7, 2019. https://www.pewresearch.org/short-reads/2019/11/07/key-findings-about-americas-military-veterans.

[301] Rachel Nostrant "Only One-Third of Military Families Would Still Recommend Service, Blue Star Families Survey Finds." *Military.com*, March 18, 2024. https://www.military.com/daily-news/2024/03/18/only-one-third-of-military-families-would-still-recommend-service-blue-star-families-survey-finds.html.

says service is, but for what it *really* is. And this reality isn't always what parents want for their children.

I grew up in the 1980s in New Jersey next to a base that was dying before my eyes as a result of a string of military downsizing decisions. Despite being right next to a foundering installation that should have fed into my community, I only knew one military family before I met and later married my husband.

My childhood best friend, Alyssa, had been a Navy brat before our families met. Her mom, "Mrs. (Melissa) Picchini," had a lot to say about her time as a military spouse. Shortly after I started dating a man who took me to the Naval Academy Chapel on our first date, I sat down with Melissa to decide if the military lifestyle was something I wanted to factor into my future.

While she shared many positive stories of her experience, the message I took away from the conversation was something to the effect of, "If he's in the Navy, you can't assume he's going to get out in four years and you'll get your life back. If you say yes, you marry the Navy too."

This conversation stuck with me and over the years helped me cope with my decision to marry the military. I chose this life too.

"When [my daughter] was due, Renny's ship was doing workups to go do a big cruise," recalled Melissa Picchini. "I said, see if you can take leave for a week because I'm going to go into labor." Renny Picchini's CO denied his leave request. This sent Melissa's blood pressure through the roof, forcing her to be medically induced. As a Navy officer, Renny was luckily able to attend the birth of his daughter, but was soon after sent out to sea for eight months.

"When I married him, I accepted that this might be my lifestyle. So it was not assumed that he would get out because I thought he should," said Melissa. She told me she was honored to be able to support her husband as he served the country. She, too, believed in the mission. It was particularly hard for her to tell him that if he wanted to continue in the military, she would not want to have any more kids.

Their decision was made even more difficult because Renny was doing well in his career. He was a lieutenant junior grade, a navigator on a ship, and a sea duty officer. His fitness reports were good. He even had an opportunity to attend the Naval Postgraduate School to further his education. But meeting all his career milestones didn't outweigh the impact military service had on his family life.

"I was in Guantanamo Bay for a seven, eight-week workup. And prior to that, I was out at sea," he recalled. "We were in and out of sea for four or five months. And when that whole workup was completed, I came back, and [my daughter] Alyssa really didn't know who I was."

This experience, combined with some advice shared by a more senior officer, challenged Renny's desire to serve. "We were going away for six months, and his teenage kids were on the pier. And he couldn't hold it back," he told me while choking back his own tears. He recalled a senior officer telling him if he had to do it again, he might not.

Ultimately, he got out of the Navy after nine years because of the impact the lifestyle had on his family. Despite the realities of service and its impact on their family, the Picchinis left military life with countless positive memories. They both told me stories of military friendships made along the way that are still flourishing to this day.

Fast forward nearly a decade later, and Alyssa, too, felt the call to serve.

"The Naval Academy may have been one of the only college campuses I had ever been on," she said. Her uncle lived in Annapolis, Maryland, the home of the Navy's military academy.

"The Naval Academy changed my dad's life," she said. "It's big and grand and everybody there is respected. And so, of course, I wanted to apply." She looked into application requirements, which included getting a congressional endorsement, and pitched joining the Navy to her dad.

Alyssa was shocked when her dad hesitated.

"My father being in the Navy was the narrative of our family throughout my whole life. It was part of our family identity," said Alyssa

Picchini Schaffer, PhD. "Going to the Naval Academy was a way for him to take a step up. He worked really hard to get there, and he worked really hard while he was there." But he did not rush to encourage Alyssa to serve.

"Alyssa was always smarter than I was," Renny shared, clearly proud of his daughter and his military connection. "She had a lot more potential than I ever did. The Naval Academy would have stifled [that], in my opinion. So I didn't encourage it. I told her that the education was superior but the opportunities after it are limited."

Renny attended the Naval Academy and was in the last class of all males. He witnessed firsthand when the Navy began offering opportunities for females to serve, but the change had only just begun.

"We trained the first women coming in. I saw what it was like in order to advance in the service," said Renny. "Opportunities for women in the Navy sucked at that point in time." He's not wrong; over the past fifty years, women have risen in the ranks, but it hasn't happened overnight.

Michelle J. Howard became the first female four-star admiral in 2014. Admiral Lisa Franchetti became the first chief of naval operations in 2023, but was fired by the Trump administration in 2025.

"I don't regret it at all," said Alyssa. Being my best friend aside, I can say it is the military's loss. Instead of going to the Naval Academy, Alyssa went to college, followed by graduate school, ultimately earning a PhD in pharmacology and training in neuroscience.

She went on to a prestigious science-policy fellowship and served as the scientific director of TEDMED before taking a position at the Simons Foundation, where she oversees groundbreaking basic neuroscience research to further understanding of how the brain works.

The reason the Picchinis' story is important goes far beyond the fact that it impacted my life. It highlights an important truth: These individual military experiences do not just inform the narratives of the families living them, but stretch far beyond the walls of their homes. These stories are the points of connection Americans have to the military. It's the story of my friend not recognizing her dad when he came home from a deployment that informed what I thought of military life. And it was this singular oral history that made me hesitate to say yes to a man I loved because he wore a uniform.

FIGHTING TO SERVE: THE RIDGEWAYS

Needless to say, I'm glad I ignored my better instincts, and that my best friend's mother softened what I'm sure was a hard experience when she shared her words of caution with a woman who had already fallen for a man in uniform. Had I not said yes, I would not have had the pleasure of meeting Vanessa Ridgeway. Unlike Alyssa's parents, who weren't sure the military could provide her with the same opportunities as a civilian career, Vanessa was convinced military service was in her son's future.

But she was worried about her son Tory. Tory Ridgeway wanted to be an aerospace engineer in the Navy, but according to his mother, the Navy didn't seem to want him because he had autism.

Tory was diagnosed with autism when he was just four years old. His mother set out to obtain help for him at a very young age by getting him the best-quality educational support she could find.

Vanessa tirelessly sought out the best education and therapies for Tory, even when it meant long commutes. Her efforts paid off—by the time Tory entered high school, he no longer needed special education services. He had gotten to know himself and what he needed to succeed. Vanessa knew Tory could do anything he set his mind to because he had already done so. She knew he just needed the tools and a runway. She knew he would fly.

When Tory was ready to graduate high school, he was accepted to Embry-Riddle Aeronautical University and was awarded a Naval Reserve Officers Training Corps (NROTC) scholarship. He was going to join the Navy like his dad. He and Vanessa knew this school would set Tory on a path toward his ultimate goal of becoming an aerospace engineer in the

Navy. He looked at the course offerings and signed up for classes. He just needed to get ready for boot camp.

Tory had done it. He had learned how to thrive. Autism was a part of his life; it no longer controlled it. That changed on June 3, 2021.

While the Navy was reviewing his medical paperwork—after being granted an NROTC scholarship—it discovered it had missed his autism diagnosis, something he did not hide, but it instantly disqualified him from being able to serve his country. Despite this, he was given orders to attend boot camp. So he went.

Autism is one of the hundreds, if not thousands, of diagnoses in the DoD's thirty-seven-page Medical Standards for Military Service: Appointment, Enlistment, or Induction.[302] If an individual has one of these conditions, they are flagged by a medical reviewer and their file is then transferred to the military service for further review. The service can offer them the opportunity to apply for a waiver.

While Tory might seem like a great candidate for a medical waiver, the Navy didn't agree. They did not even give him the chance to apply for one at first.

The thing about military parents is they know the game. In the military, there are two rule books: the official policy (including that autism is a disqualifying condition) and the workaround (the squeaky wheel that's greased to hush it up). The Ridgeways knew their son was capable of serving in the Navy, and they were willing to work hard to prove it.

Because Tory was still in boot camp, Vanessa got to work on his behalf. She tried to find out what was happening by talking to the Navy directly. She also started calling friends to ask for advice and ultimately helped Tory reach out to his congressional representatives and members of the media. Vanessa shared how much Tory had overcome and how he wanted to follow in his father's footsteps of serving his country.

---

302 U.S. Department of Defense. *DoD Instruction 6130.03: Medical Standards for Appointment, Enlistment, or Induction into the Military Services*. Washington, D.C.: U.S. Department of Defense, July 2, 2020. https://www.esd.whs.mil/Portals/54/Documents/DD/issuances/dodi/613003p.pdf.

Their work paid off. Their congressional representative, Steny Hoyer, contacted the Navy asking for clarification on their decision to disqualify Tory without the option of applying for a waiver. A few weeks later, Tory received another letter from the Navy. They were giving him another chance to show that his autism would not prevent him from carrying out his job. He was allowed to apply for a medical waiver.

But there was a catch: If he was granted a medical waiver, there were limits on what he would be allowed to do for the Navy. He couldn't be a commissioned officer. And only officers could become aerospace engineers. The job he had dreamt of since childhood was off the table.

Within the military community, there are different career pathways that a new recruit can pursue: Military Occupational Specialties (MOS). The pathways open to service members depend on the scores they receive during the recruitment period. The higher the score, the more jobs the candidate has to choose from. Once they select a specialty area, they begin training in that specialty.

In addition to taking mental aptitude tests, recruits also fill out medical screening paperwork. Medical paperwork is flagged for one of the many disqualifying conditions listed in official policy, such as taking anti-anxiety medication or listing a previous medical condition or diagnosis.

It makes sense; the DoD wants to ensure those who are put in a physically or mentally demanding situation can get themselves and their fellow service members out of it safely. Tory wanted to fill a job that the Navy believed required a score and level of fitness that Tory did not possess.

His mother was not only worried about Tory's health and safety, like other would-be military parents; she knew she had done her best to prepare him to face the world. She was worried that despite all she had already done for him, she could do nothing to prevent the military from crushing his dreams of serving simply because he is autistic.

WE DON'T WANT YOU: REDEFINING FITNESS

Tory Ridgeway's story is just one example of a larger issue with military recruiting. Because of the deference paid to the military, it gets to determine what it means to be fit, to be a member of an elite warrior class. And because it controls this measuring stick, it can change its standards at any time. Instead of telling Americans "I want you!" like Uncle Sam did during World War I, it plays hard to get and tells Americans it doesn't want them after all.

After hearing this story, I was awarded a grant by Military Veterans in Journalism to research neurodiversity in the military and find out if the DoD was discriminating against recruits on the basis of disability.[303] I learned that the DoD is exempt from many laws that the rest of America has to follow, chief among them the Rehabilitation Act of 1973. This act prohibits employers from discriminating on the basis of race, gender, and disability, to name a few examples. The intent of this deference is to allow the DoD to maintain a ready force, assuming it can meet certain legal criteria.

The deference paid to military recruiting is similar to the deference that used to be given to college admissions offices.[304] In 2023, the Supreme Court overturned a previous ruling that allowed quotas; it also said college affirmative action programs violated the Equal Protection Clause of the Constitution,[305] ruling they failed strict scrutiny,[306] a legal test requiring

---

303 What I found appeared in the following publications: Jennifer Barnhill, "The Cost of Medical Stigmas for Military Families," *Military.com*, January 2, 2024, https://www.military.com/daily-news/2024/01/02/cost-of-medical-stigmas-military-families.html, and Jennifer Barnhill, "US Military Recruitment Crisis May Hinge on Medical Waivers," *The War Horse*, August 3, 2023, https://thewarhorse.org/us-military-recruitment-crisis-may-hinge-on-medical-waivers/

304 American Bar Association. "Promoting Diversity? It's Constitutional! (Grutter v. Bollinger)." *ABA Law Student Division*, April 6, 2018.
https://www.americanbar.org/groups/law_students/resources/on-demand/quimbee-grutter-v-bollinger/#:~:text=The%20issue%20was%20whether%20a,compelling%20interest%20in%20achieving%20diversity.

305 NBC News. "Supreme Court Strikes Down Affirmative Action Programs at Harvard and UNC." *NBC News*, June 29, 2023. https://www.nbcnews.com/politics/supreme-court/supreme-court-strikes-affirmative-action-programs-harvard-unc-rcna66770.

306 Szypszak, Charles. *Understanding Law for Public Administration*. Kindle Edition. Jones & Bartlett Learning, 2012, 65.

deference to be narrowly tailored to a compelling government interest. Universities didn't meet this standard, and their precedent was overturned.

In other words, if you are going to be given permission to do something that seems like discrimination, you'd better cover your ass by following the policy exception to the letter. Universities didn't, and the legal precedent was overturned.

The military's "compelling government interest" is deployability—the ability to perform duties in any environment.[307] While all service members must be ready to be deployed, only 20 percent of jobs are combat focused.[308] Warriors can be administrators, doctors, human resources professionals, cooks, and more. I wondered whether deployability was narrowly tailored enough to withstand similar scrutiny.

Research published by the RAND Corporation in 2019 said recruiters mentioned that the required paperwork and waiver outcomes often varied for different applicants with the same medical issues.[309] Additionally, military medical standards for recruits are higher than the requirements for those who are currently serving.[310] This variation of standards all but proves that having a medical condition does not always prevent service members with a medical diagnosis from being able to do the job.

No one can live up to the elite warrior standard, not even the elite warriors. For centuries service members have done their jobs undiagnosed, serving long before science had names for their conditions. Today, many active-duty members are still getting the job done with medical waivers. But without more transparency about who gets a waiver, who doesn't, and why, the military should not be given the benefit of the doubt and the legal deference that comes with it.

---

[307] U.S. Army. "Deployment." *GoArmy.com.* Accessed August 26, 2025. https://www.goarmy.com/army-life/intro-to-army-life/deployment.html.

[308] Ibid.

[309] Lytell, Maria C., Kimberly Curry Hall, and Nelson Lim. *Improving U.S. Military Accession Medical Screening Systems.* RAND Corporation, 2019. https://www.rand.org/content/dam/rand/pubs/research_reports/RR2700/RR2780/RAND_RR2780.pdf.

[310] DoD Instruction 6130.03 Volume 1 covers recruitment and Volume 2 covers retention.

Currently, the DoD gets to choose what medical liability it is willing to assume and when. Recruiters report medical and educational recruiting standards are changed to ensure recruiting goals are met.

The military "Be all you can be" narrative says it can take any American and transform them into an elite member of the warrior class. The DoD says it doesn't want to change standards, but it regularly changes them. It just doesn't want to be told to do so.

This is not the first time military deference has been used to narrowly define fitness. The military has used its elite status to undermine the service of Black Americans, female Americans, and LGBTQ+ Americans. And it currently prevents neurodiverse Americans, like Tory Ridgeway, from serving.

I'm happy to report that despite the Navy's decision, Tory is thriving at Embry-Riddle and pursuing his dreams of being an aerospace engineer, just not for the military.

REWRITING THE RECRUITING NARRATIVE

"It turned out that from the perspective of [my] family history, [my son's] service was normal," Frank Schaeffer wrote in *AWOL: The Unexcused Absence of America's Upper Classes from Military Service—and How It Hurts Our Country*,[311] which he co-authored with Kathy Roth-Douquet. "It was only to me and to my generation . . . that it might appear strange to have a son serving his country."

Parents play a crucial role in who serves in the military. But this role is often minimized. It is hard to talk about recruiting an elite warrior class when they first have to get mom's permission to sign up. Current recruitment strategies minimize their role and instead target a small, often

---

[311] Kathy Roth-Douquet and Frank Schaeffer. *AWOL: The Unexcused Absence of America's Upper Classes from Military Service—and How It Hurts Our Country.* Harper Perennial, 2007. p. 100.

homogenous, group, which limits the diversity of the military. And Congress has noticed.

"Eighty-four percent of the current members of the professional military are from military bloodlines," said Senator Angus King of Maine at a hearing of the House Armed Services Committee. "In my town of Brunswick, Maine, we had a naval air station for forty or fifty years. Kids got to know people from the military. They got to know them as their coaches. They saw them in town. That's gone now."[312]

This was an unintended consequence of the closing of military bases in the northeast. King was responding to testimony that highlighted the importance of familiarity with the military as a key factor in recruitment. "One of the major factors is the young people growing up in a community have some contact with or familiarization with the military," said King. "This is a serious problem."[313]

In the same way military marketing slogans target a small group of Americans who have a propensity to serve, recruiting from within military families significantly narrows the pool of recruits to the same geographic, racial, and socioeconomic profiles, and opens the door for a homogenous military.

Recruiting an all-volunteer force from an ever-changing candidate pool requires a multipronged strategy. Current strategies include television commercials, social media campaigns, attending high school job fairs, and word of mouth from veterans and families. Unlike the first three strategies, the DoD has little control over veterans and families in a social media–inundated world. It can't stop all families from discouraging their children from serving. But it can do more. It can pay attention to the role military families play in recruitment and respond accordingly. It can hear stories

---

[312] U.S. Senate. *Hearings to Examine the Recruiting Challenges Facing the United States Military.* Committee on Armed Services, 118th Cong., 1st sess., March 22, 2023. Video, 5:44. Washington, DC: Government Publishing Office, https://video.snapstream.net/Play/aG1OVAOa91vhtczrTz22UX?accessToken=c95h49jkdmwde.

[313] U.S. Senate Committee on Armed Services. "In Senate Armed Services Hearing, King Stresses Need for Greater 'Geographic Diversity' in United States Military." Press release, October 5, 2021. https://www.king.senate.gov/newsroom/press-releases/in-senate-armed-services-hearing-king-stresses-need-for-greater-geographic-diversity-in-united-states-military.

like the Picchinis' and take their concerns to heart. It can review the promotion opportunities afforded to women, and it can communicate their efforts to recruits and families.

America needs military service to be a viable option for all Americans. The institution fails when it does not seek to make service universally accessible. It can't recruit conservatives and not liberals, and vice versa. The DoD has the ability and technology to train the best and the brightest. It just has to ensure the narratives it uses to recruit support this effort. This will require the DoD to get to know a broad audience.

To recruit the best and brightest, the DoD needs to make service relatable to a wider pool of Americans. Focusing on recruiting an elite warrior class alone doesn't do this. This strategy seeks to absolve the DoD from making its "product" more attractive, however it can, to younger generations and those currently serving. This military recruiting narrative refuses to admit that it is the institution itself that service members and would-be recruits are rejecting. Instead, it revamps marketing strategies (it doesn't evaluate) based on whoever is in office, pointing fingers at the failures of previous administrations.

If people are not signing up to serve, it is not exclusively because the military is woke or macho or sexist. These narratives are put into the public sphere and are part of—but not all of—the problem. Younger generations are not signing up to serve because the military has crafted a narrative that has separated the average American from an elite warrior class. As a result, the average American doesn't know enough about military service to know if it is something they should consider. What they do know is what they see in movies, or the flat messages presented by the DoD.

By contrast, military families have a front-row seat to the reality of service. This is why military families are the key to preventing a draft. If you create an environment where those serving actually want to be, word will spread—inside and, more importantly, outside military families.

How *you* can change this narrative: Listen to firsthand military stories that feature the point of view of service members, veterans, and their families. Access to more stories of service will allow Americans to walk away with a fuller impression of military life.

How the DoD can change this narrative: Take ownership of the military recruiting narrative. Military recruiting will continue to be unstable because the nation is unfamiliar with military service. The public has lost confidence in the institution because you first told them you were elite and without weakness, but social media allowed them to see this is not true. Change this unattainable narrative by embracing a more transparent recruiting process that casts a wide net. Don't wait for congressional mandates to be all you can be.

The Mission or the Man?

Listening to and accepting more than the dominant narrative asks us to confront what author Jim Collins calls the Stockdale Paradox: "You must maintain unwavering faith that you can and will prevail in the end, regardless of the difficulties, and at the same time, have the discipline to confront the most brutal facts of your current reality, whatever they might be."[314]

Military families can be resilient *and* broken. They can take care of each other *and* need help in doing so. We can and must be able to hold and accept what seems to be contradictory narratives because our lack of belief in them does not make them any less true. Doing so may feel unsettling at first, but practice opens the door to a more complete understanding of the issue at hand. As this book draws to a close, I want to present you with yet another seemingly contradictory idea.

As you read on, I want you to decide which of the two men described below is a real hero.

---

[314] Collins, Jim. "The Stockdale Paradox." *Jim Collins*, accessed August 26, 2025. https://www.jimcollins.com/concepts/Stockdale-Concept.html.

In 1519, Spanish conquistador Hernán Cortés was about to invade Aztec land—with a less than willing crew. Some men may have wanted to collect their share of booty, others wanted to return home to Cuba, and others had divided loyalties. Cortés feared they were contemplating mutiny. He had experienced a mutiny before. But Cortés didn't just need to conquer lands on behalf of Spain; he personally needed a military victory. Having violated local authorities, he could not return to his base of operations in Cuba. With this knowledge, Cortés had a choice: to fight, knowing that his men might retreat to their ships if they started losing the battle, or not to fight.[315]

Cortés went with a third option. He concocted a story that many of the ships were not seaworthy, having been damaged by the strong gales they encountered on the way to Mexico. Cortés then stripped the ships of their sails, riggings, and ironworks, and anything else that could be used on land. Finally, the hulls were then scuttled.[316] Without an exit plan, his men were motivated to fight or die. They won.

Although Cortés may have had personal motivations for his actions, his actions have since become associated with strong and decisive leadership.[317]

Over half a millennium later, in March 2020, COVID-19 had begun to spread, eventually taking the lives of millions. The military was not immune to its effects. "Sailors do not need to die. If we do not act now, we are failing to properly take care of our most trusted asset—our Sailors,"

---

[315] PBS. "Hernán Cortés." *PBS Conquistadors*. Accessed August 26, 2025. https://www.pbs.org/conquistadors/cortes/cortes_d00.html.
[316] Maya Bell, "Searching for the Lost Ships of Cortés." *University of Miami News*. January 2, 2019. https://news.miami.edu/stories/2019/01/searching-for-the-lost-ships-of-cortes.html.
[317] John Henley, "Burn Your Ships: A History Lesson About How to Be a Great Leader." *The Center for Sales Strategy*, May 31, 2018. https://blog.thecenterforsalesstrategy.com/burn-your-ships-how-to-be-a-great-leader#:~:text=If%20you%20leave%20the%20ships,committed%20as%20you%20obviously%20are.

Navy Captain Brett Crozier wrote in an email to senior leaders that was eventually leaked to the press.[318]

More than 1,200 members of his crew were sick; one died. Crozier's actions were seen by military leadership as circumventing the chain of command, because the Navy had plans to help, although those plans were not yet public. It was speculated that the email was leaked intentionally; as a result, Crozier was relieved of his duties as the commanding officer of the *USS Theodore Roosevelt*. His actions were praised by his sailors, but were denounced by the Navy.

WHO IS THE HERO: CORTÉS OR CROZIER?

Cortés was willing to sacrifice the lives of his men to save the mission. Crozier was willing to sacrifice the mission to save his men.

To answer this question, America has to ask itself which is more important: the mission or the men.

The answer is unsatisfying: They're both important.

Cortés and Crozier are simultaneously heroic and flawed leaders because you cannot achieve the mission without the men and the men serve the mission. I suspect Crozier felt his only course of action was going outside the chain of command in hopes that public pressure would help him achieve his mission. Both Cortés and Crozier effectively burned their ships, committing to a risky course of action.

This is why understanding and unpacking military narratives is important. If the average American goes through life thinking about war like Cortés—where the mission is more important than the men—it glorifies military leaders whose risky choices pay off while ignoring the military leaders who made similarly risky choices but failed to achieve the

[318] CDR Salamander, "We Are Not at War—Sailors Do Not Need to Die." *U.S. Naval Institute Blog*, April 1, 2020. https://blog.usni.org/posts/2020/04/01/we-are-not-at-war-sailors-do-not-need-to-die.

same positive outcome. We incorrectly associate risky choices with positive outcomes, to our peril.

Alternatively, if we see Crozier only as someone who did not respect the chain of command, without acknowledging the limitations of the institution and the chain of command structure, we are no better off than if we accepted Cortés' victory at face value.

The real hero? Both

The military stories you have been told are only part of the truth. The other parts are the stories you need to hear. Both narratives are true, but when we choose one at the expense of the other, we will never see the whole picture.

FINDING A MORE COMPLETE PICTURE

For me, this was a tough lesson to learn, and it took up more bandwidth than I ever expected. I am a blonde, white, Christian female married to a white male service member. On paper, I fit the stereotypical definition of what it means to be a patriotic American. My upbringing did not encourage me to question the narratives that go along with life as a white, female Christian.

Instead of questioning the truths that I accepted as fact, I was raised to think I needed to protect my beliefs. To question them was to introduce doubt, and to compromise felt like I was compromising all that I believed in. I was told it was my duty to stand up for my beliefs. It was not good enough to live them out for myself; if I wanted to prove my faith, I had to act. I was encouraged to protest gay marriage to protect straight marriage. Once I got married, though, I realized my marriage didn't need protection because no one was coming for me or my beliefs. No one told me not to be a Christian. No one made me feel bad for being white. No one judged my husband's service or our status as Americans.

My perspective changed because the military lifestyle, like other experiences that push you outside your comfort zone, challenged what I thought I knew. I met people whom I previously did not understand. As I got to know a diverse group of people—who they loved, what they were afraid of, and what they fought for—it made it hard for me to hold onto my past beliefs. I reflected on the stories I had been told and compared them to the lived experiences of those around me. I also compared what the Bible said to the stories religious leaders were sharing. I sought out more stories, stories that helped me find a better version of myself.

Finding stories that broadened my understanding was not hard. The problem I regularly encountered was not a lack of individuals who wanted to share their experiences, but systems and leaders who refused to acknowledge certain stories.

Over the years, my interview requests went unanswered. Freedom of Information Act (FOIA) requests were unanswered. When finally forced to respond to individual stories of military service members and families in crisis, leaders dismissed them as anecdotes. But this is not just a military problem.

I attended a church in California. It was a big church, which made it hard to make close connections. One thing the military community encourages to combat our role as outsiders is volunteerism. So I spoke with the military liaison at the church. I mentioned I was a reporter and familiar with military benefits and policies, and would be happy to offer whatever support I could to other military families in the congregation.

While we were there talking beside the coffee and donut table with kids running all around us, I noticed something change. Despite me being the one to offer my support and explain my knowledge about military benefits and programs, the church leader talked to my husband. My husband had no free time to volunteer; he also had little knowledge about benefits he didn't use himself.

I dismissed the church leader's behavior as that of someone from a generation gone by, but I kept it in my heart as I continue to attend church.

A few months later, we received an email from that church asking if we wanted to be mentors to other military families.

Mentorship is something we value in our household. It is something built into the military structure. It was an honor to be asked. However, while we value mentorship, we equally value and encourage questions. When we told church leaders we would be honored to help but would encourage those we mentor to ask themselves and their faith tough questions, they stopped calling.

We were left to wonder if that church was serving the men or the mission.

The mission isn't the institution *or* the people, it's the people *in* the institution. Jesus focused on loving our neighbors in the Great Commandment; our Constitution opens with "We the people"[319]; and Abraham Lincoln said it in the Gettysburg Address, proclaiming America as a government "of the people, by the people, for the people."[320]

Men and women are the mechanism to achieve the mission *and* the mission itself. When you neglect the people—when you silence their stories—you harm the mission.

To improve any institution, we must learn about its people. We need to hear stories that:

- Recognize Corporal Fred McGee's heroism, unclouded by racism.
- Acknowledge military family members are essential to the mission, not a drain on it.
- Expose politicians when they claim credit for the actions of military wives who fought for the safe return of their POW husbands.
- Ensure families of the fallen are supported, not abandoned.

---

319 *U.S. Constitution.* 1787. National Archives. https://www.archives.gov/founding-docs/constitution-transcript.
320 Abraham Lincoln. *Gettysburg Address.* Speech, Gettysburg, PA, November 19, 1863. National Archives. https://www.archives.gov/founding-docs/gettysburg-address.

- Live out the sentiment of "thank you for your service" by directing resources to those who need them.
- Reject the toxicity of faked resilience in favor of real support.
- Call out false narratives that politicize the support military families need and redirect focus to supporting those who serve.
- Acknowledge military service should be a viable option for all Americans, not just an elite few.

We all need to get better at finding stories that challenge our preconceived notions. That is why I will continue to ask questions of institutions I am part of, like the church and the military. It is not because I do not respect these leaders or institutions. I ask questions because I value the people in them more.

When we ask questions of leaders and tell our stories, we prove to these systems that they need *we the people* to function.

Because power goes back to the people when nuance and detail enter the conversation, something our nation needs right now.

I have had many conversations with my left-leaning friends who are quick to dismiss the value of the military institution, service members and their families included. They don't see themselves or their causes reflected in our population, so they assume we are all conservative warmongers. At large, they do not understand the motivations of the right, so they dismiss the right's faith-based concerns and call them stupid. This is the wrong stance.

Alternatively, my right-leaning friends and family are drawn to military narratives of strength, ones looking back at a time when men were men and strength was easier to define. However, getting back to that time requires stepping back social progress inside and outside of the military. This is the wrong stance.

I was raised to think America was great because of its people. We were hard workers who were willing to stand up for what is right, even when it was hard. Our military embodies so many of these amazing ideals, as do military spouses and kids. But contrary to the military stories you've been told, service members and their families are no different from the average American. They want to fight for something bigger than themselves. They care about this country and want to leave it a better place than how they found it. We all can and should do our part in our own ways.

To do this, we need to stop seeing each other as members of a particular group.

Civilians and military.

Left and right.

Atheists and Christians.

Black and white.

Gay and straight.

Women and men.

In many ways, writing this book has felt like my own personal burning of the ships, by calling out various institutional flaws and possibly alienating myself from my own community. I love the military community. Together we have experienced the highs and lows this life has to offer. The people in the institution have helped me grow as a human being. But I care too much about its people to let the institution stay as I found it. So I'm hoping that sharing some of the stories I have been given will not just be about exposing some aspect of our government, but offering us a plan of action—a way to burn our ships, knowing that the mission has always been the man.

While this book focuses on the military, this lesson is universal. We need to stop consuming the stories we are told by institutions or groups that look and sound just like us. We need to start asking people to tell us their stories, because individuals—not institutions—are the source of the stories we need to hear.

But don't take my word for it. Talk to people. Don't simply consume the stories you are told—find the stories you need to hear. You will know it is a story you need to hear when it makes you uncomfortable, challenging your preconceived notions.

And when you start to get too comfortable with what they are saying, start talking to different people.

Acknowledgments

This is a book I never wanted to write. I didn't see myself as an "involved" military spouse. I also didn't want to be a "dependent" or acknowledge my title of military spouse—a title that only saw me through the lens of my husband's career. Nor did I really have any aspirations to write a book, something I would prefer to leave to others. As a result, I have many people to thank for helping me to see past the things I thought I wanted for myself.

This book was written on lunch breaks, at night, and on weekends—in the hidden moments between my day job. Those moments would not have existed without the unwavering love and support of my husband and children, who often picked up the slack when I couldn't stop writing . . .

Dave, this book would not exist without you. Thank you for being strong enough for me to question everything, and stronger still to turn my questions on their head with questions of your own. You challenge me to think deeper in every way. Thank you for carving out space in our busy lives to make this book even a remote possibility. You are my answered prayer. I love you.

M, my girl who knows herself—her likes and dislikes—no matter what others may think. This is a gift you will carry into becoming the quiet leader you were born to be. Thank you for inspiring me with your passion and creativity.

A, my fearless girl who shines her light bright for all to see. You inspire me to keep chasing my dreams. Thank you for being relentlessly supportive of your fellow big dreamers.

J, my wild man who knows more about military history than most adults. Keep reminding your generation about the importance of remembering the things some want us to forget. And keep walking into rooms just to say, "I love you, Mom." You heal my heart when it is heavy.

To my extended family, thank you. To my mom, my first feminist icon, whose example showed me that women can do anything. You instilled the importance of faith in me at a young age. These lessons have shaped me as a person and as a writer and advocate. I wrote this book because my faith called me to. The person of Jesus taught me how, when, and why to flip tables to elevate the sanctity of God and those who he created in his image.

To my dad, who taught me I could push back on authority and win. To my brother for telling me I was someone who did what I said I would do until I believed it. To my aunt Mary, who opened my eyes to international travel—an essential skill set for navigating the military world.

And to Gwen, Mickey, Joe and all my family who have flown from Florida to California to Japan to Nevada to Maryland, whenever I needed help to make this lifestyle work. You have not let the logistical challenges stand in the way of showing your love and support. Thank you.

I owe similar gratitude to the publishing and journalism communities, who gave me both the skills and the platform to tell these stories.

Thank you to my publisher, Kristin Bentley, along with the entire E.P. House editing team. Kristin, your passion and enthusiasm for this project never wavered. You knew my book needed to be a book before I did.

Thank you to my friend (and editor), Maddie Dolan, for reminding me that I am a writer and pulling me out of my "journalism retirement."

Thank you for helping make Nevada (and Maryland) fun, and for reading and editing this book. You are my most trusted editor.

Thank you to my editor at *Military Families Magazine*, Bianca Strzalkowski, for assigning me to important topics like food insecurity and the "widow's tax." I would not have likely stumbled into these areas on my own and I am eternally grateful that you trusted me with those important stories.

Thank you to Zachary Fryer-Biggs, Sarah Blansett, and the team at *military.com* who identified a gap in military spouse representation and gave me the runway to fill it.

To Kelly Kennedy and the team at The War Horse, whose robust and editing process taught me so much.

So much of where this book has gone began with research at these publications.

I am also indebted to my mentors and research partners, who shaped my thinking and sharpened my craft.

Thank you to my mentor Sue Hoppin, for inspiring me to always think outside the box, while also helping check my passion and guiding me towards the achievable.

My fellow museum nerd and mentor, Heath Hardage Lee, who first introduced me to Sybil Stockdale and the *League of Wives*. Heath, your guidance throughout this writing process has made me believe I'm capable of remembering my training as a historian, after all those years my skills built up dust.

Thank you to those at the Naval History and Heritage Command who helped me shed a bit more light on Mouza Zumwalt. Thank you for recommending me to the LWMP and to its team who moved mountains and made history.

Thank you to the researchers at the Government Accountability Office (GAO), Blue Star Families (BSF), Military Family Advisory Network (MFAN), D'Aniello Institute for Veterans and Military Families at Syracuse University (IVMF), and countless others for helping to put data behind the military family story. A special shout out to Elizabeth Field, PhD, and Jessica Strong, PhD, for never saying no to my data-related questions. You helped contextualize my reporting, transforming human interest pieces from anecdotes to indicators of larger cultural shifts. Thank you to Margaret Harrell, PhD, for quantifying military spouse unpaid labor during your time at RAND, making me feel less alone in my desire to know more.

Thank you to the team at Joining Forces, under both the Obama and Biden administrations for helping to elevate the experiences of military families and to Second Lady Pence who also made listening to military families a priority.

Thank you to the Public Administration department at the University of North Carolina Chapel Hill who helped not only advise me through my master's degree, but who helped me in writing articles and research papers about special education that were eventually cited by the White House.

Thank you to Eric Fotheringham, PhD, who helped me identify what I was seeing in the military nonprofit space as sector failure.

Thank you to Chris Cody, PhD, and Maureen Berner, PhD, you taught me how to identify good survey design and interpret data, something that was invaluable in my process of decoding the military stories we've been told.

To Amy Shuman, PhD, for your partnership while at The Ohio State University. You dedicated your time to better understand military children in special education during our Partners in PROMISE collaboration. Your mentorship in qualitative research and guidance on narrative work helped shape this book.

To Alyssa Picchini-Shaffer—thank you for being my person, for telling me to be loud in a world that told me to be silent. Your professional partnership has made our friendship grow beyond our NJ childhood and our young adult life in Italy and D.C. When I come to you for (free) consultations on how to rework a research question, lead a Ted-Med-style talk, understand the mind of a funder, or ask what professional direction I should take, I know I'll get both the honesty of a friend and the rigor of the industry leader you are.

Alongside these individual mentors and friends, I must thank the organizations and advocacy networks that shaped my understanding of military family life.

Thank you to the Bush Institute's Veteran Leadership Project team and scholars who gave me access to insights I would not have had otherwise, and a balance that seeks to unify rather than divide. I especially want to thank my fellow 5x5 classmates who helped me see the story in the story.

Thank you to Lori Simmons and the entire Armed Forces Insurance Military Spouse of the Year program for recognizing countless military spouses each year and making our community feel seen. Thank you for welcoming me into this family and your tireless commitment to the issues that too often go unseen.

Thank you everyone I have worked with in the EFMP community for teaching me so much about your lives and trusting me with your stories.

And to my friends in this journey—friends who have read early drafts (looking at you MM & JH), stayed up in the early morning hours talking over solutions (HA), watched my kids so I could promote the book (Monterey family), and repeatedly reminded me why I started (HC & SS)—your belief in me carried this book across the finish line.

To my secret sources—you know who you are. You knew the risks and shared anyway, valuing service members and families over your own jobs. Thank you for your bravery. Here's hoping we don't hear those chopper blades any time soon.

Finally, I could not have written this without the trust of the countless military spouses who shared their stories with me. Since I began reporting on military families, I have recorded over 1,200 interviews.

This book is dedicated to Esther and all the military spouses who work to rescue others from drowning while treading water themselves. You are not weak when you ask for help. You do not diminish service members' stories by telling your own. Keep telling them. And remember: It is people just like you who have, through their hidden contributions, changed the face of the military. And as a historian, I can say with confidence you will do it again.

About the Author

Jennifer Barnhill, MPA, is a columnist for *Military.com*, a freelance journalist, and the host of Military Dinner Table Conversations, a monthly reverse town hall elevating the stories of military families. She was named the 2025 Armed Forces Insurance Navy Spouse of the Year and is a 2023 Bush Institute Stand-To Veteran Leadership Scholar. Her reporting on military family policy has appeared on CNN and informed discussions on Capitol Hill, and her research has been cited by the White House, featured by NPR, and presented before Congress. Drawing on her lived experience navigating the military ecosystem, Jennifer uncovers how policies affect families in practice.

Jennifer walked away from a PhD scholarship after falling in love with a service member, not realizing she wasn't just marrying a man—she was marrying the military. She unexpectedly fell in love with the military community too, but was soon shocked to discover that while military families took care of each other, the institution did not. It often made life harder. Never one to shy away from a challenge, Jennifer pursued a Master of Public Administration from UNC Chapel Hill while volunteering within the community to better understand the broken systems she was writing about. The experience gave her a front-row seat to how policies are made—and how they fall short.

Armed with this deeper understanding, she returned to journalism to spotlight some of the overlooked issues impacting the community: families facing food insecurity, surviving spouses fighting for earned death benefits and would-be recruits turned away due to outdated medical policies.

These and countless other experiences culminated in this book—an urgent examination of who gets to tell the military's story, and why that must change. Through it, Jennifer invites readers to reconsider what they think they know about military service—by listening to the hidden all-volunteer force, military families.